Misframing Men

Misframing Men

The Politics of
Contemporary Masculinities

MICHAEL KIMMEL

RUTGERS UNIVERSITY PRESS

NEW BRUNSWICK, NEW JERSEY, AND LONDON

LIBRARY OF CONGRESS CATALOGING-IN-PUBLICATION DATA

Kimmel, Michael.
  Misframing men : the politics of contemporary masculinities / Michael Kimmel.
    p.   cm.
  Includes bibliographical references and index.
  ISBN 978–0–8135–4762–6 (hbk. : alk. paper) — ISBN 978–0–8135–4763–3 (pbk. :
alk. paper)
  I. Men—Identity. 2. Masculinity. 3. Men in mass media.   I. Title.
  HQ1090.K545 2010
  305.31—dc22   2009038368

A British Cataloging-in-Publication record for this book is available
from the British Library.

Visit our Web site: http://rutgerspress.rutgers.edu

Manufactured in the United States of America

For Amy, always

CONTENTS

Preface   ix

Introduction: Misframing Men   1

PART ONE
Reframings

1   Has "A Man's World" Become "A Woman's Nation"?:
    Men's Responses to Women's Increased Equality in
    the Twenty-first Century   15

2   The Children's Hour: Masculine Redemption
    in Contemporary Film (with Amy Aronson)   38

3   Reconciliation, Appropriation, Inspiration, and
    Conversation: Four Strategies of Racial Healing
    among White Men   50

PART TWO
Reversals

4   Who Are the Real Male Bashers?   69

5   A War against Boys?   92

6   "Gender Symmetry" in Domestic Violence   99

PART THREE
Restorations

7   Profiling School Shooters and Shooters' Schools:
    The Cultural Contexts of Aggrieved Entitlement
    and Restorative Masculinity   131

8   Globalization and Its Mal(e)contents: Masculinity
         on the Extreme Right   143

9   Promise Keepers: Patriarchy's Second Coming
         as Masculine Renewal   163

10   Saving the Males at VMI and Citadel   173

11   Janey Got Her Gun: A VMI Postscript   197

PART FOUR
Resistance

12   Who's Afraid of Men Doing Feminism?   209

13   Profeminist Men: The "Other" Men's Movement   220

         Index   231

PREFACE

A collection of essays, both new and old, often causes nostalgic moments, putting an author in a reflective frame of mind—recalling the occasions for which some essays were written, or the historical events that spurred them, or the seeming urgency of the political moment to which they responded. Even the new ones are freeze-frames, individual snapshots of a moving political target.

Some of these essays, those responses to then-urgent political moments, may feel utterly anachronistic in the current climate, while others might speak to these issues as they reshape themselves in the present environment. VMI and the Citadel may be coeducational now, but the struggle for women's equal inclusion continues in firehouses and locker rooms across the country (and, indeed, in public arenas around the world). Middle-aged middle-class men may not be trooping off to the woods to chant and drum, but the malaise and uncertainty among those same men has only deepened, fueled now by right-wing blather about how "they" have taken away "your" birthright. The movements of the extreme right have only been fueled by the election of our nation's first African American president, and his liberal policies on immigration, employment discrimination, health care, and human rights.

Of course, a collection of essays on similar themes is bound to run into some degree of repetition. After all, a formulation that seemed to work when describing one issue might seem to work just as well when I touched on that same issue a year later in another context. In those cases where the article was published elsewhere first, I've left those paragraphs untouched and beg the reader's indulgence.

As a whole, though, the book has a definable shape. Between the first essay and the last two essays in this book lie a series of works about what I think are political mistakes, missteps on the way to redefining manhood in an age characterized by greater gender equality than ever before in our history. Antifeminist rants, mythopoetic retreats, evangelically based political exclusion of gays and women in the guise of embracing a more masculine Jesus—all these represent evidence that the once-solid ground of American masculinity has been so definitely shaken that it now feels, to many, like quicksand.

Marx once wrote about the amazing ability of the bourgeoisie to revolutionize everything:

> Constant revolutionizing of production, uninterrupted disturbance of
> all social conditions, everlasting uncertainty and agitation distinguish
> the bourgeois epoch from all earlier ones. All fixed, fast-frozen relations,
> with their train of ancient and venerable prejudices and opinions are
> swept away, all new-formed ones become antiquated before they can
> ossify. All that is solid melts into air, all that is holy is profaned, and man
> is at last compelled to face with sober senses, his real conditions of life,
> and his relation with his kind.

The same could be said about gender relations. Women's increasing equality
has been dramatic—and has taken place unbelievably fast. It's shaken the foundations of traditional American masculinity—a masculinity rooted in easy
camaraderie among men who were similarly situated by class or race (that is,
the casual comforts of white working-class men) and whose sense of entitlement was unchallenged by women.

In less than half a century, women's entry into the labor force has shattered
previous myths about women's "natural" lack of ambition or professionalism.
Imagine if, in only half a century, the percentage of male secretaries or nurses
had gone from less than 10 percent to more than half. Wouldn't that be *the* story
of the year—in any year? Or if the most dramatic increase in any high school
extracurricular activity were among male cheerleaders? Would that not get a
mention on ESPN? (The most dramatic change in middle and high school in the
past three decades has been girls' participation in sports, which rivals only the
introductions of computers in transforming children's lives.)

It is not in the least Pollyanna-ish to remark about how dramatic and how
sudden this transformation has been. There is, of course, still a long way to go.
These days, for example, rape is defended not as men's prerogative but as the
expression of the accumulated force of evolutionary history to be reproductively
successful. The more equal women get, the more their opponents resort to biological bases for inequality; the more similar women and men are, the more
feminism's critics resort to "natural" differences. As "all that is solid melts into
air," there are many who seek to fabricate new solid forms or to provide old glue
to newly created sand.

Despite the increasingly shrill assertions that we are Martians and
Venusians, the evidence is overwhelming that here on planet Earth, women and
men are far more similar than they are different, and that the world is increasingly gender-integrated and gender-equal.

I argue that this is not only a good thing for women, but that it is good for
children, for men, and for society as a whole. Societies always benefit when all
citizens are freed up to contribute to the best of their abilities, unconstrained by

artificial barriers established by the frightened and the arrogant. Children of married heterosexual parents benefit from dual-career parents, just as they benefit from "dual-carer" parents. Mostly, children benefit from love and support—in whatever package it appears. Gay marriage, now inevitable, will be a boon for children as well as their parents. And the evidence is overwhelming that men will benefit from women's equality—not only materially, but psychologically and emotionally as well.

That aggregate empirical evidence is certainly echoed in my own life. I daily can only glimpse the myriad ways that my life is enriched by women's increasing equality—the pleasures of daily interaction with colleagues, friends, and family. My life would be immeasurably impoverished, its richness dramatically reduced, were we to return to some imagined time when people "knew their place," and were forced to conform to ideas that others had about their "natural" abilities.

My life has always been animated by those who don't know their place—by colleagues who stretch beyond the boundaries of traditional disciplinary research, by friends who push me beyond the comforts of conventional camaraderies and bonding, by a family that is both stable and secure and constantly full of surprises.

Many people were instrumental to my work: colleagues at Stony Brook, my family, and my friends. You know who you are.

I'm grateful to my editors at Rutgers University Press, Adi Hovav and Marlie Wasserman, for believing in the project and helping me see it through.

I would like to thank my many collaborators over the past decades: Yasemin Besen, Raewyn Connell, Diane Diamond, Abby Ferber, Jeff Hearn, Rachel Kalish, Michael Kaufman, Matt Mahler, Mike Messner, Rebecca Plante, Nancy Sacks, Kirby Schroeder, Tyson Smith, and Amy Traver.

For the past fifteen years, Amy Aronson has been the best collaborator, co-author, companion, and co-parent I could have ever imagined. She's lived through all these essays, logged countless hours talking about the political moments that gave rise to them, and wrote one of them with me. This book would not have been possible without her, nor, to be honest, would anything else. This one's for her.

MSK
Brooklyn, NY
August 2009

Introduction

Misframing Men

This past decade has witnessed an extraordinary transformation in men's lives. For decades, wave after wave of the women's movement, a movement that reshaped every aspect of American life, produced nary a ripple among men. But suddenly men are in the spotlight.

Yet the public discussions often seem strained, silly, and sometimes flat-out wrong. The spotlight itself seems to obscure as much as it illuminates. Old tired clichés about men's resistance to romantic commitment or reluctance to be led to the marriage altar seem perennially recyclable in advice books and on TV talk shows, but these days the laughter feels more forced and the defensiveness more pronounced. Pop biologists avoid careful confrontation with serious scientific research in their quest to find anatomical or evolutionary bases for promiscuity or porn addiction, hoping that by fiat, one can pronounce that "boys will be boys" and render it more than a flaccid tautology. And political pundits wring their hands about the feminization of American manhood, as if gender equality has neutered these formerly proud studs.

In the nearly four hundred interviews I did for my book *Guyland*, a study of young men aged sixteen to twenty-six, I found a post-adolescent, pre-adult generation drifting purposelessly, sometimes grasping frantically at a definition of manhood not its own. Many were prematurely disillusioned, dismissing any serious engagement with their lives with a smile and a shrug. "It's all good," they'd say. Directionless, many seemed agitated at the mere thought of constructing a life plan. "I feel like I just keep hitting the snooze button on my life," one twenty-four-year-old told me.

Others were willing to go to extraordinary lengths to prove they were real men. Driven less by a "Peter Pan syndrome" and more by a "Peter Panic syndrome," they took excessive risks, flirted with alcohol-inspired sexual predation, and suffered sadistic tortures hoping to have some nineteen-year-old validate their eighteen-year-old manhood. They follow their cruel masters like young puppies, desperately eager to please.

And still others hissed with a seething resentment against women's "invasion" of "their" space. Whether the board room or the locker room, the operating theater or the theater of military operations, women's entry has also provoked an angry backlash from some men. Once, it seemed to be so easy to find an arena in which to prove one's manhood. Look at the world portrayed by the hit TV show *Mad Men*—a world where men sustained a casual affability in their homosocially pure arenas, where women were secretarial playthings (or an occasional vixen who inherited daddy's money and power). Things were so much easier when women "knew their place" (reference to the civil rights movement intentional).

Buffeted by changes not of their making, increasingly anxious in an economic and political arena that erodes their ability to be breadwinners, and confused by new demands about emotional responsiveness and involved fatherhood, men seem uncomfortable in that new spotlight, shifting uncomfortably, shielding their eyes, even railing against the glare.

The source of this malaise—this range of emotions from anxiety to anger—is that we still don't really know how to talk about masculinity in the United States. And a major reason for that is that the issues are consistently misframed in the media. Sometimes, it is because boys and men are invisible, as when we read about "teen violence" or "urban violence" or "school violence." Exactly which gender are we talking about? (It's young boys who have been virtually all the gangbangers and school shooters. In fact, two variables—age and gender—predict the overwhelming majority of all violence in our society.)

Or when gender is visible—the "boy crisis" in schools, for example—we fret and are led astray by media pundits who want us to believe that the cause of this crisis is some feminist educational cabal that has destroyed the contemporary school system. That is, we're encouraged to see the boy crisis as the school's failure to acknowledge and minister to boys' "natural" propensity for rambunctious mischief, which simultaneously ignores all differences among boys—by race, or class, or ethnicity, for example—and ignores the way that masculinity, the meaning of manhood, is a driving force of this "crisis."

This is a book about why we keep getting it wrong.

Let me be clear at the outset: I don't think this is the result of any calculated plan, any conspiracy to misframe gender issues. Some of the misframings have been so deliciously mediagenic (hundreds of middle-aged, middle-class white men donning Native American "war paint" and drumming in the woods; hundreds of thousands of evangelical men worshiping in sports stadiums; Citadel cadets celebrating the withdrawal of the first female cadet after only a few days) that it would be hard for any media outlet to resist. If it feeds (our previously held stereotypes), it leads.

In other instances political pundits with an agenda have led us astray. Four decades of feminism has been accompanied by four decades of increasingly shrill (and increasingly loud) denunciations of feminists—from bra-burners to "feminazis." Gender equality, we've been told, is really bad for women, who lose themselves in that great big world, and can only find themselves as mothers, in the home, where they belong. Gender equality is even worse for children, who somehow get the misguided idea that women can do anything that men can do—including compete on an even playing field. But underneath this is the idea that gender equality is really, really bad for men. If women can both bring home the bacon and fry it up in the pan, what does that say about men, who have been sitting impatiently at the head of the table waiting for their dinner to be served on time?

The consequences of this misframing are especially important for young men, searching for ways to be men—grown-up, adult, responsible, and reliable—in an increasingly complex and equal world. Indeed, part of the reason the young men I interviewed seemed so clueless is precisely because of the increasing power of media images in constructing their ideas of what it means to be a man.

In childhood, we rely on adults to facilitate our socialization. The classic trinity of family, church, and school comprise the three great institutions of socialization, and the agents of that socialization, the people responsible, are parents, teachers, and religious figures. To the child, of course, this translates into grown-ups, grown-ups, and grown-ups.

By adolescence, and especially into young adulthood, the centrality of adults begins to wane, and media images and peer groups take their place as the primary forces of socialization. We can pretty much count on peer groups to get it wrong much of the time: it is those same-sex groups who often set the unrealistic standards against which our performance will be measured and judged, and our manhood credited. And it is through media images that we come to know what that performance is supposed to look like. Thus, misframing masculinity will continue to lead young men away from a confident, secure sense of themselves as men.

This book examines the framings—and misframings—of men in the public eye. Some of the essays are about actual movements among men—movements to restore a masculinity that is perceived to be damaged, or to retrieve a more vital and sacred sense of masculinity that has dissolved in the warm bath of consumerism that daily washes over us. Others are movements only of words, rhetorical debates and battles over turfs in the public arena, such as schools, or debates about how to understand masculinity.

Some are composed of earnest and sincere men, and women, searching for a way to re-anchor manhood after its perceived unmooring in the modern world. Today there are social movements organized to enable men to retrieve or restore a lost sense of masculinity, or to enable men to experience fuller, richer, and happier lives. There are movements for men's rights, fathers' rights, for increased awareness of health issues or of violence. Other perspectives are offered by people who are less than sincere, wailing like sirens, hoping to lure well-intentioned vessels to their doom. Whether symbolic or real, these struggles are indeed struggles for the hearts of men.

IN ONE RESPECT, we have Anita Hill to thank for the new visibility of masculinity. Nearly two decades ago, in 1991, the confirmation hearings for Clarence Thomas's nomination to the Supreme Court brought to national attention Hill's startling revelation about her experience working with Thomas at the EEOC. (Evidence of a profound shift in our cultural understanding of masculinity may be seen in the dramatic shift in the polls about that event. In 1991, over two-thirds of Americans believed Thomas; today, less than one-fourth does.) Revelations about sexual harassment quickly proliferated—from Tailhook parties at the well-named Aberdeen Proving Ground to Senator Robert Packwood, President Bill Clinton, and a host of others. So too did accusations of date and acquaintance rape against Mike Tyson, William Kennedy Smith, Kobe Bryant, and a seemingly endless parade of potential perps. The efforts to "save the males" from feminine invasion at the Citadel and VMI ended with a Supreme Court decision in 1996. The national nail-biting over the perils of fatherlessness (and single-parent families) resulted in an avalanche of misguided books extolling the virtues of fatherhood and blaming feminist women for keeping fathers from their children; what's more, these books became the basis for equally misguided public policy in the George W. Bush administration.

As the debate about men behaving badly played out in the 1990s, there were plenty of books, both scholarly and popular, that addressed these emerging issues. From 1991, with Robert Bly's *Iron John* and Sam Keen's *Fire in the Belly*, through Susan Faludi's *Stiffed*, best-selling authors have chronicled a deep male malaise. William Pollack's *Real Boys* (and the subsequent cottage industry of "real boy" books) and *Raising Cain*, by Dan Kindlon and Michael Thompson, have chronicled the spread of this masculine discontent into the lives of boys, and encouraged society to pay more attention to boys' cries for help.

On the other side of the political ledger, David Blankenhorn's *Fatherless America* and David Popenoe's *Life Without Father* spoke not of men's needs but of society's needs for men's presence in the lives of their children. Christina Hoff Sommers's much-discussed book *The War against Boys* argued that it was not a problematic masculinity that was destroying boys' lives, but "misguided feminism" that was making it impossible for boys to be, well, boys.

By the turn of the new century, masculinity was on parade everywhere one looked, especially in the media. From the relentlessly and unapologetically sexist *The Man Show* and scores of magazines like *Maxim* and *Details*, to movies in which young children humanize stoic men (including Tom Cruise, John Cusack, and The Rock) into emotionally available—and happier—men, to the more consciously gender-bending TV shows *Boy Meets Boy* and *Queer Eye for the Straight Guy*, masculinity has been paraded before us, consciously and intentionally, as perhaps never before.

It's interesting, too, that the increased visibility of defensively unapologetic white men has been paralleled by the increased visibility of gay men—especially white urban gay men. The Supreme Court ruled that what gay people do in the privacy of their own homes is no longer subject to "the brooding interference of the state," in Thurgood Marshall's felicitous phrase. The stolid Episcopal Church has ordained its first openly gay bishop. Gay marriage is on the ascendancy—and will be legal in all fifty states by the time my ten-year-old son reaches his fiftieth birthday. (How's that for predictive social science?) Suddenly, it's almost cool to be gay.

This new visibility does have its downside—the effacement of lesbians and gay men of color, for example. But it also indicates some erosion of the homophobic edifice that serves as the foundation of heterosexual masculinity. Some of the most notable inroads have been in the media representations of gay men. By far the most mesmerizing cultural expression was the surprise hit TV show *Queer Eye for the Straight Guy*. This show revolves around the "Fab Five"—five clever, campy, and culturally sophisticated gay men—who select a forlorn, clueless, disheveled, straight guy and give him (and his apartment) a total makeover. Each of the five has a specialty: food and wine, home décor, hair styles, clothing, and interpersonal manners. And each works his transformative magic with wit and flair.

Further, while straight guys are being made over in *Queer Eye*, or reinvented as "metrosexuals," so too are entire television networks. TNN reinvented itself as "Spike TV—The First Network for Men," filled with extreme sports, adult-themed cartoons like *Striperella* (featuring the voice of Pamela Anderson), pro wrestling, and some can't-miss reruns of Chuck Norris and other action stars. Just in case all those sports channels, news shows with angry kvetching white men, and local access porn channels—heck, just in case domination of virtually every television network but Lifetime, Oxygen, and WE—wasn't enough.

As the new millennium dawned, it seemed that this angry white male was riding rather high in the saddle, reassured of his dominance after decades of assault by feminists, gay liberationists, affirmative actionists, and liberal academics. "Men Are Back" shouted more than one editorial page (and whispered several women's voices in ad campaigns for men's cosmetic products). All that defensive defiance is actually a pretty good marker of just how far we've come. It's often less the triumph of untrammeled traditional masculinity, and more the grumpy retreat to his "lair" (aka the den, garage, basement, or workshop), where he can have a few beers with the boys, belch and fart, make fun of women and gay men—in other words, have a few moments of solace from the increasing *equality* that is the dominant feature of his life. It's hardly the rage of reactionaries; it's more the resigned howl that signals eventual accommodation. The beast is slouching toward Bethlehem, all right, but he still wants to put his feet up on the coffee table and control the remote along the way.

Then came 9/11, and everything seemed to change. Again.

IN THE NEAR-DECADE SINCE 9/11, this "new-old," traditionally heroic and unapologetic masculinity has been on constant view. So insistent has been this effort to trumpet the return of the old heroic manhood—and the concomitant effort to return women to their "rightful" place in the home, from soccer moms and career gals to security moms swooning over the firefighters' biceps—that Susan Faludi made this strange cultural turn the foundation of her book *The Terror Dream* (2007).

It's often hard to remember the debates and issues before 9/11 because that moment has indelibly transformed the background against which gender is played out. On September 10, 2001, you may recall, firefighters, police officers, and soldiers represented some of the last remaining resisters of gender equality. Firehouses especially were bastions of men behaving badly, citadels of unreconstructed chauvinism. Photos of the fire department's graduating class every year looked more like the graduating class at the Citadel in 1964. In New York, as of 2001, less than one quarter of 1 percent of the city's twelve thousand firefighters was female. Statistically, that's two out of every thousand firefighters. In reality, it's fewer than thirty women. Between 1982 and 1992, the FDNY hired no women at all. (In addition, less than 3 percent of firefighters in New York City are black and 4.4 percent are Hispanic, according to the Vulcan Society, an organization devoted to promoting the interests of African American firefighters.) New York City still has the whitest and most male firefighting force in any major city in the country. How had New York City's fire department come to resemble a southern military school on the eve of integration?

On September 10, 2001, recall, firefighters weren't necessarily the bad guys—one always distinguishes between the actual individual firefighters and the structure of their organization—but they were hardly the swoon-at-their-feet heroes they were on September 12. And the organization was getting a lot of heat for their racial and gender composition.

On the other side of the class divide, the newly installed global hegemonic image of masculinity was still riding high. This despite the bursting of the dot-com bubble, the economic plunge into recession, and the complicity of some of its most prominent high flyers in corporate scandals the scale of which makes Teapot Dome look increasingly like a tempest in a teapot.

The events since 9/11 reversed the fortunes of both images of masculinity. The rehabilitation of heroic masculinity among firefighters, police, and other rescue workers was immediate. Let me be clear: I share in the reverence for those people who were willing to run into burning and collapsing skyscrapers to save others. They did behave heroically. But heroic actions in one arena should not blind us to unheroic behavior in other arenas. Despite those few writers and pundits who managed to notice that there were female firefighters, police, and rescue workers among the heroes of 9/11, the media trumpeted the revival of traditional masculinity. Real men were back—and we were told we were safer for it.

The global business class didn't fare so well either. No sooner did he stop reeling from the bursting dot-com bubble, globalization's well-dressed *Homo economicus* was pushed aside by the reemergence of *Homo Reaganomicus*—the recharged militarized masculinity of the Bush-Cheney years that proudly proclaims the United States not only as the world's only true superpower, but the axis of an emerging global empire, beholden and accountable to no one.

By the end of the first decade of the twenty-first century, Wall Street seemed to be in full retreat, an example of what can go wrong with uncontrolled corporate masculinity. The current economic crisis is the fruition of that failed notion of masculinity—a masculinity embodied by Ponzi schemers, corporate and legal frauds, and hedge fund racketeers.

Pity, then, the global entrepreneur, whose masculinity quotient has tumbled with the NASDAQ. He's still connected to transnational institutions like the global marketplace, the European Union, and the United Nations. He's a slave to the fashion designers of "Old Europe" (Rumsfeld's term for those EU nations who had the temerity to oppose the U.S. invasion of Iraq). Hey, he may even speak French.

The new American unilateralism, embodied by Bush and his senior advisers, was pitted against Old Europe's reliance on cooperative institutions and its promotion of social welfare and peace. How backward! And for a while it seemed to work. *New York Times* columnist Maureen Dowd noted that initially many women found George W. Bush's frat boy, know-it-all snicker sexier than Bill Clinton's grasp of both foreign policy and female body parts. It was tragically ironic that the idealization of military masculinity of the Bush years, coupled with the post-9/11 canonization of firefighters and police, led to the reassertion of traditional gender ideologies—in the very country that was attacked by those who found our gender ideologies too liberal and sought to impose even more traditional policies.

Much of this new visibility was defensive, some even angry. Even the late Norman Mailer weighed in on the decline of the American white male—not his actual decline, of course, but the fact that he *feels* that he's been displaced from the epicenter of American life. Mailer interpreted the rush to war and embrace of President Bush (and Donald Rumsfeld) as masculine icons in the post-9/11 era as the triumph of this masculine ressentiment.

George W. Bush was, for a time, the front-man for this new masculinity, in his photo-op flight suit proclaiming "Mission Accomplished" to the seemingly endless Iraq war. But Donald Rumsfeld was its real poster boy. The Republican hawks, like Cheney, Bush, and Paul Wolfowitz, who had collectively logged not one nanosecond in actual battle, swaggered after Rumsfeld, the nerdy warmonger whom *People* magazine called one of the "sexiest Americans alive."

With testosterone-drenched rhetoric, American policymakers strutted like bullies through the halls of the middle school—pushing inferior wimps out of the way, flouting the law and ignoring the fact that no one especially liked them, defying teachers and daring the principal to do something about it. One senior official made clear that masculinity was entirely wrapped up in this ever-escalating military escapade. "Anyone can go to Baghdad," he said. "Real men go to Tehran."

While it may be premature to fully assess whether the United States' "first feminist president" (as *Ms.* magazine dubbed Barack Obama) will embody a new media image of masculinity, the signs are indeed promising. Multilateralist foreign policy replaces unilateral bullying. Evenhanded judiciousness replaces swaggering, snickering smugness. And as a model of manhood, the happily married egalitarian husbands and involved and expressive fathers that are the current president and vice president may augur a new vision of manhood that may ripple through the culture.

THE FIRST SECTION OF THIS BOOK, "Reframings," explores some of the structural and cultural bases for the current misframing. Each essay addresses a different theme. The first outlines men's different responses to the current economic downturn. A second, shorter magazine article adds to this portrait of media-created masculinity, examining how "bad" men are transformed into "good" men in some recent films. A third essay explores some of the false framings that enable white men to avoid seriously confronting racism, false modes of "racial healing" that don't require any serious engagement with racial inequality.

The second section, "Reversals," begins with the carefully constructed and orchestrated assault on feminism that has been part of the right wing's ideological offensive over the past two decades and a constant source of inspiration for resurgent reactionary masculinity. Only a decade ago, being an "angry white man" was seen as a pathetic posture of false victimhood; now, it's worn almost as a badge of honor. Almost everywhere one looks, men are trumpeted as the new victims of feminism run amok, the new "second sex."

Several essays included here respond to this new, and I believe, false compassion for men as the new victims. (Real victims of all inequality deserve compassion, but I believe that those who shed the biggest crocodile tears for these men are less concerned with their actual lives and more concerned with scoring points against some fantasy of feminism.) This false compassion is often expressed as a sort of tit-for-tat equivalence, as if girls and women have made enormous strides in achieving equality, but only at the expense of men.

According to these critics, feminist women have twisted the facts, overstated their case, and in the process tainted men as irredeemably bad and ignored the ways in which men are themselves victims.

I begin the section with an essay taking on the growing group of feminist haters whom I call the "real" male bashers. This piece takes on evolutionary psychology and the new biologism, John Gray's and Dr. Laura's pop psychology, and some of the latest round of "boy" promoters. If you look closely at what they actually say, I believe you'll agree that feminists aren't the male bashers, but rather that those who accuse them of being anti-male have some of the most vile and negative impressions of masculinity currently on offer. According to them, men are biologically driven, violent, rapacious beasts, uncommunicative sexual predators for whom rape is synonymous with "dating etiquette" and fatherhood just another word for "absentee landlord." While they've been relatively successful in vilifying feminist women as "man haters," it's really the anti-feminists who hate men.

This sets up the next chapter, which addresses the current debate about boys directly. "A War against Boys?" examines the claims made by those who would now rescue boys from the "misandrous" reforms initiated by feminism—as if growing numbers of self-confident, assertive, and athletic girls could be anything but wonderful for boys to be around! (What could be better, after all, for guys who are themselves secure and confident to be met by girls who are their equals?)

In "'Gender Symmetry' in Domestic Violence," I address another arena in which men claim to be the "real" or the "new" victims—the gender symmetry arguments that women hit men as often as men hit women. It turns out that none of these studies is based on nationally representative samples of women and men, both in intact marriages or cohabiting as well as once-married or cohabiting, including all forms of assault (e.g., sexual assault). Political assertions of "gender symmetry" seem to be motivated far less by compassion for battered men than from rage at the worldwide struggle for gender equality. It's as if they believe that compassion is a zero-sum game, and any expression of compassion for women who are battered would somehow mean that we would be less compassionate about men. (Compassion is just as likely to be mutually reinforcing, since witnessing the pain and horror of violence to one person should make us more sensitive to the pains of others.)

Of course, we need to be compassionate toward all victims of domestic violence. Personally, my compassion for those women whose lives have been torn apart by domestic violence has made me more, not less, compassionate toward those few men who have also been victimized. Even if the "gender symmetry" advocates were right, the only logical response would be to dramatically increase funding for domestic violence prevention and intervention. None of them suggests that the number of women who are battered is too low, only that the number of men is equal to it. Why don't they argue that public funding should be doubled?

The book's third section, "Restorations," looks at various responses to the increased problematization of masculinities that has taken place over the past decade. Masculinity has become the foundation for a variety of political movements and organizations, and the basis for social action, as men seek to "restore"—retrieve, reassert—a masculinity that has become increasingly troubled.

The first essay in this section looks at the constellation of adolescent masculinity, gay baiting, and bullying in the various tragic, random U.S. school shootings since 1992. I argue that these shootings were about restoring masculinity, but that they came not only from a place of humiliation, but also from what I call "aggrieved entitlement"—that it is only boys, after all, who think that when they have been put down and harassed they have the right (if not the obligation) to make others pay. Many of the essays in this section examine political movements designed to restore masculinity to its "rightful" place as both the dominant sex and the unexamined, invisible norm against which all "others" are measured.

Another article examines the efforts by working-class white men to restore their sense of masculinity by participating in movements on the extreme right. I have interviewed nearly one hundred white supremacists, Aryan youth, skinheads, and neo-Nazis in the United States and Scandinavia, and have examined the gender politics of both the Oklahoma City bombing in 1995 and the 9/11 attack as expressions of that restoration. I include two articles about the VMI and Citadel cases, legal challenges to all-male admissions policies that went all the way to the Supreme Court. (I served as an expert witness in those cases.)

I also look at one of those organizations and movements of men that emerged in the 1990s, movements that were about retreat from engagement with politics as a way to retrieve a resonant spiritual masculinity that was submerged in the mire of consumerism. During the 1990s, I went to Promise Keeper rallies and mythopoetic men's retreats in an effort to understand their celebration of what Walt Whitman called "the manly love of comrades." I also debated with Robert Bly and other mythopoetic leaders, confronted Promise Keeper founder Bill McCartney about homophobia, and argued endlessly with proponents of men's rights. I include one essay that was a result of this search.

THERE ARE, HAPPILY, SIGNS OF CHANGE. The decline of homophobia, especially among young people, is both statistical and real. And increasingly, there are groups of young men who are the sons of feminist mothers, friends with feminist women, students of feminist professors, who understand that gender equality is not some form of politically correct brainwashing but actually a blueprint for a more resonant manhood—a manhood of involved fatherhood, loving friendships, and passionately equal relationships.

On many campuses today, there are groups called "Men Against Violence" or "Men Against Rape." White Ribbon Campaigns have spread from Canada to more than twenty countries and nearly one hundred campuses in North America. All around the world, men have begun to organize around issues of men's violence against women. The essays in the final section of the book address these changes, proposing, endorsing, and promoting a response by men that embraces gender equality.

Being pro-feminist has been an unsteady and unstable home for my political activism for the past thirty years. It's been unsteady and unstable because to organize men against sexism is to work against interests, at least as those interests have been typically defined. If men benefit so significantly from gender inequality, and in such myriad invisible ways, why would men take up the struggle to challenge it?

Part of that answer relies on the ethical imperative: gender equality is a movement for equality, and equality is good, just, fair, right, and moral. So, to the extent that men would strive to live up to those principles, men would support gender equality. This usually has as much resonance with American men as my grandmother's admonitions to finish my dinner because people were starving in Europe. Why should we share, when it's so much better to have more?

When men do embrace the ethical imperative, it's more out of a politics of guilt than a desire to do the right thing. And privileged men, straight and white, wracked by guilt, do not necessarily make great political allies. Often, there's some self-hatred projected into a politicized hatred of men and masculinity. Some men refuse to take up space, to assert themselves, for fear of being sexist. The drive for self-purification, to make ourselves worthy, may be noble in intent, but it often creates a politics of self-negation that is relentless and merciless in its denunciation of one's allies.

In the final essays, then, I suggest that the time has come for men to support gender equality. It's in our interests. Transforming masculinity will enrich our lives immeasurably, deepening our capacity for intimacy with women, other men, and children, and expanding our emotional repertoire, enabling us to be the kinds of fathers, friends, lovers, husbands, and partners that we once only dreamed we could be.

PART ONE

Reframings

1

Has "A Man's World" Become "A Woman's Nation"?

Men's Responses to Women's Increased Equality in the Twenty-first Century

"This is a man's world," sang James Brown in 1964, with a voice both defiantly assertive and painfully anguished. He starts off proudly, with a litany of men's accomplishments: men made the cars, the trains, the electric lights, and the boats that carried the loads and took us out of the dark. Men even made the toys that children play with. But lest he encourage a bit of smug self-satisfaction, Brown changes course at the end of the song. "But it would be nothing . . . without a woman or a girl." Without women, Brown ends, men are "lost in the wilderness . . . lost in the bitterness . . . lost, lost," his voice trailing off in both confusion and despair.

This essay is about that wilderness forty-five years later—a wilderness in which some men today are lost, others bitter, and still others searching for new forms of masculinity amid what they believe is the excessive feminization of American society and culture—not because of the absence of women in their lives that Brown noticed but rather, ironically, because of their increased presence. At work and at home, in private and in public, women's increasing equality has been an issue to which men have had to respond. How have men responded? While some have noisily and bitterly protested, and some continue to fight a rear-guard action to undo women's gains, most American men have simply continued to go about their lives, falling somewhere between eager embrace of women's equality and resigned acceptance.

Across the globe, of course, it still is pretty much a man's world. Men still control the overwhelming majority of the world's material, social, and cultural resources. Still, the massive changes in both economic and social life and the

This chapter is a revised version of an essay originally published in *The Shriver Report: A Woman's Nation Changes Everything*, edited by Heather Boushey and Ann O'Leary. Washington, DC: Center for American Progress, 2009.

status of women around the world have eroded the easy assumption that it was and would always be a man's world.

So if, as this essay's title suggests, the United States is becoming "a woman's nation," then as women's equality proceeds, as more and more married couples are both working full-time, what has happened to men? How are men responding to women's increased equality? In this essay, I'll argue that even if the United States is not quite yet "a woman's nation," it is just as surely no longer only a man's world.

Declaring America to be "a woman's nation," while deliberately provocative, does underscore a significant trend of the gradual, undeniable, and irreversible increase in gender equality in every arena of American life—from the public sector (economic life, politics, the military) to private life (work-family balance, marital contracts, sexuality). Women have successfully entered every arena of public life, and today many women are as comfortable in the corporate board room, the athletic playing field, the legal and medical professions, and the theater of military operations as previous generations of women might have been in the kitchen.

And they've done it amazingly fast. It is within the last half-century that the workplace has been so dramatically transformed that the working world depicted in the hit TV show *Mad Men* looks so anachronistic as to be nearly unrecognizable. For both women and men, these dramatic changes have come at such a dizzying pace that many Americans are searching for the firmer footing of what they imagine was a simpler time, a bygone era in which everyone knew their place.

The transformation of American public life announced by these changes in women's lives has, of course, had a profound impact on the lives of American men—whether or not they recognize it. Indeed, these changes have reverberated to the core of American manhood. Some of the responses received disproportionate media coverage than their number might have warranted. But a guy changing a diaper or drying a dish is far less mediagenic than a bunch of Wall Street bankers drumming as they bond around a bonfire, or some enraged divorced dad dressed up as Batman and scaling some state capitol building to promote "fathers' rights." I'll try to map a range of men's responses, but the evidence is clear that most American men are quietly and apolitically acquiescing to these changes.

The Foundations of Masculine Identity
Have Been Shaken, Not Stirred

Since the country's founding, American men have felt a need to prove their manhood. For well over a century, it's been in the public sphere, and especially the workplace, that American men have been tested. A man may be physically strong, or not. He may be intellectually or athletically gifted, or not. But the one thing that has been non-negotiable has been that a real man provides for his family. He is a breadwinner.[1]

A man who is not a provider—well, he doesn't feel like much of a man at all. Two general trends—structural and social—define the dramatic erosion of the foundation of that public arena for men, leading some men to their current malaise and confusion over the meaning of manhood. James Brown may have been right in 1964 that men made the boats, trains, cars, and electric lights. But the dramatic structural shifts that have accompanied globalization mean that there are very few cars, boats, trains—and even toys—being made domestically any longer.

In the past three decades, it has been manufacturing jobs that have been hardest hit, as layoffs in the steel, automobile, and other brick-and-mortar industries have downsized, outsourced, cut back, laid off, and closed. Add to that the gradual erosion of our social safety net (health insurance, medical benefits, retirement and pension accounts, Social Security) instituted by the New Deal and we are now living now in a new era of "social insecurity." Even Norman Mailer in 2003 noticed that men had been taking a "daily drubbing" in the economy, and that "the good average white American male has had very little to nourish his morale since the job market went bad."[2] As one sixty-two-year-old machinist told a journalist, "we went to lunch and our jobs went to China."[3]

This decline in manufacturing has been precipitous—and permanent. "The foreman says these jobs are going, boy, and they ain't coming back," sang Bruce Springsteen in "My Hometown"—a 1985 tune that resonates even more today as the Great Recession bleeds even more manufacturing jobs out of the U.S. workforce. Even in economic recovery, as President Barack Obama observed, these jobs "will constitute a smaller percentage of the overall economy," so that, as a result, "women are just as likely to be the primary bread earner, if not more likely, than men are today."[4]

If women's entry into the labor force stirred up men's ability to anchor their identity as family provider, women's emergence as primary breadwinner is a seismic shift, shaking some men's identity to its foundation.

My father tells me that when he was in college, he and his friends would occasionally pose this question to each other: "Will you let your wife work?" And, he tells me, they all answered it in pretty much the same way: "She shouldn't have to work. I should be able to support my family all by myself."

Today, among my male students, the question itself is meaningless. They expect their wives to work, and certainly do not expect that they will be asked to grant permission for their wives to do so. They expect to be part of a two-career couple, for financial, if not political reasons.

Couple this with the equally seismic shift in the structure of the workplace and we see a major reason why many contemporary observers see a "crisis" of masculinity—a general confusion and malaise about the meaning of manhood. The very foundations on which masculinity has historically rested have eroded; the entire edifice seems capable of collapse at any moment. Or so it seems to a variety of men who rail against our changing society.

"Lost in the Bitterness": The Defensive Resistance of Men's Rights

To some men, women's entry into the public arena is experienced not as "entry" but as "invasion." The men who today oppose women's entry into firehouses and police stations, military combat units and corporate boardrooms, echo those who opposed their entry into The Citadel and the Virginia Military Institute, the Augusta Country Club, and the locker room a decade ago—men who themselves echo those who opposed women's right to vote, join a union, serve on a jury, drive a car, or enter the workforce a century ago.

Demographically, they range from younger working-class guys—firefighters and factory workers who sense greater competition for jobs—to middle-class, middle-aged corporate types, who believe that the policies of women's entry (affirmative action, an end to wage discrimination, comparable worth) hurt them. Both groups mourn the loss of the casual locker-room frivolity that marked the all-male workplace, and are afraid of, and angry about, sexual harassment guidelines, which they regard as the Politically Correct police.

There have always been men who have opposed women's equality in the public sphere. Historically, that opposition came in the guise of a sort of chivalrous protectionism: Women were so frail, so delicate, that the entry into the voting booth, or the workplace, would damage these fragile physical specimens beyond repair. Women were not to be "excluded" from the public sphere as much as they were to be "exempted from certain things which men must endure," as the Rev. John Todd put it when he opposed woman suffrage in 1848. Men should soldier on, sacrificing for their families. Women shouldn't have to.

Men who oppose women's equality today often express a *defensive resistance*. They're less interested in protecting women's biological fragility, and more interested in preserving those arenas as all-male havens. Women, we might be told, are not qualified for the positions they seek; they are not strong enough, not tough enough, not (fill in the blank) enough to make the grade. This defensive resistance lies close to the surface; a gentle scratch can elicit a furious response. "I will have none of the nonsense about oppressed and victimized women; no responsibility for the condition of women . . . none of the guilt or self-loathing that is traditionally used to keep men functioning in harness," fulminates Richard Haddad, a champion of men's rights.[5]

While researching my recent book, *Guyland*, I happened on a Brooklyn bar that has been home to generations of firefighters and their pals. There's an easy ambience about the place, the comfort of younger and older guys (all white) sharing a beer and shooting the breeze. Until I happen to ask one guy about female firefighters. The atmosphere turns menacing, and a defensive anger spills out of the guys near me. "Those bitches have taken over," says Patrick.

> They're everywhere. You know that ad "it's everywhere you want to be." That's like women. *They're* everywhere *they* want to be! There's nowhere you can go anymore—factories, beer joints, military, even the goddamned firehouse! [Raucous agreement all around.] We working guys are just fucked.[6]

Not long ago, I appeared on a television talk show opposite three such "angry white males" who felt they had been the victims of workplace discrimination. They were in their late twenties and early thirties. The show's title, no doubt to entice a large potential audience, was "A Black Woman Stole My Job." All of the men described how they were passed over for jobs or promotions for which they believed themselves qualified.

Then it was my turn to respond. I said I had one question about one word in the title of the show. I asked them about the word "my." Where did they get the idea it was "their" job? Why wasn't the show called "A Black Woman Got *a* Job" or "A Black Woman Got *the* Job"? These men felt the job was "theirs" because they felt entitled to it, and when some "other" person (a black, female) got the job, that person was really taking what was "rightfully" theirs. (As is apparent, then, most anti-feminist sentiment comes from white guys, guys who expected those positions, and saw them as "theirs.")

In a column in the *New York Times*, Anna Quindlen reported the comments of a young man she interviewed. "It seems like if you're a white male you don't have a chance," he observed—even though he attended a college where only 5 percent of his classmates were black. "What the kid really meant is that he no longer has the edge," she wrote about the encounter,

> that the rules of a system that may have served his father will have changed. It is one of those good-old-days constructs to believe it was a system based purely on merit, but we know that's not true. It is a system that once favored him, and others like him. Now sometimes—just sometimes—it favors someone different.[7]

That sense of entitlement—and entitlement thwarted—is what lies beneath the surface of much of men's resistance to women's equality. These men employ what we might call a "wind chill" theory of gender politics—it doesn't matter what the temperature actually is; it matters only how it feels. Gender equality is felt to be a zero-sum game: if women win, men lose. And, to hear them tell it, men are losing.

But they rarely "tell it." Usually they scream about it. Just flip on virtually any talk radio station in America and listen in to the callers as they rail against a system that no longer favors them. Eavesdrop on the myriad "men's rights" groups that advocate for men as the new victims of reverse discrimination. Or tune into sports radio, the most gender-specific spot on your radio dial.

As women have raced onto the athletic field in record numbers, some men have run off into sports talk. Once the domain of real men—indeed, sports were prescribed to pump up the manhood of an increasingly feminized nation at the turn of the twentieth century—the participation of women and girls in sports is one of our era's most significant gender transformations. In 1971, fewer than 300,000 high school girls played interscholastic sports, compared with 3.7 million boys. By 2005, the participation of boys had increased by about half a million, but girls' participation had soared to 2.9 million. But though women may play sports, they don't tend to spend much time talking about them.

Sports talk radio often expresses the defensive male bonding that lies just below the surface of the easy camaraderie of that imaginative locker room. Here's how one regular listener explained it to communications scholar David Nylund:

> It's a male-bonding thing, a locker room for guys in the radio. You can't do it at work, everything's PC now! So the Rome Show [Jim Rome is the most famous sports talk radio personality] is a last refuge for men to bond and be men. . . . I listen in the car and can let the maleness come out. I know it's offensive sometimes . . . but men need that![8]

As the title of former Stanford basketball player Mariah Burton Nelson's book so pithily put it: "the stronger women get, the more men love football."

Sometimes, it leads to some dizzying reversals of both conventional wisdom and common sense. Are feminists concerned about domestic violence? Proclaim "gender symmetry"—and argue that women hit men as much as men hit women. Women concerned about sexual assault? "The way young women dress in the spring constitutes a sexual assault upon every male within eyesight of them," wrote one retired professor. Women seek to protect their right to choose? Attempt to establish a "man's right to choose"—and to prevent a woman from aborting "his" child, while ignoring any responsibility for the child once born. Women in the workplace campaigning against wage discrimination or sexual harassment? Insist that the wage gap favors women and that sexual harassment is actually an expression of women's sexual power; when the male boss wants his female employee, it "undermines the ability of the employer to establish boundaries because the employer often feels needy of the employee."[9]

This anti-feminist political agenda is best, and most simply, made by Harvard political scientist Harvey Mansfield, in an op-ed essay in the *Wall Street Journal*. "The protective element of manliness is endangered by women having equal access to jobs outside the home," he writes. "Women who do not consider themselves feminist often seem unaware of what they are doing to manliness when they work to support themselves. They think only that people should be hired and promoted on merit, regardless of sex."[10]

While it can't be true that only feminists actually believe in meritocracy, some who would support men evidently want to keep that playing field as uneven as possible. That's certainly what groups such as the National Organization for Men, Men's Rights International, and others seek as they organize men around perceived injustices against men by the feminist cabal that supposedly now rules Washington.

One recent case is particularly representative. In 2008, New York City attorney Roy Den Hollander brought a suit against Columbia University, alleging that its Women's Studies program discriminated against men, and that teaching feminism, a "religion," violated the constitutionally protected separation of church and state. (He had earlier brought a suit against nightclubs for favoring women with "ladies' nights.") Judges threw out both cases as utterly without merit.

And that's the point, Hollander argues. Of course those feminist-inspired judges—one was a woman!—wouldn't hear his case. "Feminazis have infiltrated institutions, and there's been a transfer of rights from guys to girls."[11] In the eyes of these anti-feminist men's rights groups, James Brown was dead wrong. It's no longer "a man's world." They share the perception that America has become a "woman's nation." And, in their view, it's time to take it back.

"Lost in the Wilderness": Masculinist Retreat

To other men, women's increased empowerment only highlights the loss of masculine vigor among American men. Their response is not to attempt to roll back women's gains but rather to return to a nostalgic notion of masculinity, one rooted in ostensibly natural, primal, sacred, or mythic qualities. If women have indeed invaded all the previously all-male institutions, men need to find, as Virginia Woolf might have put it, "a room of their own"—an all-male space where men can relax with other men, free from the constant policing that accompanies political correctness, and retrieve their inner sense of their own masculinity, in the presence of other men. For these "masculinists," gender politics are a project of reclamation, restoration, and retrieval—not of some lost power over women, but of a lost sense of internal efficacy and sense of power.

In the last decades of the twentieth century, thousands of middle-aged, middle-class white men found themselves literally "lost in the wilderness" as they trooped off dutifully on what were called "mythopoetic" retreats with poets such as Robert Bly and storytellers such as Michael Meade. These "weekend warriors" sensed that men had lost their vitality, their distinctively male energy in a world of alienating office cubicles, yucky diaper-changing, and sappy date movies.

For masculinists, power is not about economic or political aggregates or different groups' access to resources. Nor is it to be measured by comparing wages or representatives on corporate boards or legislative houses. Rather, power is an interior experience, a sense of dynamic energy. As a result, they tend not to engage with policy initiatives designed to push women back. At their best, they are indifferent to women's collective experience; they may even take inspiration from women's empowerment. They seek instead to combat their sense of emasculation not with impotent rage against feminized institutions, but rather by restoring their sense of power in reclaiming masculine myths.

Other guys find that lost all-male Eden in cyberspace. While cinematic and pornographic fantasies of men's power have long been with us, the proliferation of video and computer games in which avatars wreak havoc on women, gays, and other "others" is still somewhat shocking. For significant numbers of younger men, remote corners of cyberspace have become the newest incarnation of the Little Rascals' "He-Man Woman Haters Club," the tree house with the sign that says "No Gurls Allowed."

These types of masculinists tend to rely on archaic notions of the essential, natural, and binary masculine and feminine. As a result, they may become momentarily enamored with anti-feminist policy initiatives, such as the re-segregation of schools into single-sex classes, ostensibly to promote boys' engagement with education, but often to set back decades of feminist efforts to make classrooms and athletic fields more equal. (These anti-feminists are not to be confused with those popular voices in minority communities [backed by many policy analysts] who are engaged with the crisis facing many *minority* boys in school, which is both real and serious.) For these mostly white masculinists, their zeal to support fathers' connection with family life and especially with the experience of fatherhood often draws them into "angry dad" campaigns against custody or divorce laws, in which men are said to be the victims of reverse discrimination.

Among the most interesting arenas of contemporary masculinism, however, are some of America's churches. In part, this is fueled by a well-known gender disparity in church attendance and religiosity. Simply put, women are more religious, both in thought and in practice, than men. According to some, American Protestantism needs to be re-masculinized.

This has a long history in the United States. In the middle of the nineteenth century, one observer commented he had never seen a country "where religion had so strong a hold upon the women or a slighter hold upon the men" than the United States. By the turn of the twentieth century, Protestant ministers worried that religion had become a women's domain, that the sentimental piety and sanctimonious moralism were well-suited for female churchgoers. "Have we a Religion for men?" asked one disgruntled guy.[12]

His prayers were quickly answered. A new movement was born: Muscular Christianity, designed to revirilize the image of Jesus and thus to masculinize the Church. Jesus was "no doughfaced, lick-spittle proposition," proclaimed evangelist Billy Sunday, but "the greatest scrapper who ever lived." Books such as *The Manhood of the Master* (1913), *The Manliness of Christ* (1900), and *The Manly Christ* (1904) all sought to refashion Jesus as more Hans and Franz than girly-man.

All-male revivals celebrated Jesus as he-man with colorful language and spirited services. Sunday proclaimed that mainstream ministers had become "pretentious, pliable mental perverts." "Lord save us from off-handed, flabby cheeked, brittle-boned, weak-kneed, thin-skinned, pliable, plastic, spineless, effeminate, ossified three-karat Christianity!" Sunday thundered in "The Fighting Saint," his most famous sermon. "Don't tell me about the peaceful gentle Jesus!"[13]

As then, now. "Christ wasn't effeminate," grumped Jerry Falwell. "The man who lived on this earth was a man with muscles . . . Christ was a he-man!"[14] The most visible of these renewed revirilization efforts has been the Promise Keepers, who held massive 50,000-to-75,000-attendee men-only rallies in sports stadiums (because it was where men felt comfortable gathering), with ministers (called coaches) and their assistants (dressed in zebra-striped shirts as if they were football referees) who sought to return men to the church.

Founded in 1990 by Bill McCartney, former football coach at the University of Colorado, the Promise Keepers are an evangelical Christian movement that seeks to bring men back to Jesus. Virtually entirely white and middle class, from the South and Midwest, they wedded what you might think is a more "feminine" notion of evangelical Christianity—ideals of service, healing, and racial reconciliation—with a renewed assertion of man's God-ordained position as head of the family and master of women.

In return for men keeping their promises to be faithful husbands, devoted fathers, and general all-around good men, the movement's "bible," *The Seven Promises of a Promise Keeper*, suggests that men deal with women this way:

> [S]it down with your wife and say "Honey, I've made a terrible mistake. I've given you my role in leading this family and I forced you to take my place. Now I must reclaim that role." . . . I'm not suggesting that you ask for your role back. I'm urging you to take it back. . . . There can be no compromise here. If you're going to lead you must lead.[15]

Others have followed suit, from "The Power Team," hyper-muscular zealots who pump up their gendered theology along with their biceps, performing feats of strength like breaking stacks of bricks, to "J-B-C Men" who promise a "shock and awe" gospel and bonding at the movies. (J-B-C stands for "Jesus—Beer—Chips!") Or Seattle evangelist Marc Driscoll who rails against the "Richard Simmons, hippie, queer Christ" offered by mainline Protestant churches.[16]

To the new masculinists, it may no longer be a man's world, but they'd like, at least, to find small pockets of all-male purity in which they can, again, be men among men.

"The Baby Girls and the Baby Boys": Fatherhood as Politics

After enumerating men's accomplishments in the workplace in his hit song, James Brown shifts his tone to a softer, more yearning and plaintive tone. "Man thinks of our little baby girls, and the baby boys / Man makes them happy, 'cause he makes them toys." Here Brown signals the other defining feature of American manhood: fatherhood. After all, if one's identity is wrapped up in being a family provider, one has to have a family to provide for.

The transformation of the American economy and women's entry into the paid labor force have combined to provide both opportunity and motive for a reevaluation of American fatherhood. This isn't the first time. At the turn of the twentieth century, fears of feminization of American boyhood, coupled with a growing critique of enervating office work, spawned a "fatherhood movement" designed to shift Dad's focus back to the home. If modern society had "imprisoned" women in the home, as Betty Friedan would one day put it, it had also "exiled" men from it, and men were admonished to come back in from the cold.

In the twenty-first century, reconnecting men to family life has become a politicized terrain, filled with moral urgency, legalistic outrage, and social movement organization. Some advocates of the new fatherhood paint with far broader strokes than simply enabling married couples to better balance work and family. David Blankenhorn's *Fatherless America* credited absent fathers with causing myriad social problems, ranging from juvenile delinquency, drug taking, sexual irresponsibility, crime, and violence to unemployment. "Boys raised by traditionally masculine fathers generally do not commit crimes," adds David Blankenhorn. "Fatherless boys commit crimes."

As divorce rates climb, one arena in which fatherhood has become highly politicized is during and after divorce. Many of the organizations promoting involved "fatherhood responsibility," especially in communities of color, seek to keep men engaged in family life because it's good for the children, good for women, and good for the men themselves. For other men, mostly white and middle class, the stroke of the pen finalizing divorce turns hordes of doting daddies into furious fathers who feel aggrieved by a process they believe denies them access to their children to whom they feel entitled.

These "fathers' rights" guys blend easily into more general anti-feminist organizations in advocating for public policy reforms. Case in point: Fred Hayward, founder of Men's Rights Inc., argued that women were "*privileged* because they are more frequently *allowed* to raise children, while men are being *oppressed* by denial of access to children."[17]

Fathers' rights groups use a language of equality to exact their revenge against their ex-wives, their ex-wives' lawyers, and the entire legal system, demanding mandatory joint custody and an end to alimony and child support payments. "Society cannot take away a father's right to his children and expect him to cheerfully pay child support," writes one activist. "Society cannot expect a father to make enough money to support two separate households. Society cannot afford to support mothers who choose not to work."[18] Fathers must have equal rights—the right to custody and the right to financial freedom without burdensome alimony and child support. Here is one man, interviewed by Jocelyn Crowley:

> [Child support] reduces the other parent to slavery and starvation. My ex-wife lives in a palace and I live in a trailer house. What made me decide to go to [the state where my children live now] is I had one can of pork and beans left, I ate them, and then I had no food left. I said, why am I staying here? When my kids were here with me in the summer, we went to the day-old bread store. I turn my air conditioner off during the day. [I am] living like a Nicaraguan and she is living in a plush palace, which is fine. That is wonderful and my children are living there during the school year against my will and their will. They lose half of their family and I am languishing in this little trailer house. That is all I can do. It is slavery. I am in a slave cabin.[19]

In reality, the fathers' rights groups are tapping into a problem that few men report having. Most parents get the custody arrangements they say they want, and while, all things being equal, the legal system does tend to privilege ex-wives' claims over ex-husbands' claims, all things are rarely, if ever, equal. In a recent study of 1,000 divorces in two California counties, for example, psychologist Eleanor Maccoby and law professor Robert Mnookin found that about 82 percent of mothers and 56 percent of fathers received the custody arrangement they wanted, while 6.7 percent of women and 9.8 percent of men requested more than they wanted and 11.5 percent of women and 34.1 percent of men requested less than they wanted.[20] This suggests "gender still matters" in what parents ask for and what they do to get it. That mothers were more likely to act on their desires by filing for a specific request also indicates that men need to ask for more up front to avoid feeling bitter later.[21]

But one consequence of current custody arrangements is paternal withdrawal. Whether this is because the father is bereft about losing regular contact with his children, or because once the marital bond is severed he considers himself to have escaped from a conflict-ridden family situation, it appears that many men "see parenting and marriage as part of the same bargain—a package deal," write sociologists Frank Furstenberg and Andrew Cherlin. "It is as if they stop being fathers as soon as the marriage is over."

In one nationally representative sample of eleven sixteen-year-old children living with their mothers, almost half had not seen their fathers in the previous twelve months. Indeed, American dads pay child support less often than their European counterparts: less than half of all divorced fathers in the United States pay child support compared to about three-fourths in Europe.[22] We see a widespread "masculinization of irresponsibility"—the refusal of fathers to provide economically for their children, which has led to the "feminization of poverty" with excruciatingly high poverty among single-mother families. What predicts continued paternal involvement in their children's lives after a divorce is the quality of the relationship between the ex-spouses prior to the divorce.

"And the Baby Boys" (Again): The Politics of the "Boy Crisis"

If the emphasis isn't on fathers, it's on their sons. Here's a place where, it appears, girls' increased equality has had serious negative consequences for boys. The data seem convincing: From elementary school onward boys get lower grades, lower class rank, and fewer honors than girls. They're 50 percent more likely to repeat a grade in elementary school, one third more likely to drop out of high school, and about six times more likely to be diagnosed with Attention Deficit and Hyperactivity Disorder.[23] By the time they get to college—if they get there at all—they're seriously outnumbered and outranked.

Doomsayers lament that women now outnumber men in the social and behavioral sciences by about 3 to 1, and how women have invaded such traditionally male bastions as engineering (where they now make up 20 percent) and biology and business (virtually par).[24] To many of the current critics, this is all women's fault—either as feminists, or as mothers, or both.

Feminists, we read, have been so successful that what was once a "chilly classroom climate" has now become overheated. By the time they get to college, they've been steeped in anti-male propaganda. "Why would any self-respecting boy want to attend one of America's increasingly feminized universities?" asks George Gilder in the *National Review*. The American university is now a "fluffy pink playpen of feminist studies and agitprop 'herstory,' taught amid a green goo of eco-motherism . . ."[25]

So, what's wrong with this picture? For one thing, it creates a false opposition between girls and boys, assuming that educational reforms undertaken to enable girls to perform better actually hindered boys' educational development. But these reforms—new initiatives, classroom arrangements, teacher training, increased attentiveness to students' individual learning styles—actually enable larger numbers of *boys* to get a better education.

Though the current boy advocates claim that schools used to be more "boy friendly" before all these feminist reforms, they obviously didn't go to school in those halcyon older days, like the 1950s, when the classroom was far more regimented and teachers far more authoritarian; they even gave grades for "deportment." Rambunctious boys were simply not tolerated; they dropped out.

Gender stereotyping hurts both boys and girls. There is no zero-sum game, even though it often feels like it. The net effect of the No Child Left Behind Act has been zero-sum competition as school districts scramble to stretch inadequate funding, leaving them little choice but to cut all non-curricular programs to ensure that their curricular mandates are followed. This disadvantages boys, since many of these programs were after-school athletics, gym, and recess. And cutting "unnecessary" school counselors and other remedial programs also disadvantages boys, who compose the majority of children in behavioral and remedial educational programs.

The problem of inadequate school funding lies not at feminists' door, but in the halls of Congress. This is further compounded by changes in the insurance industry, which often pressure therapists to put children on medication for ADHD, rather than pay for expensive therapy.

Another problem is that numbers themselves don't add up. More *people*— that is, males and females—are going to college than ever before. In 1960, 54 percent of boys and 38 percent of girls went directly to college; today the numbers are 64 percent of boys and 70 percent of girls. It is true that the *rate of increase* among girls is higher than the rate of increase among boys, but the numbers are increasing for both. As Jacqueline King put it in a 2006 report from the American Council on Education, "it does not appear that women's success is coming at the expense of men, but rather that women's college participation is rising faster than men's."[26]

Most critically, the imbalance is not uniform across class and race. It remains the case that far more working-class women of all races go to college than do working-class men. Part of this is a seemingly rational individual decision: A college-educated woman still earns about the same as a high-school-educated man.

By race, the disparities are even starker. Among middle-class white high school graduates going to college this year, half are male and half are female. But only 37 percent of black college students are male, and 63 percent female, and 45 percent of Hispanic students are male, compared with 55 percent female. The numerical imbalance turns out to be more of a problem of race and class, than about gender. It is what sociologist Cynthia Fuchs Epstein calls a "deceptive distinction"—a difference that appears to be about gender, but is actually about something else (in this case, class and race).

Found, Not Lost: "Acquiescence and Acceptance"

The anti-feminists may shout loudest, and the new masculinists may be the most mediagenic of men's responses to increased gender equality, but they represent only a small fraction of American men. The largest, if least acknowledged, response to women's equality has been the quiet acceptance of gender equality at both the public and private level. In the public sphere, the majority of American men support wage equality, comparable worth, and women's candidacies for public office.

On the domestic front, surveys consistently show "substantial and persistent" long-term trends increasing the endorsement of gender equality in families. With only modest attitudinal adjustment, most American men have acclimated to the dual-career couple model that now characterizes most marriages. Some are even delighted to have the additional family income. Most American men subscribe to a general "ethical imperative" and see women's equality as right, just, and fair. They just don't think it has all that much to do with them as men.[27]

But it does. As I will show below, when fatherhood is transformed from a political cause to a personal experience, from an ideological position or an existential state of being to a set of concrete practices, men's lives are dramatically improved. As are their children's.

This acceptance isn't the result of some grand ideological transformation in the meaning of manhood. Some part of it is simply financial. "These days, Ward Cleaver wouldn't be able to afford a house in the suburbs or Beaver's tuition—unless June went to work too," writes Nicholas Kulish in the *New York Times*. Indeed, despite dire warnings that the current economic recession will spur increases in reactive defensiveness among men, it may, in fact, propel the trend toward greater acceptance of equality. One recent survey found that a decline in men's breadwinner status tends to promote egalitarian gender ideologies.[28]

Plus, it is the inevitable result of countless micro-level decisions made by families every day: about their daughters' and sons' education, an increased intolerance for bullying or harassment, a sense of fairness about wage equality and reducing discrimination. It's not that men woke up one morning and decided to scrap their traditional definition of masculinity. Rather, they gradually, and without fanfare or struggle, drifted into more egalitarian relationships because they love their wives, partners, and children.

Support for gender equality begins at home. Across race, class, and (non-evangelical) religious ideologies, support for the more conventional male-breadwinner/female-homemaker ideology has fallen dramatically since the late

1970s. A new report by the Families and Work Institute finds that while 74 percent of men (and 52 percent of women) subscribed to that conventional model in 1977, just over two-fifths of men (42 percent) and fewer than two-fifths of women (39 percent) subscribe to it today.[29]

What's more, men's attitudes about women's ability to balance work and family have also shifted in a decidedly positive direction. In 1977, less than half of men (49 percent) agreed with the statement "a mother who works outside the home can have just as good a relationship with her children as a mother who does not work." Thirty years later—a short time in attitude shifts—two-thirds of men agree (as do 80 percent of women). The media-celebrated claim that many Ivy League women graduates are "opting out" of the labor force altogether—an empirically dubious claim at its class-biased best (students who *say* they plan to opt out often do not, and those who do, opt back in relatively quickly)—finds little support among their male Ivy League counterparts. "[S]ome of you may want to be Harriets again," wrote Kulish, "but we men may not be prepared to become Ozzies."[30]

This change is more pronounced the younger the respondent. Just over a third of "Millennials" (employees who were twenty-eight or younger in 2008) support that model today, while slightly more than half (53 percent) of mature workers (sixty-three and older in 2008) support it—though 90 percent of mature workers subscribed to the conventional model in 1977. And while 70 percent of men in dual-career couples still subscribed to the more conventional model in 1977, only about 37 percent of them subscribe to that today.[31]

While most American men's participation in family life, that is doing housework and child care, tends to be expressed by two two-word phrases—men "help out" and "pitch in"—men's share of housework and especially child care has also increased significantly in the past few decades. Men are both more likely to do more housework, and more likely to hug their children and tell them that they love them than in previous decades. It took several decades for the norm to be a dual-career couple; it will take several more decades before the norm is also a "dual-carer" couple.

The average father today spends three hours a day on the weekend with his family, up significantly from estimates in earlier decades. While women still do the majority of routine housework, "husbands of working wives are spending more time in the family than in the past." In 1924, 10 percent of working-class women said their husbands spent "no time" doing housework; today that percentage is less than 2 percent. Between the mid-1960s and the mid-1970s, men's housework increased by 26 minutes a day (to 130 minutes from 104 minutes per day), while women's share decreased by about 30 minutes (to 6.8 *hours* per day).

In another survey of 4,500 married dual-career couples between the ages of twenty-five and forty-four, the median amount for men was about five hours a

week; for women it was about twenty hours. Men reported that they did 10 percent of the housework in 1970, and 20 percent in 1990, which, depending upon
how you look at it, represents double the percentage in only twenty years, or,
still, only one-fifth the amount that needs to be done.[32]

When couples were asked to keep accurate records of how much time they
spent doing which household tasks, men still put in significantly less time than
their wives. The most recent figures from the National Survey of Families and
Households at the University of Wisconsin show that husbands were doing
about fourteen hours of housework per week (compared with thirty-one hours
for wives). In more traditional couples in which she stays home and the husband is the sole earner, her hours jump to thirty-eight and his decline slightly to
twelve. Reasonable, since they've defined housework as "her" domain. But when
both work full-time outside the home, the wife does twenty-eight hours and the
husband does sixteen. This is four times the amount of housework that
Japanese men do, but only two-thirds of the housework that Swedish men do.[33]

Though we tend to think that sharing housework is the product of ideological commitments—progressive, liberal, well-educated middle-class families
with more egalitarian attitudes—the data suggest a more complicated picture
that has less to do with ideological concerns. In every single subcategory (meal
preparation, dishes, cleaning, shopping, washing, outdoor work, auto repair
and maintenance, and bill paying), for example, black men do significantly
more housework than white men. In more than one-fourth of all black families,
men do more than 40 percent of the housework. Men's "share" of housework
comes closer to an equal share.

In white families, only 16 percent of the men do that much. And blue-collar
fathers, regardless of race (municipal and service workers, policemen, firefighters, maintenance workers), are twice as likely (42 percent) as those in professional, managerial, or technical jobs (20 percent) to care for their children
while their wives work. This difference comes less from ideological commitments and more from an "informal flex time," a split-shift arrangement with
one's spouse, which is negotiated by about one-fourth of all workers in the
United States, and one-third of all workers with children under age five.[34]

Such findings are echoed among Mexican-origin families. There, fathers
did more housework when the family income was lower or when wives contributed a larger share of family income, an indication that there, too, economic
reality can modify ideological assumptions.[35] Among immigrant groups, class
position tends to be more important than ethnicity as well—though it might
tend in a different direction. Taiwanese immigrant men, for example, in the
professional class tend to hold more egalitarian attitudes and perform more
housework and child care than do Taiwanese men in the working class.

As a result of these complex findings, researchers increasingly adopt an
intersectional approach—exploring how race, class, ethnicity, and immigrant

status interact to produce distinct patterns. It may be that class position—regardless of race, ethnicity, or immigrant status—may be the best predictor of both ideological orientations and actual behaviors, though the two may be contradictory or mutually reinforcing.[36]

Housework aside, when it comes to being fathers, men are evidently willing to do more. A poll in *Newsweek* magazine found that 55 percent of fathers say that being a parent is more important to them than it was to their fathers, and 70 percent say they spend more time with their children than their fathers spent with them. What's more, they are actually *doing* it. According to the 2009 study by the Families and Work Institute, the amount of time fathers spend with their children under thirteen on workdays has increased from two hours a day in 1977 to three hours a day in 2008—an increase of 50 percent. (Women's rate has remained constant over that thirty-year period, at 3.8 hours per workday.) Millennial fathers spend 4.3 hours per workday (their wives spend 5 hours). Men are not merely walking their talk; they almost seem to be jogging it.[37]

And they've got some support from the nation's trusted advice-givers. Dr. Benjamin Spock's multi-decade best-selling book *Baby and Child Care* noted (and perhaps even encouraged) the shift in thinking about fathers' involvement. In the first edition, published in 1946, Dr. Spock suggested that men could be somewhat involved in child care:

> Some fathers have been brought up to think that the care of babies and children is the mother's job entirely. This is the wrong idea. You can be a warm father and a real man at the same time. . . . Of course I don't mean that the father has to give just as many bottles or change just as many diapers as the mother. But it's fine for him to do these things occasionally. He might make the formula on Sunday.

In its most recent 1998 edition, however, Dr. Spock records the shifts his work has helped to bring about:

> Men, especially the husbands of women with outside jobs, have been participating increasingly in all aspects of home and child care. There is no reason why fathers shouldn't be able to do these jobs as well as mothers. . . . But the benefit may be lost if this work is done as a favor to the wife, since that implies that raising the child is not really the father's work but that he's merely being extraordinarily generous.[38]

President Obama has also weighed in on the state of American fatherhood. In June 2008, prior to the presidential election, he took African American men to task for high rates of absenteeism in the lives of their children. And, as we've seen, after the dissolution of a relationship, many fathers dramatically reduce, or lose altogether, contact with their children. But while the couple is together, in both black families and white, native-born or immigrant, religious or secular, men are, today, more involved in child care than possibly any other generation in American history.

And yet, American men's participation in child care lags behind the rates of participation in other industrial countries—countries where public policies provide adequate health care, child care, and paid parental leave. In Australia, Canada, and the Netherlands, for example, men's rates are about double the rates in the United States, while in Britain the rates are about 40 percent higher.[39]

Men's increased participation in child care has its dangers, of course. Men are reporting significantly higher levels of work-family conflict than they did thirty years ago (and their rates now surpass women's). Three of five fathers in dual-earner couples report significant work-family conflict, up from just over a third (35 percent) in 1977.[40]

What's more, with men's child care participation increasing so much faster than their housework, a dangerous disequilibrium is developing in which Dad is becoming the "fun parent." *He* takes the kids to the park and plays soccer with the kids; *she* stays home. "What a great time we had with dad!" the kids announce as they burst through the kitchen door to a lunch that she prepared while also folding the laundry and vacuuming the living room.

But when men do share housework as well as child care the payoff is significant. Sociologists Scott Coltrane and Michele Adams looked at national survey data and found that when men increase their share of housework and child care, their children are happier and healthier and do better in school.[41] They are less likely to be diagnosed with ADHD, less likely to be put on prescription medication, and less likely to see a child psychologist for behavioral problems. They have lower rates of absenteeism and higher school achievement scores.

"When men perform domestic service for others, it teaches children cooperation and democratic family values," said Coltrane. "It used to be that men assumed that their wives would do all the housework and parenting, but now that women are nearly equal participants in the labor force, men are assuming more of the tasks that it takes to run a home and raise children."[42]

Perhaps the most telling correlation is that when school-aged children do housework with their fathers, they get along better with their peers and have more friends. And they show more positive behaviors than if they did the same work with their mothers. "Because fewer men do housework than women," said Adams, "when they share the work, it has more impact on children." Fathers model "cooperative family partnerships."

When men share housework and child care, it turns out, their wives are happier. This is intuitively obvious. Historically, working mothers reported higher levels of self-esteem and lower levels of depression than full-time housewives. Yet they also reported lower levels of marital satisfaction than did their husbands, who were happier than the husbands of traditional housewives. This was because under such arrangements, women's workload increased at home, while the men benefited by having almost the same amount of work done for them at home and having their standard of living buttressed by an additional income.[43]

But wives of egalitarian husbands, regardless of class or race and ethnicity, report the highest levels of marital satisfaction and lowest rates of depression, and are less likely to see therapists or take prescription medication. They are also more likely to stay fit, since they probably have more time on their hands.[44]

The benefits for the men? Men who do more housework and child care are healthier, physically and psychologically. They smoke less, drink less, and take recreational drugs less often. They are more likely to stay in shape and more likely to go to doctors for routine screenings, but less likely to use emergency rooms or miss work due to illness.

They're also psychologically healthier. They are less often diagnosed with depression, see therapists, or take prescription medication compared to men who do not share housework. They report higher levels of marital satisfaction. They also live longer, causing the normally staid British financial magazine *The Economist* to quip, "Change a nappy, by God, and put years on your life." "When males take full responsibility for child care," sociologist Barbara Risman points out, "they develop intimate and affectionate relationships with their children." Nurturing their children is good for men's health.[45]

And they have more sex. Research by psychologist John Gottman at the University of Washington found higher rates of marital sex among couples where men did more housework and child care. This last finding was trumpeted by *Men's Health* magazine with the headline "Housework Makes Her Horny" (although I suspect that is not true when *she* does it). It is probably worthwhile pointing out that there is no one-to-one correspondence here; I would advise male readers of this essay against immediately rushing home to load the washing machine. Instead it points to wives' lower levels of stress in balancing work and family, coupled with a dramatic reduction in resentment that they alone are doing the second shift.

"Nothing Without a Woman or a Girl": Toward the Enthusiastic Embrace of Gender Equality

There's an old adage that the Chinese character for "crisis" is a combination of the characters for "danger" and "opportunity." While many men see increased gender equality as a dangerous reversal of traditional gender arrangements, most men are going along for a rather apolitical ride, seeing neither danger nor opportunity. They're doing more housework and child care, supporting their wives' career aspirations, sharing the decision-making about family life and career trajectories, not because of some ideological commitment to feminism, but because of a more quotidian commitment to their families and loved ones.

In a sense, the fix is already in. Women are in the labor force—and every other public arena—to stay. So the choice for men is how we will relate to this transformation. Will we be dragged kicking and screaming into the future? Run off to some male-only preserve, circle the masculine wagons, and regroup?

Some men, though, see through the media's misframing, and see, instead, the opportunity for "enthusiastic embrace" of gender equality—not only because it is inevitable (which it is) and not just because it's right and just and fair (which it is). But also because we see that men who embrace equality will live happier, healthier lives, lives animated by love and connection with our wives, our partners, our children, and our friends. And so do the children of these and most other men, who grow up with working mothers—and have sisters, friends, and girlfriends who expect to be equal at work and at home.

Becoming a "woman's nation" may be a vast improvement for everyone over remaining a "man's world." Gender equality is not a zero-sum game at all, but a win-win.

NOTES

This essay was commissioned by Maria Shriver for her book *A Woman's Nation*, published by the Center for American Progress. I am grateful to Maria Shriver, Ann O'Leary, and Heather Boushey for their comments on earlier drafts.

1. See, for example, Michael Kimmel, *Manhood in America: A Cultural History*, 10th anniversary edition (New York: Oxford University Press, 2006).

2. Norman Mailer, "The White Man Unburdened," *The New York Review of Books*, 50 (12), July 17, 2003; available at: http://www.nybooks.com/articles/16470.

3. Cited in Richard Goldstein, "Butching Up for Victory," *The Nation*, January 26, 2004; available at: http://thenation.com/doc.mhtml?i=20040126&s=goldstein.

4. Obama is cited in Reihan Salam, "The Death of Macho," *Foreign Policy*, June 22, 2009; available at: http://www.foreignpolicy.com/articles/2009/06/18/the_death_of_macho.

5. Richard Haddad, "Feminism Has Little Relevance for Men," in *To Be a Man: In Search of the Deep Masculine*, ed. Keith Thompson (Los Angeles: Jeremy Tarcher, 1991), 100.

6. See *Guyland: The Perilous World Where Boys Become Men* (New York: HarperCollins, 2008).

7. Anna Quindlen, "The Great White Myth," *New York Times*, January 15, 1992.

8. David Nylund, *Beer, Babes, and Balls: Masculinity in Sports Talk Radio* (Albany: SUNY Press, 2008).

9. Warren Farrell, *The Myth of Male Power* (New York: Simon and Schuster, 1992), 301, 298.

10. Harvey Mansfield, "Why a Woman Can't Be More Like a Man," *Wall Street Journal*, November 3, 1997, A22.

11. See Lauren Collins, "Hey La-a-a-dies!" *The New Yorker*, August 6, 2007; available at: http://www.newyorker.com/talk/2007/08/06/070806ta_talk_collins; see also John Del Signore, "Columbia Sued for 'Bigoted' Women's Studies Courses," *The Gothamist*,

August 19, 2008; available at: http://gothamist.com/2008/08/19/columbia_sued
_for_offering_bigoted.php. A copy of his complaint may be found at: http://www
.roydenhollander.com/.

12. Cited in Ted Ownby, *Subduing Satan: Religion, Recreation, and Manhood in the Rural South*
(Chapel Hill: University of North Carolina Press, 1991), 14.

13. Cited in Roger Bruns, *Preacher: Billy Sunday and Big-Time American Evangelism* (New
York: Norton, 1992), 16, 121, 122, 138; William G. McLaughlin, *Billy Sunday Was His Real
Name* (Chicago: University of Chicago Press, 1955), 175.

14. Cited in Frances Fitzgerald, *Cities on a Hill* (New York: Simon and Schuster, 1986), 166.

15. Randy Phillips, "Spiritual Purity," in *The Seven Promises of a Promise Keeper* (Colorado
Springs: Focus on the Family, 1994), 79–80.

16. Molly Worthen, "Who Would Jesus Smack Down?" *New York Times Magazine*, January 11,
2009, 22.

17. See Anna Gavanas, *Fatherhood Politics in the United States* (Urbana: University of Illinois
Press, 2004); and Jocelyn Crowley, *Defiant Dads: Fathers' Rights Activists in America*
(Ithaca, NY: Cornell University Press, 2008). Fred Hayward is quoted in Marcy Sheiner,
"What Do Men Really Want . . . and Why Should We Care?" *East Bay Express*, July 10,
1992, 11.

18. Jon Conine, *Fathers' Rights: The Sourcebook for Dealing with the Child Support System*
(New York: Walker, 1989), 2.

19. Crowley, *Defiant Dads*, 119.

20. Eleanor Maccoby and Robert Mnookin, *Dividing the Child: Social and Legal Dilemmas of
Custody* (Cambridge: Harvard University Press, 1992).

21. Robert L. Griswold, *Fatherhood in America* (New York: Basic Books, 1993), 263; Nancy
Polikoff, "Gender and Child Custody Determinations: Exploding the Myths," in
Families, Politics, and Public Policy: A Feminist Dialogue on Women and the State, ed.
I. Diamond (New York: Longman, 1983), 184–185; Robert H. Mnookin, Eleanor
Maccoby, Catherine Albiston, and Charlene Depner, "Private Ordering Revisited:
What Custodial Arrangements Are Parents Negotiating?" in *Divorce Reform at the
Crossroads*, ed. S. Sugarman and H. Kaye (New Haven: Yale University Press, 1990),
especially 55; Maccoby and Mnookin, *Dividing the Child*, especially 101.

22. Maccoby, quoted in Dirk Johnson, "More and More, the Single Parent Is Dad," *New York
Times*, August 31, 1993, A15; Frank F. Furstenberg and Andrew J. Cherlin, *Divided Families:
What Happens to Children When Parents Part* (Cambridge, MA: Harvard University Press,
1991); Frank Furstenberg, "Good Dads—Bad Dads: Two Faces of Fatherhood," in *The
Changing American Family and Public Policy*, ed. A. Cherlin (Lanham, MD: Urban Institute
Press, 1988); William J. Goode, "Why Men Resist," in *Rethinking the Family: Some Feminist
Questions*, ed. B. Thorne and M. Yalom (New York: Longman, 1982).

23. See, for example, Brad Knickerbocker, "Young and Male in America: It's Hard Being a
Boy," *Christian Science Monitor*, April, 29, 1999.

24. Tamar Lewin, "American Colleges Begin to Ask, Where Have All the Men Gone?" *New
York Times*, December 6, 1998; Brendan Koerner, "Where the Boys Aren't," *U.S. News
and World Report*, February 8, 1999.

25. George Gilder, "The Idea of the (Feminized) University," *National Review*, December 31,
2005.

26. Jacqueline King, "Gender Equity in Higher Education" (Washington, DC: Council on
Education Center for Policy Analysis, 2006).

27. See, for example, Arland Thornton and Linda Young-DeMarco, "Four Decades of Trends in Attitudes toward Family Issues in the United States: The 1960s through the 1990s," *Journal of Marriage and Family* 63 (November 2001): 1009–1037.

28. Nicholas Kulish, "Changing the Rules for the Team Sport of Bread-Winning," Editorial Observer, *New York Times*, September 23, 2005; see also Jiping Zuo and Shenming Tang, "Breadwinner Status and Gender Ideologies of Men and Women Regarding Family Roles," *Sociological Perspectives* 43 (1) (2000): 29–43.

29. Ellen Galinsky, Kerstin Aumann, and James T. Bond, "Times Are Changing: Gender and Generation at Work and at Home" (New York: Families and Work Institute, 2009), 10.

30. Ibid., 12; Kulish, "Changing the Rules for the Team Sport of Bread-Winning."

31. Galinsky et al., "Times Are Changing," 11.

32. On men's involvement in family work, see Joseph Pleck, "Men's Family Work: Three Perspectives and Some New Data," *The Family Coordinator* 28 (1979): 481–487; "American Fathering in Historical Perspective," in *Changing Men: New Directions in Research on Men and Masculinity*, ed. M. S. Kimmel (Beverly Hills, CA: Sage Publications, 1987); *Working Wives/Working Husbands* (Newbury Park, CA: Sage Publications, 1985); "Families and Work: Small Changes with Big Implications," *Qualitative Sociology* 15 (1992): 427–432; "Father Involvement: Levels, Origins, and Consequences," in *The Father's Role*, ed. M. Lamb, 3rd ed. (New York: John Wiley, 1997).

33. Lisa Belkin, "When Mom and Dad Share it All," *New York Times Magazine*, June 15, 2008, 47.

34. See Bart Landry, *Black Working Wives: Pioneers of the American Family Revolution* (Berkeley: University of California Press, 2001); see also Scott Coltrane, "Research on Household Labor: Modeling and Measuring the Social Embeddedness of Routine Family Work," *Journal of Marriage and the Family* 62 (2000): 1208–1233; Margaret Usdansky, "White Men Don't Jump into Chores," *USA Today*, August 20, 1994; Julia Lawlor, "Blue Collar Dads Leading Trend in Caring for Kids, Author Says," *New York Times*, April 15, 1998.

35. Katy Pinto and Scott Coltrane, "Divisions of Labor in Mexican Origin and Anglo Families: Structure and Culture," *Sex Roles* 60 (2009): 482–495. See also B. Shelton and D. John, "Ethnicity, Race, and Difference: A Comparison of White, Black, and Hispanic Men's Household Labor Time," in *Men, Work, and Family*, ed. Jane Hood (Thousand Oaks, CA: Sage, 1993); Yen Li Espiritu, "Gender and Labor in Asian Immigrant Families," *American Behavioral Scientist* 42 (1999): 628–647.

36. Scott Coltrane and Kristy Y. Shih, "Gender and Household Labor," in *Handbook of Gender Research in Psychology*, ed. Joan C. Chrisler and Donald R. McCreary (forthcoming); see also H. Dillaway and C. Broman, "Race, Class, and Gender Differences in Marital Satisfaction and Divisions of Household Labor among Dual-Earner Couples: A Case for Intersectional Analysis," *Journal of Family Issues* 22 (2001): 309–327.

37. Jerry Adler, "Building a Better Dad," *Newsweek*, June 17, 1996; Tamar Lewin, "Workers of Both Sexes Make Trade-Offs for Family, Study Shows," *New York Times*, October 29, 1995, 25; Galinsky et al., "Times Are Changing," 14.

38. Benjamin Spock and Steven J. Parker, *Dr. Spock's Baby and Child Care*, 7th ed. (New York: Pocket Books, 1998), 10.

39. United Nations, *The World's Women, 1970–1990: Trends and Statistics* (New York: United Nations, 1991).

40. Galinsky et al., "Times Are Changing," 18.

41. Scott Coltrane and Michele Adams calculation based on the Child Development Supplement of the Panel Study of Income Dynamics, personal communication from Scott Coltrane.

42. "When Dads Clean House, It Pays Off Big Time," press release, University of California Riverside, June 9, 2003, courtesy of Scott Coltrane.

43. Arlie Hochschild, *The Second Shift* (New York: Viking, 1989); Paul Amato and Alan Booth, "Changes in Gender Role Attitudes and Perceived Marital Quality," *American Sociological Review* 60 (1995): 58–66.

44. See Katy Pinto and Scott Coltrane, "Divisions of Labor in Mexican Origin and Anglo Families: Structure and Culture," *Sex Roles* 60 (2009): 482–495; and especially Coltrane, "Research on Household Labor."

45. "Sex, Death, and Football," *The Economist*, June 13, 1998, 18; Robert D. Mintz and James Mahalik, "Gender Role Orientation and Conflict as Predictors of Family Roles for Men," *Sex Roles* 34(1–2) (1996): 805–821; Barbara Risman, "Can Men 'Mother'? Life as a Single Father," *Family Relations* 35 (1986): 95–102; see also Caryl Rivers and Rosalind Barnett, "Fathers Do Best," *Washington Post*, June 20, 1993, C5.

2

The Children's Hour

Masculine Redemption in Contemporary Film

(WITH AMY ARONSON)

During her reign as resident feminist on the op-ed page of the *New York Times*, Anna Quindlen once asked her women readers which man they'd prefer for a mate: a short, thin, reedy man, careful, committed, and chivalrous, always sexually faithful; or a dark, roguishly handsome self-interested scoundrel, who would never be faithful. Readers, of course, chose the former (though when the question was posed to our students, several women always note that they wouldn't mind having sex with the latter before they got married).

But what if, Quindlen asked, you gave them names. Call the first one Ashley Wilkes, the second Rhett Butler. Now whom would you choose?

"Well, that's different," said one woman student. "Rhett Butler's never been loved by me. When I love him, he'll change."

In a heartbeat, Quindlen had exposed the consequences of women's romantic fantasies: a woman's love can change a bad man into a good man. When Rhett is loved by that woman, he may physically remain Rhett (indeed, he'd better), but emotionally he'll become Ashley.

This romantic fantasy—"the angel in the house," in Virginia Woolf's famous phrase—is the centerpiece of feminine fiction;[1] Charlotte Bronte's *Jane Eyre* (1847), which many see as the great mother of all women's novels, is a *locus classicus*. And it's been a Hollywood staple for decades; *Eyre* itself has been made into a film an astounding eight times. Think of *Magnificent Obsession* (1954) in which Rock Hudson renounces his wastrel ways and dedicates himself to medicine for the love of Jane Wyman. (And this was a remake of the 1935 film with Robert Taylor and Irene Dunne.) Or *San Francisco* (1936), where the bad gin-joint

---

Originally published in *Masculinity: Bodies, Movies, Culture*, edited by Peter Lehman. New York: Routledge, 2001.

proprietor (Gable again) is transformed in his battle with the saintly priest (Spencer Tracy) for Jeanette MacDonald's soul (and other body parts).

Like Gable, Humphrey Bogart made a virtual career out of this transformation. In *Casablanca* (1942) his infernal abiding love for Ingrid Bergman leads him to act heroically, the renunciation of love as its ultimate confirmation. In *African Queen* (1951), it's Katharine Hepburn who elicits the move; in *To Have and Have Not* (1944), it's Lauren Bacall (who is also the vehicle for the plunge into depravity and ruin in *The Big Sleep* [1946]).

Feminism and the Transformation of Women's Lives

The transformative power of women's pure love has been one of America's most resilient cultural tropes. Except it doesn't work any more. Because it wasn't really femininity that transformed those bad guys. It was innocence. And once upon a time, women embodied that innocence—on screen and in real life.

Not anymore. Feminism changed all that.[2] Over the past thirty years, women's lives have changed dramatically—with enormous consequences for men. This transformation sets the historical and social context for these new media representations.

For one thing, women made gender visible. Women have demonstrated the centrality of gender in social life; in the past two decades, gender has joined race and class as the three primordial axes around which social life is organized, one of the primary building blocks of identity. This new visibility of gender has transformed the university, where virtually every curriculum has a women's studies program and every university press boasts a women's studies book list. It's transformed the culture, as now everyone has to pay attention to gender in some way.

Most evident has been women's transformation of the workplace—and every public arena. Women are in the workplace to stay. Almost half the labor force is female. Far more of the new jobs created in the 1990s went to women. In college classrooms, this is easily illustrated. When we've asked women students how many intend to have full-time careers outside the home after graduation, virtually all the women raise their hands. But when asked if their mothers have or had full-time careers outside the home for at least ten years without an interruption, about half the hands go down. Grandmothers? Perhaps 5 percent of the hands are raised now. Students can clearly see that over three generations, women's experience in the workplace has been utterly transformed.

The full-scale entry of women into the public arena, and especially the workplace, has created a third arena of change in women's lives: the efforts to balance work and family life. Historically, women were not able to balance work and family, but were instead forced to choose between them. Today, of course, women "want it all" in that infelicitous phrase of the kinder, gentler first Bush era. But can women have the glamorous rewarding careers they want and also the warm loving family? Can women have it all?

Actually, until now, it's been men who have "had it all"—the careers outside the home and the emotionally satisfying family lives. In fact, women have been unable to have it all precisely because men do have it all! And men have it all because women have been doing the "second shift," the household shift that has traditionally been their task, after the workplace shift is over.[3]

Finally, women have changed the sexual landscape. As the dust is settling from the sexual revolution, what emerges in unmistakably finer detail is that it's been women, not men, who are our era's real sexual pioneers. Men often think that the sexual revolution, with its promises of more access to more partners with less emotional commitment, was tailor-made for male sexuality's fullest flowering. But, in fact, it's been women's sexuality that's changed in the past two decades, not men's. The summary statement about such changes is simple: Women now feel empowered to claim sexual desire. Women can like sex, want sex, seek sex, and even—gasp!—get horny. Women feel entitled to pleasure. They have learned to say yes to their own desires, claiming, in the process, sexual agency.

There is a mountain of sex research that might illustrate such a point. Let me suggest only two examples. About fifty years ago, Alfred Kinsey found that fewer than one-half of all women under twenty-five had masturbated to orgasm—sexual self-pleasuring being a pretty good indicator of one's entitlement to pleasure. In 1995, the major sex survey published by the National Opinion Research Center at the University of Chicago found a figure closer to 90 percent. About half of all women surveyed in 1994 had masturbated during the preceding year. Here's another indicator of sexual entitlement. Twenty-five years ago, sociologist Lillian Rubin found that three-fourths of the white working-class women she interviewed said that they faked orgasm at least "sometimes" if not more often. In 1995, she returned to that same neighborhood and interviewed working-class women, some of whom were the daughters of the women she had interviewed a quarter century earlier. Then she found that fewer than two in ten had *ever* faked it. In the most recent sex survey, a maximum of 15 percent of women might have faked an orgasm during the previous year.[4]

While women's lives have changed dramatically, what's been happening with men? The easy answer is "not very much." Sure, some men have changed in some ways, but most men have not undergone a comparable revolution. Men have experienced a stalled revolution, and in the growing gender gap, men lag increasingly behind women in feeling empowered to implement change in their lives. This is, I think, the reason that so many men seem so confused about the meaning of masculinity these days, and why so many books and magazines can generate sales by dispensing bad advice.

Actually, of course, men's lives have changed just as dramatically. The problem is that many men are not aware of it. For example, our fathers lived in world where they could go to an all-male college, serve in an all-male military, and spend virtually their entire working lives in an all-male working environment. That world, however, has forever disappeared. There are only three private all-male colleges in America today; the military is gender-integrated, as is every single workplace in the country.

What has not changed, though, are the ideas we have about what it means to be a man. The *structure* of our lives has changed, but not their *culture*, the ideologies that give that structure meaning. This is what social scientists used to call "culture lag," where the technology and institutional framework of a society changes more rapidly than the culture's stock of meanings and interpretations of social structure, which then spend some fitful decades catching up with those institutions. That's where men are these days: our lives have changed dramatically, but the notions we have about what it means to be a man remain locked in a pattern set decades ago, when the world looked very different.

The 1990s found men constantly bumping up against the limitations of that traditional definition, but without much of a sense of direction about where they might go to look for alternatives. Alan Alda never replaced Rambo, and neither is today seen as an adequate role model for today's men. We chafe against the edges of traditional masculinity, but seem unable or unwilling to break out of the constraints we feel from those rules. Thus the defensiveness, the anger, the confusion that is everywhere in evidence.

From Reality to Fantasy

This dramatic shift in women's lives has been embraced by Hollywood. Sometimes, women's new public sphere activities have been celebrated in film, more often derided. Feminism promised more than equal opportunities for individual women and an end to discrimination against them in all public arenas; it also promised the possibility of a transformation of gender relations, a promise of a transformation of *men's* lives. In the Hollywood rendition—as in real life—women were successful in obtaining the end to barriers to public sphere equality, but the transformation of gender relations—the change in men's lives—was its price.

After all, consider the ways in which Hollywood addressed the possibilities of the men's transformation. From *Rebel without a Cause* (1955), when an aproned Jim Backus attempts to tell his confused and errant son, James Dean, about how to be a man, to *Mr. Mom* (1983), when Michael Keaton, a newly unemployed auto executive, is so addled by the technology of housework (a technology that is typically advertised as so simple that even a woman can understand it!) that he nearly destroys his home and family, the transformation of *men's* lives has been cast as feminizing, emasculating.

So it is with all social movements for social transformation: the larger vision of transformation is the cost of the opening of opportunities for disaggregated individuals. The larger social context of those opportunities remains unchallenged, the gender of institutions more stable than before.[5]

Translated into celluloid, the equal opportunity promised by feminism has changed good girls, innocent and pure, into worldly women—corrupted by power (*Disclosure*, 1994), tainted by greed (the bony climber Sigourney Weaver compared to the zoftig wannabe Melanie Griffith in *Working Girl*, 1988), immune to the needs of their children (*Kramer vs. Kramer*, 1979). Some have even become murderous (*Thelma and Louise*, 1991.)

In some films, women's political struggle for equality has been mistaken for a struggle to obliterate all gender distinctions and to masculinize women. In *G.I. Jane* (1997), Demi Moore refuses "women's" standards and tests, separate barracks and latrines; she wants the real deal. And so, after we watch the country's highest paid film actress shave her own head, and after she has been bloodied and brutally and savagely beaten with her hands tied behind her back, her Master Chief training officer asks if she's had enough, if she's ready to quit, if she gives up. Her response? Moore shouts, "Suck my dick!" which, of course, he cannot do, and not just because he's heterosexual. Of course, Moore does not possess a penis, but at that moment she possesses something even more valuable. Standing tall and erect, bloodied but unbowed, joining a long line of American male warrior heroes, Moore possesses the phallus, not a penis, the signifier if not the thing signified.

When women aren't trying to become men, they've got better things to do with their time than changing bad men into good ones. In *An Unmarried Woman* (1978), Jill Clayburgh opts to stay that way, while in *Waiting to Exhale* (1995), the ensemble waits for men who are already good. In *She's Gotta Have it* (1986), girls just wanna have fun too.

About the only 1990s movie in which good women turn bad men into good men is *The First Wives Club* (1996)—but that's after they've been dumped, and against the men's wills. About the best today's women can get from men these days is grudgingly ethical behavior, which, fortunately, is more than compensated for by sisterly solidarity.

If feminism has been translated into equal opportunities for women, whatever the moral and political valences that entails, it has left men's lives unchanged. If women "escaped" from the prison of their suburban homes following Betty Friedan's tocsin in *The Feminine Mystique*, men are still "exiled" from them, unable to return to the virtuous world of hearth and home without being utterly emasculated. Since feminism has thus far failed to liberate men, men still need some external agent to transform them from bad men into good men. And if women won't do it, who will? What force is innocent and virtuous enough to change him? In Hollywood these days, it's a little child who will lead them.

Only young children embody the virtuous innocence that can change bad men into good men.[6] This is easily observable in several Hollywood hits in the 1990s. In *Liar Liar* (1997), for example, it's shyster corporate attorney Jim Carrey's revelation that he's a bad father to his five-year-old son that leads him to the righteous path. His Dantean descent into the depravity of unbridled honesty, occasioned by Justin Cooper's birthday wish that his father couldn't lie for twenty-four hours, transforms a bad father into a good man, literally overnight.

And the pivotal scene in *Jerry Maguire* (1996), the Oscar-nominated smash hit, comes not through a magical romantic moment or ecstatic sexual passion between Tom Cruise and Renee Zellweger, and not even in the racial healing generated by his friendship with Cuba Gooding Jr. It's when Cruise is sitting on the sofa with Jonathan Lipnicki, Zellweger's adorably bespectacled and nerdy son, that he realizes the meaning of life and the importance of acting like a mensch.

It's doubly significant that in both cases, the guy then gets the girl. Not only must he prove himself worthy as a father figure to their children, but he can only accomplish that—he can only be changed—by the boys.

And what about some other "classics," like *Vice Versa* (1988), in which Judge Reinhold is changed from a demanding workaholic to an understanding boss, and a from bumbling boyfriend into a loving mate, by walking a mile in his son Fred Savage's moccasins and listening to his sage advice. Or *Made in America* (1993), in which the conniving cracker used car salesman Ted Danson becomes a smoke-free, teetotaling, virtuous father to his black daughter. And what about *Bye Bye Love* (1995), in which three divorced dads (Randy Quaid, Paul Reiser, and Matthew Modine) suffer more from being away from their children than from their divorces, and after painful revelation, become better fathers, and therefore better men. Even Oskar Schindler (*Schindler's List*, 1993) is haunted by that little girl in the red coat, whose terror transfixes and then transforms him. (In case viewers missed the point, Spielberg colorizes her image in the stark black-and-white world of the Holocaust.) Spielberg has made a virtual cottage industry celebrating childhood innocence against the corruptions of adulthood. In *E.T.* (1982), only the love and faith of children enables that elfin extraterrestrial to escape from the prodding and poking invasions of grownup researchers. And then there's *Three Men and a Baby* (1987), in which gurgling infantile innocence tames three devoutly philandering bachelors the way no women ever could.

This trope shows no signs of fading out. One of the first big summer movies of the new millennium was *The Kid* (2000), starring that diehard action hero, Bruce Willis. In this film, he plays a middle-aged jerk who gets his shot at redemption when he meets a ten-year-old boy who reminds him of himself.

In a sense, *Kramer vs. Kramer* is the touchstone text of this new genre. There, Dustin Hoffman, an absentee landlord of domestic patriarchy, is converted to devoted daddydom by making breakfast and sitting by the playground, while his ex-wife, Meryl Streep, is climbing the corporate ladder. Not only can men be nurturing fathers, the film suggested, but they can be better *mothers* than modern women.

And Kramer evokes another timeless theme: it is the sons who will heal the pain of the fathers. Fatherhood is thrust upon him unwittingly, with no preparation, and he gradually transforms himself in the role to become a nurturing parent. Far more than in *Tootsie* (1982), it is in *Kramer vs. Kramer* that Dustin Hoffman "learns to do it without the dress." He learns not to be a woman, whom he can merely imitate, but to be a "mother." As, of course, does Robin Williams, in *Mrs. Doubtfire* (1993), although he also needs the asexuality of the frumpy British nanny in order to get in touch with his "feminine" side.

Nowhere is this theme of the son healing his father's wounds—and, in the process, healing his own "father wound"—more evident than in *Field of Dreams* (1989), a film that ushered in a new genre, the male weepie. (This film was a perfect cipher for the sexes, a John Gray interplanetary gender difference moment: women watched, almost stupefied, at the ending, saying, "I don't get it, they're having a catch?" while their husbands/dates/boyfriends/friends wept openly and said, "they're having a catch!") It is through baseball, America's game, that father and son are reconciled, that the pain of both father and son is finally healed.

Taken together, these fatherhood fables can be read as part of the "backlash-bind" against women. Women have abandoned their role as nurturing mother in their rush toward self-fulfillment in the labor force or, even, sexually. If women would only leave the workplace and go back home, where they belong, they could do their job of taming men and raising children, who would not be placed at such risk that they have to transform a man. (Of course, women can keep working and being independent, but they'll never get a man that way.) Women can either be powerless, long-suffering saving graces (as of old), or powerless, man-less figures on the margin—ultimately to be rescued by their children as well. Writing men in can mean writing women out.

What's more, men still require some external agent to facilitate their transformation from violent, rapacious beast or bumptious ne'er-do-well. Sisters may be doin' it for themselves these days, but their brothers still need a significant amount of help.

Women's Return to Virtue

Women can no longer be counted on to transform bad men into good men, since they have abandoned their natural roles. So who is going to help them return to innocence, to their naturally virtuous state which they abandoned when they left the home and went off to the workplace? Men obviously can't do it: they're programmed to be violent, rapacious beasts without some force to constrain them. And children failed at the task, or at least they can't be counted on since feminism—the glamorous world of work, sexual fulfillment, and individual identity—has seduced women away from their families, homes, and, most importantly, motherhood.

To be sure, there are exceptions, such as *Baby Boom* (1987), the yuppie-becomes-mommy confection starring Diane Keaton. There, the necessity of childcare transforms a corporate career climber into a nurturing mother-substitute, whose business savvy suddenly makes her more successful than she could ever have dreamed earlier. Kids are good for business when you make kids *the* business.

But these days, children can be counted on only to help teach bad men to be good men, but not bad career women into good, nurturing, maternal figures. It would have to be someone who really knows the values of domesticity, someone who can really express feelings and has their priorities straight. Of course, it's gay men! Gay men have stepped into the breach and are teaching straight women how to hold onto their men, their families, and reset their priorities so that domestic bliss comes before career hustles.

Like feminism and the civil rights movement, gay liberation promised more than simply the end of discrimination against gays and lesbians; it promised the transformation of sexual relations themselves—the liberation of sexuality from the yoke of marriage and procreation, and, more importantly, as gay men and lesbians challenged the gender binary, the obliteration of gendered sexuality entirely. Men could behave sexually like both "men" and "women," as could women. Often at the same time! This held the potential to transform the gendering of sexuality at its core.

And like feminism, the gay liberation struggle has sacrificed that larger transformative vision for the acceptance of gay and lesbian individuals, disaggregated and decontextualized. Gay liberation has become the tolerance and acceptance of gays and lesbians within a cultural context and sexual regime that remain as gendered as before. Gay men and lesbians are "normalized," almost "heterosexualized." They, too, want to get married and have families. Hey, they're just like us!

In Hollywood's new rendition, gay men are not the sex-crazed near-maniacal predators of *Cruising* (1980); nor even the genuinely maniacal feminine-wannabes of *The Silence of the Lambs* (1991). Gay men are kind, considerate, nurturing, and, most importantly, domestic. They like the home, they know how to decorate it, and they know that domestic bliss is the only real happiness. Gay men have become today's women.[7] And like women, they may be an object of desire, but they are not its subject—these gay men do not have gay sex.

Their goal is not to change men—men are far too homophobic for that!—but to help women realize the errors of their ways and come back to the home.

This is evident in several other films.[8] For example, in *Four Weddings and a Funeral* (1994), while the feckless Hugh Grant stumbles toward amorous rapprochement with Andie MacDowell, it is the caring committed relationship between the two gay male characters that illustrates the kind of love and caring that straights can only envy.

But in that film, gay male intervention is only indirect, by way of illustration. In *My Best Friend's Wedding* (1997), it is Rupert Everett (an openly gay man playing an openly gay man) who shows the relationship-phobic Julia Roberts that she can balance work and family. Only with his guidance can Roberts, portraying a food critic, have her (wedding) cake and eat it too.

The gay man–straight woman model pairing appears to be a cinematic match made in heaven. Or at least, the act won't be breaking up soon. In *The Next Best Thing* (2000), Everett teams up with Madonna, who portrays a thirtysomething single woman who convinces her best friend, Everett, to be the father of her child before time runs out on her biological clock. Alas, five years later, she falls in love with another man. (This is said to be a work of fiction, and not at all based on the life of the pop diva.)

In the hit comedy *In and Out* (1997), after her fiancé, Kevin Kline, comes out as gay, it's another gay character, the television reporter played by Tom Selleck, who helps Joan Cusack find a man who loves her for exactly who she is— without myths, lies, and illusions. And in *The Object of My Affection* (1998), Jennifer Aniston learns what she really needs in a husband and father for her child—someone with whom she won't have sex!

It is interesting, and perhaps not coincidental, that the emergence of gay men as the nurturing role models who can teach heterosexual women how to keep their priorities straight almost always takes place in the anticipation of a heterosexual wedding. Every one of these films centers on a forthcoming nuptial ceremony, in which the bride's ambivalence, or some other equally contrived plot device, signals the need for gay male intervention. (Even in *The Birdcage* [1996], it's Robin Williams's son's impending wedding that leads to the relationship crisis—in which, as we find out, it is the relationship between Williams and Nathan Lane that provides the real role model to those amorous lovebirds, not that between Gene Hackman and Diane Wiest.) What gay men represent is clear priorities—relationships always come first, before commitment to work.

Even television, long a holdout against gay characters who were remotely sympathetic, has jumped on the gay bandwagon. Several spin-offs of the successful *Will and Grace* are still planned—each one pairing a confused heterosexual career woman and her happy, healthy gay male roommate. It's not coincidental that in these shows gay people are shown mostly hanging around with heterosexuals. Gone is the gay "community," gay "culture," gay "institutions." Like any "good" man, Will wants to get married and settle down. The price for inclusion as gay individuals is the effacement of the social and sexual context in which those individuals exist in real life.[9]

Whereas gay men and lesbians were virtually invisible only a few years ago, by 2003 there were thirteen gay men (one lead, seven regular, and five recurring) characters on major television shows, and nine lesbians (one regular and eight recurring).[10] The flip-side of this increasing visibility, Josh Gamson argues in his book *Freaks Talk Back*, is the removal of the threat posed by gay liberation, its power to transform the lives of heterosexuals (just as the visibility of independent autonomous women also included the removal of feminism's power to transform men). This visibility has been a staple of recent television comedies, like *Will and Grace* or *Ellen*. In order for Will (played by Eric McCormick) to be a credible lead, he must play off his far more flamboyant sidekick Jack (played by Sean Hayes), who so exaggerates camp stereotypes of gay masculinity that Will seems so . . . well, normal. That normalization is crucial to his ability to transform Grace—or at least provide ongoing relationship counsel. Will is far closer to the man of Grace's dreams, which explains why she can't seem to find a straight man who has all of Will's virtues.

What makes gay men such good advisors to straight women is that they both know the pleasures of the home, and they are uncorrupted by lust for women, which, as we all know, is the major thing that makes men behave badly. Gay men are the men we seem to want heterosexual men to be.

(One cynical possibility, however, is that the increase in gay male characters is due to the notion that gay characters are safe enough to use—as long as they don't have sex, safe or otherwise—but that producers can also employ more white male actors and still fulfill their multicultural, identity politics–driven mandates for "diversity.")

Making children and gay men the repository of Rousseauian innocence and virtue may make plots simpler, but also blurs the politics. Gone are the little monsters of Puritanism, whose wills must be broken; gone too the Freudian bundles of sexual energy and infantile aggression. In the depoliticized world in which everything you really needed to know you learned in kindergarten, compassionate politics has become a form of infantile regression. And the costs for gay men are simple: they can never fall in love or have sex themselves. In order for gay men to reorient heterosexual women's botched priorities, they must, themselves, be as virtuous as children, innocent and asexual.

We've argued that the costs for individual inclusion in the public arena have been the decontextualization of those individuals from the community context in which they would ordinarily be embedded, and the effacement of larger visions of social transformation. Gay men and women are "normalized" in the heterosexual and masculine public arena, without any transformation of those men's lives nor the lives of heterosexuals. The gender and sexual regimes of male domination and heteronormativity remain unchallenged, indeed are reinforced. Such fables thus fit snugly into a right-wing family-values agenda, almost suggesting that children need fathers more than they need mothers. (If not fathers, at least patriarchs.) There are no "feminist" marriages here, with two good parents balancing career and family, working as equals for the good of all concerned. And as the Christian Coalition counsels, we're able to "love the sinner and hate the sin," separating homosexuals from homosexuality, because we don't ever allow them to express their own sexuality.

Of course, *Ellen* (Ellen DeGeneres) breaks that mold, and, in so doing, reinforces it. It is permissible (with much right-wing squawking of course) for a woman to kiss another woman. But such a passionate kiss still seems a long way off for two men in a major television show.

In these films and TV shows, both heterosexual women and heterosexual men are in desperate need of transformation. Women have been seduced by the workplace and have abandoned their natural nurturing roles; men never had those roles to begin with and have no way to get in touch with their feelings. Yes, it's true that such films show that men can love children, and even do housework and child care, without sacrificing their masculinity. And they also show that women can remember that it is love and family that provide the center of one's life. But they also show that men and women require some external agent to prompt the transformation, something outside themselves. Men and feminist women won't get better unless they are pushed, we're told; but despite all the prodding and shoving toward heroism and glory, left to themselves they can barely manage a nudge toward being better fathers and mothers, husbands and wives. Nary a whiff of compassion or nurturing wafts upwards from these men or women on their own. In the world of Hollywood masculinity and post-feminist femininity, ethics seem still to reside in some mythic "other," waiting to be inhaled.

NOTES

1. See Virginia Woolf, "Professions for Women," in *Virginia Woolf: Women and Writing*, ed. Michele Barrett (New York: Harcourt, Brace, Jovanovich, 1979), 57–63.
2. One book that in some ways anticipates this discussion is Tania Modleski, *Feminism without Women* (New York: Routledge, 1991).
3. See, for example, Arlie Hochschild, *The Second Shift* (New York: Viking, 1989).
4. See Alfred Kinsey, Wardell B. Pomeroy, and Charles E. Martin, *Sexual Behavior in the Human Female* (Philadelphia: W. B. Saunders, 1953); Alfred Kinsey, Wardell Pomeroy, and Charles Martin, *Sexual Behavior in the Human Male* (Philadelphia, W. B. Saunders, 1948); Edward Laumann, John Gagnon, Robert Michael, and Stuart Michaels, *The Social Organization of Sexuality* (Chicago: University of Chicago Press, 1995); Lillian Rubin, *Words of Pain* (New York: Basic Books, 1976); Lillian Rubin, *Erotic Wars* (New York: Farrar, Straus and Giroux, 1990).

5. One recent case may provide a useful example. In the recent litigation to open Virginia Military Institute (VMI) and The Citadel to women, the only question that could be discussed was whether or not individual women could enter those homosocial state-supported bastions of military masculinity. The larger question of whether or not VMI and The Citadel's brutal educational regime, what they called "the adversative method," was a useful method to develop competent men of integrity for the next century could never be raised. The gendered institution remains unchallenged, despite the entry of women into it.

6. Vivian Sobchack, discussing the role of the child within the genres of contemporary horror film and the family melodrama, argues that the child in the horror film "shows us the terror and rage of *patriarchy in decline* . . . ," while the "popular family melodrama shows us a sweetly problematic *paternity in ascendance.*" See Sobchack, "Child/Alien/Father: Patriarchal Crisis and Generic Exchange," *Camera Obscura* 15 (1986): 7–36. See also, Thomas DiPiero, "The Patriarch Is Not (Just) a Man," *Camera Obscura* 25–26 (1991): 101–124.

7. The literary critic Leslie Fiedler has elaborated a related trope, wherein gay men function as a form of female surrogate, thus releasing straight men from the confines of marriage and letting them off the hook for generations of oppressing the Other. Several other literary scholars have usefully explored this theme, particularly Richard Slotkin, *Regeneration through Violence: The Mythology of the American Frontier, 1600–1800* (Middletown, CT: Wesleyan University Press, 1973); and Richard Volney Chase, *The American Novel and Its Traditions* (Baltimore: Johns Hopkins University Press, 1980).

8. Sharon Willis further elaborates Fiedler's trope, and does so in terms of contemporary film genres. In her chapter, "Mutilated Masculinities and Their Prostheses: Die Hards and Lethal Weapons," she argues that "what these films put forward as the central figure of masculinity in crisis is really white heterosexual masculinity desperately seeking to reconstruct itself within a web of social differences, where its opposing terms include not only femininity but black masculinity and male homosexuality." See Willis, *High Contrast: Race and Gender in Contemporary Hollywood Film* (Durham, NC: Duke University Press, 1997), 31.

9. On this issue see Josh Gamson, *Freaks Talk Back* (Chicago: University of Chicago Press, 1998).

10. Tallies come from GLAAD website, http://www.GLAAD.org/.

3

Reconciliation, Appropriation, Inspiration, and Conversation

Four Strategies of Racial Healing among White Men

Racial inequality is one of America's most persistent and pervasive social problems. Its effects have generally been examined by social scientists in terms of its institutional structure—the institutional and ideological apparatuses that create, legitimate, and reproduce inequality—and by social and behavioral scientists in terms of its corrosive effects on the identities of and relations among those who are adversely affected by it. This is, of course, how it should be—that is, we need to understand the effects of structured social inequality in order to understand the context for the formation of identity, ideologies of masculinity and femininity, relations between and among women and men, and family dynamics.

But seeing the effects of racial inequality on those who are discriminated *against* ought not leave unexamined the effects on those who are discriminated *for*, those who benefit from racism. That is, we need to see also that the persistence of racial inequality in the United States can be the source of ambivalence, discomfort, and guilt for white people as well. After all, with few exceptions, white people do not want to be considered racist. They want to be considered "non-racist." And so the persistence of racism must be absorbed into an identity that is non-racist.

This is typically accomplished through the twin processes of disaggregation—reducing structures to the sum total of the individuals within those institutions—and what we might call "attitudinalization"—the rendering of structural relationships between groups into a problem of individual attitude formation. Thus, racism is assumed to be a psychological variable; racism is defined as holding racist values. So, too, is being "non-racist" a psychological disposition, a collection of individual attitudes and behaviors. One is not a

---

Original to this volume.

racist if one has never owned slaves—a ubiquitous evasion one often hears from contemporary students, even though slavery has been outlawed for nearly 150 years. "Some of my best friends are black," is another common retort to blanket claims about racism. An individual is not a racist if he or she does not hold racist stereotypes or hasn't recently participated in a lynching, "high-tech" or otherwise.

Take, for example, the recent outpouring of self-congratulation *among white people* with the election of Barack Obama as the nation's first African American president. Suddenly, the nation had declared itself to be "post-racial," as if centuries of deep-seated racism could vanish instantly, like a drawing on an Etch A Sketch tablet. And individual people now *knew* they were not racist, that the United States wasn't racist. "How can I be racist when I voted for a black man?" they seemed to be asking. It was the Bradley effect in reverse: instead of feeling safe enough, in the privacy of the voting booth, to vote their hearts and vote against the black candidate, many American voters seem to have voted for Obama as a way to convince themselves that they/we are beyond racism. Call it "premature self-congratulation."

Such psychological responses to structural problems always discomfit sociologists, who see racism not simply as the aggregation of individual racist attitudes or behaviors, but also as a set of structural relationships between groups, discursively maintained through the normative apparatuses of social institutions.

In this essay, I examine four strategies that white men have used in recent years to both dissociate from racism and adopt a non-racist identity. These strategies range from the heartfelt and genuine effort to heal a racial divide to disingenuous efforts to again use men of color to retrieve some lost sense of self or to at least demonstrate one's association with men of color—because of what it affords white men. That is, in several of the examples below, white men again use black men to confirm their own (white) masculinity at the same time that they sustain identities as non-racist.

It is for this reason that I focus specifically on white *men's* responses to racism. My efforts in this essay are a complement to my recent research on the extreme right, where white men use their racism to reaffirm their masculinity. Here, I'm going to suggest, white men seek to use their *non-racism* to reaffirm their masculinity.

I argue that by using men of color to validate their masculinity, however, they reproduce the very racism from which they seek to dissociate. First, they project onto men of color the masculine qualities that they perceive themselves as lacking. Second, they assume the entitlement to retrieve those qualities through their interactions with—or their interactions about—men of color. Third, by offsetting the question from one of race to one of gender, white men can avoid any substantive confrontation with racial privilege. Fourth, white men's efforts to decontextualize racism into a set of attitudes puts men of color, either symbolically or materially, in the position of validating white men's masculinity. Finally, this disconnection of racism from racial inequality—that is, of racist attitudes from the institutional apparatuses that reproduce racial inequality—means that white masculinity can be reaffirmed without any actual confrontation with racial inequality.

For these reasons, I argue that these efforts at racial healing are also moments of "dominance bonding" among men across race. Dominance bonding, as initially defined by sociologist Katherine Farr, is a "process of collective alliance through which the group and its members affirm and reaffirm their superiority." Bonding is central to reaffirm identity, and central to that bonding is a shared sense of superiority to others. Dominance bonding is the glue that holds the powerful together. Sociologist Mike Messner argued that dominance bonding becomes the way that men often experience emotional connection with each other based on shared sense of superiority, conferred by sexism or homophobia. Men reaffirm their masculinity—both their distance from women and their unalloyed heterosexuality—through such bonding. Dominance bonding can be anything from two (apparently) straight men nodding with lascivious smirks as a beautiful woman passes by along a continuum to public sexist or homophobic comments or humor—or worse.[1]

The foundation of this dominance bonding between white men and men of color is also often sexism and homophobia. Shared contempt for and rage at women and gay men is the field on which men of different races are invited to bond as brothers. As a form of psychological theory, sexist and homophobic dominance bonding requires the assumption of an essentialist worldview that sees categorical differences between women and men, gays and straights. As a form of political practice, it uncouples the struggles against racism from the struggles against sexism and heterosexism.

Reconciliation

"Eleven o'clock on Sunday morning is the most racially divided hour of the week."

—Bill McCartney, founder of Promise Keepers

The first strategy I call reconciliation. Reconciliation is based on an understanding of racism as a set of bad or wrong attitudes. White people need to change their attitudes in order to heal the racial divide. While this strategy does place the responsibility for ending racism on the shoulders of white people, it disaggregates the problem, and suggests that if all white people were to change their attitudes, then racism would disappear.

Among the best examples of this strategy is the evangelical Protestant men's movement, Promise Keepers. (I discuss the organization at greater length in chapter 9.) Promise Keepers' message of racial reconciliation is as compelling as it is troubling. On the one hand, reconciliation means that white people must take responsibility for racism and take the initiative in seeking fellowship with men of color. Racism will not end until white people act. Promise Keepers seeks to heal racial divisiveness by bringing black and white men together under the canopy of patriarchy. At a rally I attended, McCartney, the grandfather of two biracial children (both of his daughter Kristyn's lovers were black), declared that a "spirit of white racial superiority" maintains "an insensitivity to the pain of people of color." It is the privileged who must act.

Such a position may make Promise Keepers the single largest virtually all-white group in the nation to make racism a white people's problem. It was a message that energized the overwhelmingly white crowd at the stadium rally I attended. Rich, who is thirty-nine and white, is a single parent from New Jersey, who brought his two sons. He feels that the racial component is important. "In Christ we're all the same," he says. Daniel, a white twenty-seven-year-old, from a working-class neighborhood in Queens, came with another man from his Baptist church, Joseph, a thirty-five-year-old black man originally from Ghana. "As a white person, you kind of take race for granted, you don't see it," Daniel says. "I'm not the one being hurt, but my people have done some terrible things to blacks. As a white person, it's important to take responsibility."

So, what's wrong with this picture of white people taking responsibility for racism, of men becoming more loving, devoted, and caring fathers, friends, and husbands? For one thing, there's the message of reconciliation itself. Theirs is not a call to support those programs that would uplift the race and set the nation on a course toward racial equality. This is not about anti-discrimination legislation or affirmative action; it's not even about integration. (Indeed, most of the white men I asked said that they did not support affirmative action or school busing to achieve integration. The black men did.) Ending racism is about being kinder and more civil. It's about hearing their pain, not supporting its alleviation. It's about choosing to be nicer, but not about policies that force us to be fairer. In the Promise Keeper worldview, racial reconciliation is an individual posture, not a collective struggle.

Being less racist in one's personal life may be laudatory, but without a program of institutional remedies, it leaves untouched the chief forces that keep that inequality in place. That also means that racial reconciliation has no intersectional relationship with the other forms of inequality, such as sexism or heterosexism.

Actually, it is *through* sexism and heterosexism that racial healing is to take place. The inclusion of men of color comes at an exorbitant multicultural price— lopping off several bands of the rainbow through continued exclusion. Gays and lesbians, for example, don't get near the pearly gates. Gay men do not get to sit at the table of brotherhood. McCartney pronounced homosexuality "an abomination against Almighty God," and homosexuals "a group of people who don't reproduce yet want to be compared to people who do." Echoing familiar "love the sinner, hate the sin" rhetoric, McCartney told me at the rally's press conference that homosexuality is "like lying. God doesn't like lying but he loves liars." Perhaps, but would God support a constitutional amendment banning marriages between liars? Would God sanction discrimination against confessed liars?[2]

Even more central than a shared homophobia, white and black men are invited to come together over a shared interest in biblically based patriarchy. The core of masculine spiritual renewal is a return to mid-nineteenth-century separation of spheres as divinely sanctioned roles for men and women. For instance, in return for their keeping their promises to be faithful husbands, devoted fathers, and general all-around good men, the movement's "bible," *The Seven Promises of a Promise Keeper*, suggests that men deal with women this way:

> Sit down with your wife and say "Honey I've made a terrible mistake. I've given you my role in leading this family and I forced you to take my place. Now I must reclaim that role." Don't ask for your role back, take it back. There is to be no compromise on authority and women must submit for the survival of our culture.

The restoration of domestic patriarchy—ceded, they believe, to women by spineless men and harridan feminist women—is the foundation of gender reconciliation. As with race, a truce in the war between the sexes is possible only when one sees that move as an individual outpouring of concern, however heartfelt, for individual women, while ignoring collective efforts at building a new society together. Good, kind, decent men (and white people) can indeed develop better, more emotionally resonant and caring relationships with women and people of color, and then support precisely those policies that perpetuate their pain.

Racial reconciliation, then, is grounded on a notion of responsible manhood that is, in turn, grounded on patriarchy's second coming. Christian soldiers, black and white, must always secure the domestic front.

But such a disaggregated understanding of racism—racial attitudes minus institutionalization—demands little more of white men than that they be nicer to men of color. And in exchange white and black heterosexual men can share in all the entitlements of an unchallenged, indeed, restored, patriarchy.

Appropriation

All across the country in the 1990s, hundreds of thousands of men headed off to the woods and wilderness retreats and workshops to rediscover their "deep" manhood. Spurred, in part, by poet Robert Bly's book, *Iron John*, these "weekend warriors" donned totemic animal symbols and retold ancient myths of male bonding to tap a primitive stream of essential masculinity, long buried by the feminizing worlds of work and home. They called themselves "mythopoetic" after their use of myth and poetry, and they spoke eloquently to men's spiritual hunger, a deep longing for lives of meaning and resonance. Their weekend retreats allowed men to break down the isolation and emotional repression. Here they gave voice, perhaps for the first time, to emotional needs for closeness and friendship with other men, to pain, confusion, and vulnerabilities that were long suppressed in the confused efforts to prove their masculinity.

Underneath all the trappings of mythopoetic manhood—the mythology, faux traditionalism, appropriated Native American and nonindustrial ritualism, bowdlerized Jungian archetypes, and evocations of non-Western initiation—lay a language that sounded more like the recovery movement than the strenuous life. Men, we heard, were also searching for their inner child, healing childhood wounds, and recognizing the addictive patterns characteristic of adult children.

But the movement's search for that authentic masculine center often came at a price: the effacing of gender inequality and a certain unintended and unacknowledged racialized appropriation of the cultural idiom of the other.

Mythopoets embraced an essentialist model of gender identity in which men and women each "suffer" equally by the constraints of their socially defined roles. In most cases, mythopoetic men were respectful of feminist women's efforts to challenge gender inequality, although they believed that such struggles had nothing to do with them, and they therefore were exempt from participating.

Some, though, went further, and argued that women's "power" was actually a source of men's feeling of powerlessness. For example, men "suffered," argued Shepherd Bliss, partly because women maintained a monopoly on themes like oppression and powerlessness. "But women aren't victims," he insisted. "We all know the power of women." In his best-selling book, *Fire in the Belly*, Sam Keen argued that traditional life was harmonious and cooperative: Male and female, each in his or her sphere, living lives of meaning and coherence. Each gender was "half of a crippled whole." Men got the "feeling of power" and women got the "power of feeling"; men got the "privilege of public action" and women got the "privilege of private being," Keen quipped as if these were equivalent. In fact, some argued, men needed to become *more* powerful. Robert Moore and Douglas Gillette urged men to become kings—"aggressive, masculine, potent, . . . a warrior who enforces order within his kingdom and who may take military action to extend his kingdom."[3]

The search for the wild warrior within led men's movement scions to wander through anthropological literature like postmodern tourists, as if the world's cultures were arrayed like so many ritual boutiques in a global shopping mall. These archetypes were then slapped together in a ritual pastiche—part Asian, part African, part Native American. And all totally decontextualized. And yet it was promoted as utterly respectful of those nonindustrial cultures.

Drumming, chanting, "talking sticks," and bonfire dances led one writer to call mythopoetic retreats an example of "spiritual colonialism." But how was it different from the Improved Order of the Red Men at the turn of the twentieth century, wearing war paint while whooping it up during fraternal initiation? Or from the Tomahawk Chop of the Atlanta Braves fans?

Perhaps the turn of the twentieth century analogy is useful in another sense. In nineteenth-century minstrel shows, white performers would don blackface in order to express racial anxieties as well as to gain access to emotions—longing for home and family (especially mother), urban loneliness from spatial displacement, confusions about modern life—that were denied expression by the rigidity of white manhood. Here were all these young Italian, Irish, and Jewish boys trying to make their way in a cold and unfriendly country, repressing their loneliness and voicing a nearly "universal lamentation for homeland and birthplace." Blackface gave them access to those repressed emotions, as they sang of "Mammy," the Swanee River, "de ol' folks at home"— in short, the simple joys of home and hearth.

Of course, such behaviors would be seen as transparently racist today. But the mythopoets adopted what we might call "Redface"—the appropriation of putatively Native American rituals to allow privileged white men access to that set of emotions—community, spirituality, communion with nature—that they felt themselves to have lost and therefore displaced onto Native American cultures.

Inspiration

A significant number of young, white, suburban males see black men as role models. They are inspired by black resistance to authority, by the flirtation with violence and misogyny, and by the arrogant defiance imagined in gangsta rap videos. According to market researchers and music impresarios, between 70 percent and 80 percent of hip-hop consumers are white.[4] What does it mean that so many suburban white guys appropriate inner-city musical genres—as well as the fashion, language, and physical gestures and idioms? Mark Anthony Neal argues that "hip hop represents a space where they work through the idea of how their masculinity can be lived—what they literally take from the hyper-masculine 'black buck' and indeed it is an integral part of the cash and carry exchange."[5]

For the young white men I interviewed for *Guyland*, I found the dominant element of their inspiration was the authenticity of black ghetto masculinity.[6] As with the mythopoets, their position was simultaneously a critique of their own sanitized suburban masculinity and a racialized projection onto the masculinity of the "other." "We spend our entire days trying to fit into a perfect little bubble," said one young suburban father to author Bakari Kitwana. "The perfect $500,000 house. The perfect overscheduled kids. . . . We love life, but we hate our lives. And so I think we identify more with hip-hop's passion, anger and frustration than we do this dream world."[7]

Projecting that authenticity onto inner-city black youth, white youth then consume it in the form of hip-hop music, Sean Jean clothes, and appropriation of ghetto jargon. Think of how some of these terms—"you da man," "keep it real," "pimp my ride"—have become standard young *white* people's lexicon.[8]

At its most extreme iteration, white suburban teenagers become "wiggers." Wiggers seem to spend a good percentage of their time asserting their own authenticity by critiquing the obviously inauthentic posturing of other wiggers. There's even a website—http://www.wiggaz.com/—where they can put each other down to gain credibility points. One white guy says that wiggers' appropriation of African American styles "just look really goofy." They may "try and be all fresh . . . like . . . 'yeah you talking that shit now, watch me and my homies roll up on yo' ass.'" One especially prolific wigger, William "Upski" Wimsatt, describes another as "an effeminate wimp who shrieks 'Sang it Sistaa Soujahhh!' as he traces the cul-de-sacs of suburban St. Louis in his parents' car . . ."[9]

While it is young white guys who buy the majority of the gangsta rap CDs, those same young white guys are in rather scarce supply at hip-hop concerts. There is nary a white face in the crowd when Nelly or Ludacris performs. Consumption of the inner city stops at the borders of the ghetto. As Kevin Powell puts it, white fascination with hip-hop is "just a cultural safari for white people."[10] It's safe; you can "take it off. White hip-hop kids can turn their caps around, put a belt in their pants, and go to the mall without being followed," said one observer.[11]

Wiggaz reduce struggling against racism to styling, to a fashion statement, a consumer choice. It demands little; indeed, this "Afro-Americanization of White youth," as Cornel West puts it in his best-selling book, *Race Matters*, turns out to coexist easily with white guys' opposition to affirmative action. Cultural identification need not lead to political alliance.

The alliance of black and white youth as consumers of hip-hop music and fashion posit that it is class, not race, that is the yawning problem in America anyway. And while there may be some validity to this position, it also lets working-class and middle-class whites off the hook of having to claim any form of privilege.

Which may explain the meteoric rise of Eminem to the pop pantheon. Eminem has become a superstar by being an angry white guy who pretends to be an angry black guy. Anointed by hip-hop performer and impresario Dr. Dre, Eminem is no fabricated product of white music promoters like Vanilla Ice.

Eminem's credibility is based on class, not race. His impoverished downwardly mobile white working-class Detroit background matched that of many other whites who had drifted to the far right; but Eminem took himself into the urban ghetto rather than into the woods with the Michigan Militias. In his autobiographical film, *8 Mile*, his ultimate success comes as he defeats a middle-class black rapper—who goes to prep school!—thus asserting class solidarity over racial divisiveness.

But the foundation of Eminem's credibility is also misogynist and homophobic rage. And while he has recently backed off the vicious homophobia of his early career, he continues to draw from a deep well of class-based, gendered rage directed largely at his mother and girlfriend, as well as adolescent declarations of manhood that were part protest and part phallic fluff. Poverty was emasculating; reclaiming manhood required confronting those who were his competitors.

Taking musical or sartorial inspiration from poor urban black youth is hardly a strategy for young white men to challenge racism. It asks little of white people, save a racialized identification with the "other." And, as the inspiration confirms every racist stereotype of black men—violent, out of control, sexual predators—it may even reproduce the very racism its proponents believe they are transcending.[12]

Conversation

Every evening during his commute from work, Jim, twenty-six, joins nearly a million other guys as he tunes into WFAN ("The Fan") radio in New York, and listens to *Mike and the Mad Dog*—a 5½ hour call-in sports-talk show that he listens to on his computer during slow moments at work, and then all the way back on his commute to the Long Island suburban house he shares with his wife and their two-year-old daughter. "I love listening to *Mike and the Mad Dog*," he tells me.

> The guys who call are great, really knowledgeable, and Mike always steers the conversation away from nasty comments about women or about athletes' private lives. You know, I mean sex lives. I think that's why the athletes themselves go on the show, because they know he respects them. I've even called in a couple of times, you know. Pulled over on the fucking LIE to mouth off about the Jets or the Mets. And he completely agreed with me.

Sports talk is a place of retreat, a defensive circling of the rhetorical wagons. Once, guys liked sports in part because they assumed girls did not. Sports could identify them as men, validate their masculinity, and take them to that all-male bonding place that feels like it's theirs alone. But since girls have entered the playing field, men now retreat to a place that women don't typically go: the radio dial, the TV, the sports pages, the sports bar. The places where we talk about sports. If girls can now compete *on* the field, then sports talk—and talk radio, ESPN Zone, and the host of sites and blogs and commentary—is the new boys' club, the place where the homosocial purity of the locker room is reproduced. ESPN knows its target demographic; SportsCenter devotes less than 2 percent of air time to the coverage of women's sports.[13]

The most popular sports radio show, *The Jim Rome Show*, boasts about two million daily listeners. The announcement heralding his show suggests a slightly older demographic than eighteen- to twenty-six-year-olds, but allows for significant cross-generational bonding as well: "Your hair is getting thinner, your paunch is getting bigger, but you still think the young babes want you! That's because you listen to Sports 1140AM. It's not just sports talk, it's culture."

It's as homosocial a space as you are likely to find on your radio dial—or, indeed, virtually anywhere in the country, real or digital. Between 85 and 90 percent of the audience is male.[14] Communications scholar David Nylund has been interviewing guys who listen to sports talk radio, and especially to Jim Rome. Here is what one twenty-seven-year-old told him:

> It's a male-bonding thing, a locker room for guys in the radio. You can't do it at work, everything's PC now! So the Rome Show is a last refuge for men to bond and be men. It's just in your car, Rome, and it's the audience that you can't see. I listen in the car and can let the maleness come out. I know its offensive sometimes to gays and women . . . you know . . . when men bond . . . but men need that! Romey's show gives me the opportunity to talk to other guy friends about something we share in common. And my dad listens to Romey also. So my dad and I bond also.[15]

Male bonding in a purified all-male world. Bonding with father.

Sports radio depends on listener participation; listeners call in with comments, criticisms, and observations. It's the pure democracy of the New England town meeting. It's the pure meritocracy that you were supposed to be experiencing in the workplace, but aren't. If you know your stuff, you get to participate in the conversation. If you are the informed citizen, you win the admiration and respect of your community.[16]

Sports talk is filled with as many masculine virtues as an all-night bull session with Alexander the Great. But its function, I believe, is somewhat less than heroic. Sports radio provides what so many other venues, now lost to the steamroller of political correctness, used to provide. Notice that sports talk is decidedly *not* politically correct. It's offensive—especially to women and gays. That's because much of sports talk turns out not to be about sports but about those other groups. Joking about gays and women, putting them down, this is the ground on which male sports bonding often takes place. It's hardly innocent;

in fact, it has a kind of defensively angry tone to it. "This is our space, dammit, and it's the last place where we can say what we really feel about them!" In sports radio, guys have permission to be as sexist and homophobic as they want to be, with no guardians of the Nanny State policing them.

But the one thing that is out of bounds is racism. Say what you want about women and gays—but since sports radio is also the ground for racial healing among men, racism is not tolerated. This is what fabulously popular and defensively politically incorrect talk show host Don Imus found out to his eternal discredit. It wasn't the sexism in his comment that the Rutgers women's basketball team (which made an unpredicted run to the national finals in the NCAA basketball tournament) was "a bunch of nappy-headed ho's" that got him in trouble. Everyone calls women bitches and ho's on talk radio. It was the "nappy-headed" part—that old-school racism—that immediately mobilized everyone from the Rev. Al Sharpton to New Jersey's governor.

As guys talk about sports, there may be many other conversations taking place. But none is more important than the conversation about race. Sports talk brings men of different backgrounds together, bridging a racial or class divide that would otherwise be hard to breach. In the sports bar, or on sports talk radio, white and black men share a similar love for a team, or a player, and find out that they have a lot in common. Their gender—being men—is suddenly more important than being black or white. It's not that race is off-limits, but racism is.

Sports talk "can temporarily break down barriers of race, ethnicity, and class," as literary scholar Grant Farred put it. "White suburbanites, inner-city Latino and African-American men can all support the New York Knicks or the Los Angeles Dodgers."[17] And the rage expressed at women (especially "feminists") and gays is the *lingua franca* of that cross-racial bonding. Here's an example of racial healing based on the dictum that the enemy of my enemy is my friend.

For black men, this cross-racial bonding through sports talk may serve as a way to assert their intelligence, their ticket for entry into a white-dominated world. Black guys are accustomed to white scrutiny of their physical prowess on the athletic field; talking about sports is a way for them to also assert that they can exercise the muscle between their ears.

Sports talk also enables white guys to enter what they often perceive as a black-dominated arena. Like those legions of white suburban guys who listen to gangsta rap, talking about sports with black guys is a form of self-congratulatory racial reassurance, a way of demonstrating to yourself and others that you are not a racist. Talking about sports with black guys is often the only time they talk with black guys at all. It's a moment of racial healing, a way to feel that they are part of the solution, not part of the problem.

But the problem with this is that it often expresses the very racism it's supposed to undermine. Consider one recent example. After Los Angeles Lakers star Kobe Bryant was accused and arrested for sexual assault, every console in sports talk radio America lit up for days with guys eager to defend Kobe and vilify his accuser. His fans seem to have felt betrayed—by his being accused in the first place. "After all, we know Kobe, and this is totally out of character for him," was the way one sports-radio talk show host put it when Bryant was first accused. (It is almost certain that the speaker had never met Bryant.) "These women are out there, and it's a dangerous world for these guys." (We might more accurately say, "These entitled predatory guys are out there and it's a dangerous world for these women.")

Why were his legions of white fans so eager to defend Bryant? One might see this in a bit starker relief if we try a thought experiment. Imagine that Allen Iverson or Latrell Sprewell, two talented black basketball players, had been accused of sexual assault. Would there have been such a comparable outcry, such rage at their accusers? It's unlikely, because Iverson and Sprewell are already seen as "thugs"; few, therefore, would rise to their defense. In fact, both have been involved in assaults and neither got much public sympathy. Or take Michael Vick, who pled guilty in August 2007 to gambling and other crimes related to his sponsorship and participation in dog fighting. Vick turned out to be a "bad black man" and so his legions of supporters ran for cover. Who can possibly defend a guy who is accused of sadistically murdering Huckleberry Hound? Now, try a different example. Imagine that the accusations were leveled against Tiger Woods or Derek Jeter. Millions of fans—most of them white—would instantly rise to their defense. And it's not because Woods and Jeter are of multicultural parentage and therefore not "really" black. Rather, it's because, in the eyes of white fans, they're not really "black." They're not "bad" black men like Vick, Iverson, and Sprewell. They're "our" blacks, "good" blacks, the kind of blacks that white fans love to cheer for. They're the kinds of blacks we can emulate, and then congratulate ourselves that we're not racist—see, I even wear a Jeter jersey!

In part, this separation harks back to the nineteenth century, to the difference between field slaves, imagined as defiant and violent, needing to be subdued, and house slaves, well-trained, subservient to the wishes of the master. Accusing Kobe Bryant of sexual assault undermines the white fans' self-serving division of black athletes into "good" blacks and "bad" blacks, which, in turn, exposes the racism that creates such divisions in the first place. After all, if Kobe is guilty, then this difference between black men would dissolve, and white fans might be left with no other conclusion than the obviously racist "they're all the same" argument. In their eyes, acquitting Kobe Bryant was an act of racial healing.

Supporting Kobe Bryant on sports radio, bonding with their black brothers over shared information, exposes the fantasy that sports talk—or even athletic participation—can exert a permanent palliative effect on racial politics in

America. Those moments on the radio, or in the sports bar, are transient at best, fraudulent at worst.

Indeed, all four strategies of racial healing are doomed to fail. Abandoning racist attitudes is a necessary, but insufficient, element of ending racial inequality. That also will require that white men and men of color work together to transform those institutions which sustain and reproduce racial inequality. The field of racial healing cannot also be a field on which the equality of women or gays and lesbians is sacrificed. As in all illnesses, healing can only come when the full extent of the sickness is revealed and treated.

NOTES

1. Katherine Farr, "Dominance Bonding in the Good Old Boys' Sociability Group," *Sex Roles* 18 (1988): 259–277; see also Michael Messner, *Taking the Field* (Minneapolis: University of Minnesota Press, 2003), 31–37; and Peter Lyman, "The Fraternal Bond as a Joking Relationship: A Case Study of the Role of Sexist Jokes in Male Group Bonding," in *Men's Lives*, ed. Michael Kimmel and Michael Messner, 8th ed. (Boston: Pearson, 2008).

2. I borrow this formulation from my essay on PK, reprinted here as chapter 9.

3. See Sam Keen, *Fire in the Belly* (New York: Bantam, 1991).

4. Julie Watson, "Rapper's Delight: A Billion Dollar Industry," *Forbes*, February 18, 2004; available at: http://www.forbes.com/2004/02/18/cx_jw_0218hiphop.html; accessed December 24, 2005; see also figures cited in Bill Yousman, "Blackophilia and Blackophobia: White Youth, the Consumption of Rap Music, and White Supremacy," *Communication Theory* 13(4) (November 2003): 367.

5. Mark Anthony Neal, "Hip Hop's Gender Problem," *Africana*, May 26, 2004; available at: http://archive.blackvoices.com/articles/daily/mu20040526hipgender.asp; accessed December 20, 2005.

6. See *Guyland: The Perilous World Where Boys Become Men* (New York: HarperCollins, 2008).

7. Cited in Bakari Kitwana, *Why White Kids Love Hip Hop: Wankstas, Wiggers, Wannabes, and the New Reality of Race in America* (New York: Basic Books, 2005), 4.

8. See, for example, the interesting discussion of this among linguists like Mary Bucholtz, "'You da man': Narrating the Racial Other in the Production of White Masculinity," *Journal of Sociolinguistics* 3(4) (1999): 443–460; Cecelia Cutler, "'Keeping It Real': White Hip Hoppers Discourses of Language, Race, and Authenticity," *Journal of Linguistic Anthropology* 13(2) (2003): 1–23; Cecelia Cutler, "Yorkville Crossing: White Teens, Hip Hop, and African American English," *Journal of Sociolinguistics* 3(4) (1999): 428–442; Mary Bucholz, "Borrowed Blackness: African American Vernacular English and European American Youth Identities" (PhD dissertation, University of California, Berkeley, 1997).

9. William "Upski" Wimsatt, *Bomb the Suburbs* (New York: Soft Skull Press, 1994), 19; cited in Artemis Leah Brod, "Ironic Appropriations: Creating White Masculinities through Hip-Hop" (BA thesis, Reed College, April 2005), 6. I am grateful to Artemis Brod for lending me her stunning thesis, though I am afraid I treat the subject far less ironically than she would suggest. See also Charles Aaron, "What the White Boy Means When He Says Yo," *Spin*, November 1998.

10. Powell is cited in Kitwana, *Why White Kids Love Hip Hop*, 53. Unfortunately, I'm not in the slightest persuaded by Bakari Kitwana's argument that white suburban consumption of hip-hop heralds the arrival of new racial politics in America, a new inclusiveness and opposition to racism on the part of white music consumers. Consumption of the "other's" culture may easily coexist with discrimination against the other in real life; indeed, the consumption of the other's culture may make such discrimination less transparent, and thus more palatable to the white majority.

11. Melvin Donaldson, cited in Kitwana, *Why White Kids Love Hip Hop*, 148.

12. Nelson George, *Hip Hop America* (New York: Penguin, 1998), xi.

13. Michael Messner, *Out of Play: Critical Essays on Gender and Sport* (Albany: SUNY Press, 2007), 3.

14. Adams, "Sports Talk Radio."

15. See David Nylund, *Beer, Babes, and Balls: Masculinity and Sports Talk Radio* (Albany: SUNY Press, 2007).

16. See, for example, Christopher Burke, "Fans Find a Voice on the Airwaves," *Yale Daily Herald*, January 17, 1997; available at: http://www.yaleherald.com/archive/xxiii/1.17.97/sports/elitorial.html.

17. Grant Farred, "Cool as the Other Side of the Pillow: How ESPN's SportsCenter Has Changed Television Sports Talk," *Journal of Sport and Social Issues* 24(2) (2000): 96–117.

PART TWO

Reversals

- When women said they wanted to go to work, they were accused of being anti-motherhood.
- When women said they wanted men to become more involved as fathers, they were accused of being anti-male.
- When women said they wanted to create positive programs for girls in schools, they were accused of being anti-boy.
- When women said they were pro-motherhood, and wanted to enable women to be able to be both workers and mothers, they were accused of being selfish and wanting to "have it all."
- When women said they wanted the violence to stop, that they wanted to live free of fear of sexual assault and domestic violence, they were accused of ignoring the legions of men who were equally the victims of domestic violence.
- When women said they were angry that gender inequality holds them back, they were accused of hating men.

That's pretty much how the sustained assault on women's equality has gone over the past few decades. It's interesting that every time women claim something for themselves, the backlash always insists that it's actually about men. Thus anger at inequality becomes hating men. Being "for women" is equated with being anti-male. Such a sleight of hand is how gender inequality works: it's always about us. Even when it's not, even when it's about something else.

This section includes three essays that debunk some of these current mis-framings. In "Who Are the Real Male Bashers?" I try to show that, contrary to deliberately manufactured popular opinion, feminist women have a far more positive view of men than several of the anti-feminist crusaders, whether they originate in pop biology, self-help pop psychology, or in general anti-feminist claims. Anti-feminists believe that males are hardwired to be violent, rapacious predators, and when confronted with evidence of men acting like . . . well, acting like violent, rapacious predators, they throw up their hands and sigh, resignedly, "Boys will be boys." "What did you expect?" they seem to ask. That's just how men are. By contrast, feminists believe that boys and men can do better than that, that men are also hardwired for compassion and love, and that boys and men can be human beings, not uncontrollable animals.

"What about the Boys?" addresses the "crisis" of boys in school. While it's true that many colleges and universities have greater female than male enrollments, the cause of this shift has hardly been a feminist cabal that has made being a boy just short of being a felony. It has to do instead with structural issues that have nothing whatever to do with feminist efforts: an economy that still encourages far more boys than girls to go straight into the workplace in construction, manufacturing, and other blue-collar jobs (although the current economic crisis makes this decision even more fraught); the unleashing of women's ambitions from centuries of being stifled; and dramatic changes in school accountability due to the No Child Left Behind Act, which, by mandating achievement standards and providing no funding, has led many schools to cut back on those non-curricular activities, such as recess, gym, and organized sports, that tend to enhance boys' school experience.

More than that, boys' lack of success in schools, ranging from primary school through college (fewer honors and the like), has less to do with women's gains in some zero-sum calculus than in the definition of masculinity itself—a definition that relies on both anti-intellectualism and anti-authoritarianism—and the perceived feminization of the educational curriculum. That is, the zero-sum calculus exists elsewhere, not between girls and boys, but in the minds of boys themselves. Put most simply: boys can either succeed at school or succeed at masculinity, but they cannot succeed at both. Such a cruel calculus, enforced in classrooms and playgrounds in virtually every school in the country, pushes boys away from school success as if in a centrifuge.

"'Gender Symmetry' in Domestic Violence" provides an empirical riposte to another claim, that women are violent toward men at rates that are pretty much equal to the rates at which men are violent toward women. It turns out that these sorts of claims are possible only if one massages the categories of analysis (severity of the violence, frequency, who initiates it) into an unrecognizable shape. Most studies that find gender symmetry are based on the Conflict-Tactics Scale (CTS), which asks some questions, doesn't ask others, and then only asks one spouse or the other. It turns out that the CTS is less a reliable instrument and more like the massage school for data on interpersonal violence.

The entire argument about gender symmetry rests on a contradiction. The very pundits who insist that women hit men as often as men hit women are the same people who also insist that male and female behavior is biologically fixed, genetically programmed, or an evolutionary imperative. Thus, the people who insist that there is gender symmetry turn out to be the same people who insist that boys will be boys, and that boys are biologically driven to be wild, rapacious animals.

I realize that a foolish consistency has never been the hallmark of anti-feminist crusaders from Rush Limbaugh and Lionel Tiger to Camille Paglia and Christina Hoff Sommers, but how could anyone possibly believe that this innate propensity for violence and predation (which Paglia actually celebrates) simply stops cold at the bedroom door? Talk about magical thinking! And besides, none of these people actually claims that the rates of violence against women are artificially inflated; rather, they claim only that the rates for women hitting men are equally high (not that the rates for women are equally as low as men's). Even if that were true, then the only sensible policy implication of the gender symmetry crowd would be to advocate doubling the funding for all domestic violence programs nationwide. I could definitely get behind that! Alas, that isn't what they suggest at all. They actually propose cutting funding to women's shelters. Why? So that women would be equally badly served?

I say let's assume the gender symmetry crowd is right. Double the funding. Open up twice the number of shelters. And let's just see who comes. My guess? Battered women will finally get the resources they've needed all along.

4

Who Are the Real Male Bashers?

Ask a group of college women these days if any among them is a feminist. No one will volunteer. The predictable litany then begins. "I like being a woman." "I'm not a lesbian." "I want to be attractive." And, most telling, "I don't hate men. Feminists are all male bashers."

This is the other side of "I'm not a feminist but . . ."—which these same women also utter. After all, an overwhelming majority of college women support what would be the key policy issues of feminism—the right to choose, the right to enter any school, occupation, or profession they choose, the right to be safe in those workplaces, in their homes, or on dates.

But, they'll still insist, they're not feminists. Asked for some evidence of these ostensibly damning qualities, and they'll trot out some line they heard on Rush Limbaugh, or some hyperbolic line, quoted out of context, by Andrea Dworkin to the effect that feminists believe "all men are rapists."

Do feminists actually believe that all men are rapists? It's common to read that radical feminist author Andrea Dworkin thought so.[1] In fact, all manner of furious male-bashing, man-hating, and anti-sex ideas have been projected onto her. In reality, Dworkin didn't say that all men are rapists and that all sex is rape. She said something far more subversive: it's *men* who think so, not her.

"If one has eroticized a differential in power that allows for force as a natural and inevitable part of intercourse," she writes in the preface to the paperback edition of her book *Intercourse*, "how could one understand that [I do] not say that all men are rapists or that all intercourse is rape? Equality in the realm of sex is an antisexual idea if sex requires domination in order to

---

Original to this volume.

register as sensation." In an interview with a British journalist, she made it clearer:

> Most men and a good number of women experience sexual pleasure in inequality. Since the paradigm for sex has been one of conquest, possession, and violation, I think many men believe they need an unfair advantage, which at its extreme would be called rape. I don't think they need it. I think . . . sexual pleasure can and will survive equality.

Dworkin believes that something terrible happens to boys as they become men, and that something is that they are poisoned by inequality, and come to believe that their humanity depends on denying humanity to women. "How does it happen that the male child whose sense of life is so vivid that he imparts humanity to sun and stone changes into the adult male who cannot grant or even imagine the common humanity of women?" she asks. Not exactly the words of a man-hater, are they?[2]

Well, if not radical feminists like Dworkin, then who? Does anyone in their right mind hate men so much that they believe all men are rapists? Yes.

There are several bunches of male bashers running around these days—and they're not at all who you might think. Some of them, in fact, are the same folks who loudly and vociferously denounce feminism. Take, for example, "evolutionary psychology," that dressed-up-with-no-scientific-place-to-go "theory" that purports—in what must be the ultimate triumph of form over content—to explain all social behavior from the basic "facts" of size and number of male and female reproductive cells. Claiming the mantle of Darwinian pseudo-science from the now-discredited sociobiologists, evolutionary psychology also now informs the misguided policy recommendations of conservative policy analysts like Christina Hoff Sommers, Charles Murray, and David Blankenhorn. And, of course, bad science and bad politics add up to really bad pop therapy—as in the books by Dr. Laura and John Gray, who turn those pseudo-scientific stereotypes into pop psychology.

Charles Darwin, "Misandrist"

It may come as a shock to you, but Charles Darwin hated men. Or so it would appear from reading those evolutionary psychologists who claim to base their theories on his writings.

"Feminists, Meet Mr. Darwin" was how Robert Wright titled his exposition of the field in a well-circulated article in *The New Republic*[3]—as if a confrontation with Darwinian evolution would dispel feminist myths and discredit efforts to implement gender equality. Evolutionary psychology is not a natural science, but a social science, which is to say it is an oxymoron. It cannot conform to the canons of a science like physics, in which falsifiability is its chief goal, and replication its chief method. It does not account for variations in its universalizing pronouncements, nor does it offer the most parsimonious explanations. It is speculative theory, often provocative and interesting, but no more than that. It is like—gasp!—sociology. And, as in sociology, there are some practitioners who will do virtually anything to be taken seriously as "science," despite the fact that individual human beings happily confound all predictions based on aggregate models of behavior.

In the evolutionary psychological worldview, all human nature, and all gender-based differences, are encapsulated in the differences between males and females in the mating game. Males and females, we learn, have different reproductive "strategies" based on the size and number of their reproductive cells. From the cellular—sperm and egg—we get the psychological—namely motivation, intention, perhaps even cognition. Presto, "evolutionary psychology." Male reproductive success comes from impregnating as many females as possible; females' success comes from enticing a male to provide and protect the vulnerable and dependent offspring. Sex, you see, is "something females have that males want," according to Donald Symons.[4] Forget all that distracting stuff about female agency or desire; assumptions gleaned from advanced consumer society—sex as a commodity—are read back onto cultures for which sex could be "about" any number of things.

Thus males have a natural predisposition towards promiscuity, sex without love, and parental indifference; females have a natural propensity for monogamy, love as a precondition of sex, and parental involvement. "It is possible to interpret *all* other differences between the sexes as stemming from this one basic difference," writes Richard Dawkins in his celebrated work, *The Selfish Gene*. "Female exploitation begins here."[5]

These arguments have been effectively exposed as ideology masquerading as science by primatologist Sarah Blaffer Hrdy, who has used the exact same empirical observations to construct an equally plausible case for females' natural propensity toward promiscuity (to seduce many males into believing the offspring is theirs and thus ensure survival by increasing food and protection from those males) and males' natural propensity toward monogamy (to avoid being run ragged providing for offspring that may—or may not—be their own).

If I were a female at the mythic Darwinian moment of origin, Hrdy suggests, and if I knew that I had to invest a lot of time and energy in reproduction, I'd do the following: I'd "decide" to conceal ovulation so that any male I mate with would believe he is the father of my children and would then have to protect and provide for the reproduction of his genetic material. Then I'd promptly go out and have sex with as many males as possible, so that each would believe the offspring to be his, and then each would work his butt off to feed and protect all the children who might—or might not—be his. Hoggamus higgamous, woman's polygamous! Female exploitation actually *ends* there; that is, it's a present-day phenomenon read back into a mythic history, a faux-Darwinian "just-so" story.

In an effort to insure successful reproduction, a reasonable man, by contrast, probably calculates the likelihood of any particular mating resulting in a healthy live offspring. Do the math, as journalist Natalie Angier does in her marvelous book, *Woman: An Intimate Geography*: let's say that I am able, somehow, to "know" when a woman is ovulating (unlike other mammals who go into heat, human females conceal ovulation, thus masking their periods of fertility) and therefore likely to conceive. The odds are still nearly two-to-one against fertilization *on the day she is ovulating*. Even if conception occurs, the embryo still has nearly a one-third chance of miscarrying at some point. Thus, as Angier puts it, "each episode of fleeting sex has a remarkably small probability of yielding a baby—no more than 1 or 2 percent at best."[6]

But if a man were to invest a lot more time with one woman, mating with her often, and preventing her from possible matings with others (what animal behaviorists call "mate guarding"), then his odds of successful reproduction would significantly increase. Higgamus hoggamus—it's man who's monogamous!

And just to keep her in her place, he would surround his sexual control over her with an ideological veneer (let's call it "love") and by legally sanctioning it by church and state (let's call that "marriage"). What gender invented love anyway? And given that men control all other arenas of social, economic, and political life, why would they ever cede the single most important arena—successful reproduction, the raison d'etre of all life—to women?

While the feminist critique successfully exposes evolutionary psychology's ideological view of women, their view of men is even more noxious. "Human males are by nature oppressive, possessive, flesh-obsessed pigs," writes Wright. "Giving them advice on successful marriage is like offering Vikings a free booklet titled 'How Not to Pillage,'" he writes in his best-selling book, *The Moral Animal.*[7] Seriously, had Gloria Steinem or Catharine MacKinnon penned these lines, conservative pundits would be howling with derision at such feminist male bashers.

A brief look at one of evolutionary psychology's canonical books provides some insight into exactly how vile is their view of men. Randy Thornhill and Craig Palmer's *A Natural History of Rape: Biological Bases of Sexual Coercion* (1999) represents evolutionary psychology's finest hour.[8] Having been professionally trained to study scorpion flies, Thornhill now pronounces on all animal species. And in all animal species, these authors argue, rape is "a natural, biological phenomenon that is a product of human evolutionary heritage."[9]

You see, the male's biological predisposition is to reproduce, and his reproductive success comes from spreading his seed as far and wide as possible; women are actually the ones with the power, since they get to choose which males will be successful. "But getting chosen is not the only way to gain sexual access to females," they write. "In rape, the male circumvents the females' choice."[10] Rape is the evolutionary mating strategy of losers, males who cannot otherwise get a date. Rape is an alternative to romance; if you can't always have what you want, you take what you need.

Let's be sure we have this right. In their eyes, all men are violent, rapacious predators, seeking to spew their sperm far and wide, at whatever creature happens in their testosterone-crazed evolutionary path. Oh, sure, they try and sugarcoat it:

> human males in all societies so far examined in the ethnographic record possess genes that can lead, by way of ontogeny, to raping behavior when the necessary environmental factors are present, and that the necessary environmental factors are sometimes present in all societies studied to date.[11]

All men have the "motivation" to rape; all they need is social permission. Who says no one in his or her right mind could possibly believe that all men are rapists? These guys do.

Such male-bashing rhetoric is based on some assumptions that few, if any, would subscribe to today. Thornhill and Palmer assume that rape is about sex—"Rapists are sexually motivated," they write[12]—and that sex is about reproduction.

To be sure, rape *can be* about sex. Surely, three decades of feminist advocacy and social science research on date and acquaintance rape indicates that some rapes are a product of a combination of sexual desire, contempt for women's bodily integrity, and sexual entitlement. Few feminists or social scientists would, today, argue that rape is *never* about sex.

But if rape can sometimes also be partly about sex, it is rarely *only* about sex. Gang rape, prison rape, military rape of subject populations, rape prior to murder, rape *after* murder—these don't necessarily admit to rape-as-alternate-strategy-to-express-sexual-desire. Rape may also be about sexual repulsion, about rage and fear, about domination. Rape of women may be a homosocial event, by which one group of men expresses its domination over another group of men. Rape is a multidimensional phenomenon, offering a large amount of variation. Thornhill and Palmer's view of rape is monochromatic, and embraces only a small fraction of its remarkable variety.

Men use their penises for many motivations, and they are not all reproductive. Sex can be about play, about pleasure, about cementing bonds between females and males, or even between males or between females. It may—or it may not—have anything to do with reproduction. (I would bet that neither Thornhill nor Palmer has more than three children each, and would hope that both have made love more than three times. I would hope that their partners would tell a story of two men who know sex is not only about reproduction.) The clitoris, for example, seems to have evolved strictly because of its capacity for pleasure. Since it evolved, then, it means that pleasure has something to do with reproductive success in humans.

Since "selection favored males who mated frequently," they argue, then "rape increased reproductive success."[13] But why should this be true? Might it not also be the case that being hardwired to be good lovers and devoted fathers enabled us to be reproductively successful? One might argue that selection favored males who mated *well*, since successful mating is more than spreading of seed. After all, human males are the only primates for whom skillful love-making, enhancing *women's* pleasure, is normative, at least in many societies. (Don't go talking about "her pleasure" to those pesky little scorpion flies!)

Being an involved father assured reproductive success far better than rape. After all, babies are so precious, so fragile, that they need extraordinary—and extraordinarily long!—care and devotion. Infants conceived during rape would have a far lower chance of survival, which is probably one reason why we invented love. Infants conceived in rape might well have been subject to infanticide—historically, the most common form of birth control before the modern era.

Is rape "natural"? Of course it is. As is *any* behavior or trait found among human primates. If it exists in nature, it's natural. Some "natural" beverages contain artificial—"social"—additives that give them their color, their texture, their taste, their "meaning" or "significance." This is equally true of rape. Telling us that it is natural tells us nothing about it except that it is found in nature.

But Thornhill and Palmer's political hand is revealed when they move from nature to culture, and tell us what we can do to alleviate the problem of rape. The press release that accompanied my copy of the book notes that the authors recommend that "young women consider the biological causes of rape when making decisions about dress, appearance, and social activities." "But where is the evidence that women in mini-skirts are more likely to be raped than women in dirndls?" asks Barbara Ehrenreich. "Women were raped by the thousands in Bosnia for example, and few if any of them were wearing bikinis or bustiers."[14] Many rapes—in war, in prison—have nothing to do with ensuring reproductive success and everything to do with domination and humiliation of other men. Rape may be far more of a homosocial act than a heterosexual one.

They also propose that we institute "an evolutionarily informed education program for young men that focuses on increasing their ability to restrain their sexual behavior." "Restrain"? Is it that bad? How about "express"—their equally evolution-based biological drive to experience pleasure, mutuality, and fun? Might we not be "hard-wired" for that as well? Education for restraint is perhaps the second most politically bankrupt policy initiative around, and utterly ineffective. (The first is demanding that women "just say no.") If Thornhill and Palmer were right—and of course they are not—then the only sensible solution would be to lock all males up and release them for sporadic, reproductive mating after being chosen by females.

Thornhill and Palmer offer a far more "misandrous" account of rape than anything offered by radical feminists. To them, men are driven by evolutionary imperatives to rape, pillage, and destroy in order to insure that our seed gets planted. If women are not compliant, we men are hard-wired to take what we want anyway. They have the power of choice, but when we're not chosen—well, we get testy. "They made us do it because we can't get them any other way. And we simply *must* have them."

I've heard that before. From rapists! That's who will really find Thornhill and Palmer's arguments comforting. I can imagine that Thornhill's phone has been ringing off the hook with attorneys defending men accused of rape, asking him to be an expert witness for the defense. "You see, your honor, as I wrote, 'rape has evolutionary—and thus genetic—origins.'"

"Aha!" comments the defense lawyer. "So he was driven by his biological imperative to reproduce? How could he be held accountable for some behavior that he was compelled to do by his body? He simply had to have her!"

To them, men can make no choices, have no agency, are propelled by the dust of our ancestors to be marauding, murderous animals.

Me, I'll side with a friend who had a set of "splash guards" devised for Rape Awareness Week at his university. (For those who don't know, a splash guard is the plastic grate that is placed in men's public urinals that prevents splatter.) He had thousands made up with a simple and hopeful slogan. It says simply: "You hold the power to stop rape in your hand."

Boys Will Be Boys: Watch Out!

Reliance on such bad biology is all the rage among the pundits of the right. Driven by testosterone, propelled by natural aggressiveness and predation, men simply must be tamed. And that's women's job. By abandoning their natural roles as wives and mothers in the home, seeking satisfaction in the workplace in some vain imitation of men, women, encouraged by feminism, have reversed nature's plan and wreaked social havoc. Absentee fathers, sexual promiscuity, gang rape, and homosexuality are the inevitable result.

It takes a certain funhouse genius to turn such slanders against men into an anti-feminist screed. And that inspirational genius seems to have come from George Gilder, the guru of the New Right's sexual philosophy, such as it is. Gilder's 1973 book, *Sexual Suicide*, caused a few ripples; but its repackaging and republication in 1986 as *Men and Marriage* reads now like the ur-text of right-wing male bashing.[15]

To say that Gilder's view of men is not particularly pleasant would be a massive understatement. Hobbes's view that in the state of nature, the life of man is "solitary, poor, nasty, brutish and short," is an apt description, Gilder believes, of *gendered* human nature—that is, of men's lives.

> Men are, by nature, violent, sexually predatory, and irresponsible: Men lust, but they know not what for; they wander, and lose track of the goal; they fight and compete, but they forget the prize; they spread seed, but spurn the seasons of growth; they chase power and glory, but miss the meaning of life.[16]

An "importunate, undifferentiated lust . . . infects almost all men." Male sexuality is haphazard, irresponsible, non-procreative; intercourse is "the only male sex act."[17] Sexually inferior, we compensate with sexual aggression and predation.

Gilder reserves his fiercest animus for younger men and boys who are, in his eyes, untamed beasts:

> Every society, each generation, faces an invasion by barbarians. They storm into the streets and schools, businesses and households of the land, and, unless they are brought to heel, they rape and pillage, debauch and despoil the settlements of society.[18]

Who are they? "These barbarians are young men and boys," Gilder informs us, who are "entirely unsuited for civilized life." Without marriage, the single man is "poor and neurotic. He is disposed to criminality, drugs and violence. He is irresponsible about his debts, alcoholic, accident prone, and susceptible to disease."[19]

These young men, single, unattached, must be brought into the civilizing project by women. It is women's job to "transform male lust into love; channel male wanderlust into jobs, homes, and families." It is women who "conceive the future that men tend to flee; . . . [and] feed the children that men ignore."[20]

Even young boys must be kept away from girls. Gilder opposes coeducation, arguably the most successful educational reform of the twentieth century, because "[b]oth sexes will be damaged by the continuous disciplining that the rebellious and unsuccessful boys require."[21]

If they stay single, the sexual demons reign, leading to the worst scourge of all, Gilder suggests: homosexuality. In an interesting reversal of all homophobic stereotypes, gay men are, in Gilder's view, untamed sexual beasts—"with their compulsive lust and promiscuous impulses," gay men "offer a kind of caricature of typical single male sexuality."[22] Gay men are real men after all; in fact they're more "real" than straight men. In Gilder's view, straight men would have as much sex as gay men—if only women would let them.

Which is exactly why they shouldn't. Let them, that is. By falling for the seduction of sexual liberalism, which promised sexual fulfillment to women, and coupled with their feminist-induced desire to leave the home and go to work, women have abandoned their traditional, biologically determined, and time-honored role as the brakes on the masculine sexual locomotive. "The woman's place is in the home," he argues, taking a page out of Freud's terror-stricken and cancer-induced final opus, *Civilization and Its Discontents*, "and she does her best when she can get the man there too, inducing him to submit most human activity to the domestic values of civilization."[23]

Many other conservative policy analysts continue to build on Gilder's shaky foundation. For example, Charles Murray, co-author of *The Bell Curve*, holds that young males are "essentially barbarians for whom marriage . . . is an indispensible civilizing force." Christina Hoff Sommers, author of *Who Stole Feminism?* and *The War Against Boys* [about which I will have more to say in the next chapter], told an audience at a conference at which we appeared that "masculinity without morality is dangerous and destructive."[24] And David Popenoe warns that "[e]very society must be wary of the unattached male, for he is universally the cause of numerous social ills."

Popenoe is one of the chief academic proponents of a position that holds that irresponsible men are the cause of a current crisis in the institution of marriage. Fathers must remain attached to their families. "Men are not biologically as attuned to being committed fathers as women are to being committed mothers. Left culturally unregulated, men's sexual behavior can be promiscuous, their paternity casual, their commitment to families weak," he writes.[25]

This can be accomplished by making divorce harder for women to obtain (since women initiate the lion's share of divorces), not by challenging ideals of masculinity (which seduce men into believing they can "get away clean" from messy entanglements like paternity and commitment). David Blankenhorn makes a similar case in his book, *Fatherless America* (1995), in which he amasses a mountain of unsubstantiated correlations to blame virtually every social pathology on absent fathers.

Blankenhorn, Popenoe, and others remind us how central are fathers to family life, and how fatherlessness is the cause of innumerable social problems, from crime and delinquency, to drug taking, sexual irresponsibility, poverty, and the like. Blankenhorn's *Fatherless America* reads like a catalog of such specious correlations; fatherlessness is far more often the *consequence* of poverty, for example, as it is the cause.[26]

This entirely created fear of fatherlessness actually rests on the triumph of form over content. Fathers, by virtue of being men, bring something irreplaceable to the family, something "inherently masculine" notes Wade Horn, former director of the National Fatherhood Initiative, who became President George W. Bush's assistant secretary in the U.S. Department of Health and Human Services,

Administration for Children and Families. (It was Horn who promoted the idea that marriage-based programs will alleviate poverty, despite the overwhelming evidence of the opposite causal sequence: that alleviating poverty would lead to an increase in marriages.)

But do not mistake this for rage against the male machine. Blankenhorn and the others do not issue a clarion call for a new fatherhood, based on emotional receptivity and responsiveness, compassion and patience, care and nurture (which are, after all, the *human* qualities one needs to be a good father in the first place). Instead he rails against this new fatherhood:

> He is nurturing. He expresses his emotions. He is a healer, a companion, a colleague. He is a deeply involved parent. He changes diapers, gets up at 2:00 A.M. to feed the baby, goes beyond "helping out" in order to share equally in the work, joys, and responsibilities of domestic life.[27]

How utterly "selfish" of him. Obviously, this sensitive New Age father does all this because he "reflects the puerile desire for human omnipotentiality in the form of genderless parenthood, a direct repudiation of fatherhood as a gendered social role for men."[28] Let's assume for the moment that this sentence is actually sensible. It means that the *real* father is neither nurturing nor expressive; he is neither a partner nor a friend to his wife, and he sleeps through most of the young baby's infantile helplessness, oblivious to the needs of his wife and child. This guy is so selfless and giving as a father simply because he has a Y chromosome. Men are fathers, but they are not to actually *do* any real parenting. To be is to do.

Making sure that men are fathers is a way, Blankenhorn concludes, to "resocialize" and "domesticate" masculinity—away from all those "hard male values" like "toughness, competition, instrumentalism and aggression" and towards only certain virtues of fatherhood.[29] The father, for example, "protects his family, provides for its material needs, devotes himself to the education of his children, and represents his family's interests in the larger world"—all valuable behaviors, to be sure. And behaviors that do not require that he ever set foot in his child's room.[30]

The notion that men should be exempt from mundane housework and child care, which should be left to their wives, is, of course, deeply insulting to women. Feminism taught us that. But it's also deeply insulting to men, because it assumes that the caring and nurturing of life itself cannot be our province, but, given how clumsy and aggressive we are, had better be done at a distance.

But don't blame us. We can't help it. Our wives, however, can. It's predictable that these "pro-family" thinkers all end up blaming women for failing to extract that commitment from men. Women left the home, in search of work and fulfillment, abandoning their natural role of taming men and rearing children. Feminism declares war against nature. Rutgers anthropologist and advocate of "male bonding," Lionel Tiger, speaks of "the mammalian fact that small children should be raised by their mothers."[31]

This anti-feminist political agenda is best, and most simply, made by Harvey Mansfield, Harvard political scientist, in an op-ed essay in the *Wall Street Journal*. "The protective element of manliness is endangered by women having equal access to jobs outside the home," he writes. "Women who do not consider themselves feminist often seem unaware of what they are doing to manliness when they work to support themselves. They think only that people should be hired and promoted on merit, regardless of sex."[32] And Lionel Tiger's argument that "the principal victims of moving toward a merit-based society have been male" is indeed sad. Imagine that: feminists actually believe in meritocracy.

Right-wing thinkers invariably bump up against inconvenient facts that dash their anti-feminism—and, I like to think, it's because they have such an unyielding view of men as irredeemably awful.

They also have some internal divisions about the dimensions of male sexuality. Like Gilder, Camille Paglia, the anti-feminist vixen, claims that "[h]unt, pursuit and capture are biologically programmed into male sexuality. Generation after generation of men must be educated, refined and ethically persuaded away from their tendency toward anarchy and brutishness."[33] But while Gilder bemoans this, Paglia relishes it. To her, feminism is making women more like men, not making men more like women. Women, she wants us to know, are equally capable of sexual predation and thrill-seeking.

She and Gilder also agree that gay men are hypermasculine—without female restraint they become sort of masculinity squared, and all the evils of male sexuality are doubled for them. (Again, Paglia wonders why women can't be more like that.) Lionel Tiger, on the other hand, takes the more traditional homophobic view that gay men are hypo-masculine, effeminate non-men. But what is the cause of this? In one of the more bizarre arguments from even this rather ungrounded crowd, Tiger suggests that women's use of barbiturates during pregnancy in the 1950s and 1960s caused the spike of male homosexuality in the 1960s and 1970s. Since the claim is so preposterous, you have to read it for yourself:

> The sons of women using barbiturates are much more likely to be "feminized," to display bodies and behavior more typically female than male. Millions of American mothers of boys, an estimated eleven million in the 1950s and 60s, used barbiturates, and millions still do. A compelling thought is that this may have something to do with the evident increase in the number, or at least prominence, of male homosexuals.[34]

Now, aside from the fact that there is not a scintilla of evidence that those same women who took barbiturates had gay sons, nor even a correlation between barbiturate use and *having* a gay son, Tiger goes even further than a simple "correlation does not imply causation" fallacy. He thinks barbiturates not only explain the cause, but the "prominence" of gay men. One can only imagine that causal reasoning: gay sons of barbiturate-using mothers support liberalized drug laws which bring them into public policy arenas and make them more prominent? Remember, the aptly named Lionel Tiger is the "Charles Darwin Professor of Anthropology" at Rutgers. (Rutgers allows recipients to choose the names of their endowed chairs; rarely can one find a better case of compensatory nomenclature.)

Tiger's reputation rests on his long-discredited 1969 work, *Men in Groups*, which recycled 1950s functionalism into normative policy analysis. Over the centuries, men had developed all-male enclaves, retreats, and refuges from women, where they could relax in an affable homosociality. Since these arenas had developed, they must serve some inner collective psychic need for men, that men "need some haunts and/or occasions which exclude females." Tiger was so concerned about androgynous gender blending that he suggested that urban planners include male-only clubs in their civic projects, to provide some surcease from female invasion of the formerly all-male workplace.[35]

Tiger's book *The Decline of Males* a mystifying and confused tome, argues topsy-turvy that "the male and female sex in industrial societies are slowly but inexorably moving apart," just at the moment when all available evidence—epidemiological, economic, social, and psychological—suggests precisely the opposite.[36]

Tiger jumps on the men-as-new-victims-of-reverse-discrimination bandwagon, whose drum majors include Warren Farrell and a host of male liberationists.[37] Males are in decline, he argues, because women now control sexuality. By gaining control over birth control, they claimed all the sexual power. (Gilder thinks that since women control sexual access, they had the power all along; contraceptive technology is but an expression of that power, not its cause.) Now that women are the captains of the social ship, men are listing badly.

Thirty-eight percent of men paying child support "don't have access to their children," he tells us, as if it were the fault of their ex-wives. It's true that over half of all divorced fathers have no contact with their children, but non-custodial mothers almost never lose contact. Why is that? Do they love their children more? And while he notes that "all the data about occupational injuries and deaths are profoundly skewed against the interest of males," he seems to have forgotten that women have been demanding entry into the most hazardous occupations (police, firefighter, the military, construction) for quite some time. And guess which gender so fiercely resists their entry?

So, are males really in decline? Hardly. Less than half the world's population, we perform far less than half the world's labor and control—what?—about 90 percent of the world's resources. And while it's true that we once held virtually *all* positions of power—every seat on every corporate or university board, and every national, local, and state electoral position—we now occupy probably 80 percent of them.

Nor has this political shift resulted in the "feminization" of political or economic life. Quite the contrary—the state has never been more "masculinized" as welfare, national health care, and parental leave initiatives remain but dreams, there has been no reduction in spending for the military, and massive increases for the police and prisons. School bonds routinely fail, but municipalities blithely tax themselves into the next millennium for new sports complexes or new Supermax prisons.

Conservative policy analysts are furious at men—more furious, in fact, than any radical separatist feminist. They're so furious that they insist that women simply must leave the labor force and return to their homes, where they can constrain men's sexual lust and civilize men and boys. In this way, male bashing is the province not of feminism, but the ideological foundation of *anti*-feminism.

And, in the process, this "misandrous" view of men is transformed into a vigorous scolding of women—for being seduced by the lures of the public sphere into abandoning their homes and families, and being seduced by the possibility of sexual pleasure and agency into forsaking their role as sexual restraint. It's the women who have to wise up.

Pop Psychology: The "Doctors" Are Out (to Lunch)

And that's where the pop psychologists come in. Both "Dr." Laura Schlessinger and "Dr." John Gray have become modest-sized industries that manufacture light equipment for successful relationships, building multimillion-dollar psychological empires by scolding women into scaling back their expectations and accepting men just as they are—the lunks.

But first a word about the "doctor" part. Schlessinger has no formal training as a psychologist; her degree is in kinesthesiology. And Columbia Pacific University, where Gray received his graduate "training," was actually a correspondence school, offering degrees via what is called "distance learning," in which students receive course packets, read the materials, and then take open-book exams and receive degrees—until it was shut down, that is, by California's Department of Consumer Affairs, which called it a "giant scam" and a "diploma mill."[38]

Schlessinger, the nationally syndicated talk show host, has made her mark by dispensing pop psychological bromides like bitter little pills. She confronts her listeners, yells at them, and makes fun of their foibles. And they love it! She has done for male-female relationships what Rush Limbaugh has done for politics—steamrolling it into convenient, bite-sized little nuggets of half-truths, unsubstantiated opinions, and flat-out falsehoods.

She's also been the target of a very successful boycott by gay rights groups over her unapologetic homophobia, and the butt of a hilarious e-mail message that has circulated widely on the Internet for the past few years. Here, the contradictions of her, or anyone else's, biblical literalism are easily exposed, as the writer plaintively inquires, for example, about the appropriate price one should receive for selling a daughter into slavery, or the proper means of execution for those who cut their hair (Lev. 19:27), or those who wear cotton and polyester clothing (Lev. 24:10–16), or work on the Sabbath (Exodus 35:2).

Her advice book for women, *Ten Stupid Things Women Do to Mess Up Their Lives* (1995), was a best seller, another on an already sagging shelf of volumes that blame women for the inconstancies, infidelities, and inadequacies of the men in their lives. Its companion volume, *Ten Stupid Things Men Do to Mess Up Their Lives* (1998), also spends a good amount of time chastising seemingly smart women for their foolish choices. (As does the final volume in the trilogy, *The Stupid Things Couples Do to Mess Up Their Relationships* [2001]. Guess which member of the "couple" she addresses?) But she also goes after men. Basically, men are total losers. But they can't help it, the lovable oafs. They're biologically driven toward violence, aggression, and making dumb choices in love.[39]

They're also tired of hearing what jerks they are from feminists. So Dr. Laura adopts perhaps the most brilliant rhetorical strategy this side of Jonathan Swift: She dispenses classically feminist advice to men in the guise of bashing those awful feminist harpies who are so bitter and angry all the time. She goes out of her way to bash "overgeneralizing, incredibly negative, hysterical, man-loathing" feminist ideas held by "insanely radical contemporary feminists."[40] You might be interested to learn, for example, that "one of the most insidious negative influences on our nationwide loss of responsible fathers is contemporary feminism."[41] Must be the same feminists who urge men to refuse to share housework and child care, and counsel them to never pay child support after a divorce.

So, what *are* the things that men do to mess up their lives? They get involved with damaged women and then try and rescue them, don't admit dependency needs, get seduced by material rewards and miss the pleasures of home and hearth, think masculinity is measured by the size of the paycheck, don't respect their wives, try and conquer every woman they meet, do too little housework and far too little child care.

Confused? You should be. Dr. Laura offers exactly the same critique of men that radical feminists have given for the past thirty years—men are not caring, nurturing, loving, attentive, and emotional enough with their wives, their children, and their friends. She urges men to end rape, to stop beating up their wives, and to be more present in the home. (Gay men have apparently done only one thing to "mess up their lives"—but I guess it was a really big one!—so Dr. Laura does not pay any attention to them here.)

Here, then, is an uncommonly bitter feminist screed couched in anti-feminist terms that she believes men can embrace without ever feeling bad about themselves. But women can—and should—feel bad about their choices. "Men would not do half of what they do if women didn't let them," she told an interviewer for *Modern Maturity* magazine. "That a man is going to do bad things is a fact. That you keep a man who does bad things in your life is your fault."[42]

Now part of the reason that Schlessinger targets female readers, whether talking about men or women, has to do with simple demographics. Most books in America—and nearly all books about relationships—are bought by women. This may be because when men have relationship problems they are more likely to retreat into their caves, to try and come up with a practical solution to the problem—at least according to John Gray. A much simpler explanation is that reading is largely considered unmanly (men want action, not words) and reading about caring and nurturing a relationship is simply women's work. Real men don't read—and they certainly don't read about relationships!

This cave stuff is the central trope of Martian life, according to Gray. Gray may be the most successful self-help author of all time; his eight self-help books have sold tens of millions of copies worldwide; the flagship book alone, *Men Are from Mars, Women Are from Venus*, has sold more than 10 million copies in the United States. And then there's the CD-ROM version, dozens of audiotapes, calendars, and date books with pithy inspirational homilies, even a magazine, a movie, and television show. He's designed his own line of Hallmark greeting cards, and his self-appointed acolytes run dozens of franchised workshops and seminars around the world. And don't forget the baseball hats, pens, and other souvenirs that proclaim the title of his most famous book—all available at public events and to be purchased at his website.

Gray's central conceit is that men and women are completely different. To read *Men Are from Mars* . . . or its identical cousins, you'd think we were different species, like, say, lobsters and giraffes. Gray believes that not only do women and men communicate differently, but they also "think, feel, perceive, react, respond, love, need, and appreciate differently." We're "from different planets, speaking different languages, and needing different nourishment."[43]

The interplanetary differences in Gray's astronomy are hard-wired into maleness and femaleness, the result, he says, of "DNA programming."[44] To demonstrate this, Gray recites a list of physical differences, aside from the rather obvious ones. Men, you may be interested to know, have thicker skin, longer vocal cords, and heavier blood with more oxygen to enable us to breathe more deeply.

None of that "social constructionism" here, none of those "variations" depending on class, race, sexuality, age, or nationality. No, forgive the pun, shades of Gray. All males and females are the same—and what that "same" is means that we are different from each other. All his books are liberally sprinkled with statements about how men "automatically" do some things, and women "instinctively" do something else, how our "natural cycles" make communication difficult.

These biological differences are the origin of the fundamentally different personalities that men and women everywhere have. For example, men value power, competency, efficiency, and achievement; women value love, communication, beauty, and relationships. Women are "more intuitive, are more interested in love and relationships, and experience different reactions to stress," while men have a "greater interest in producing results, achieving goals, power, competition, work, logic, and efficiency."[45]

In relationships, a man is like a rubber band—he pulls away, stretching only so far and then springing back; he "automatically alternates between needing intimacy and autonomy." A woman is like a wave, her self-esteem rising and falling depending upon whether she feels loved.[46]

Women are afraid of receiving; men are afraid of giving. "Women have an incredible capacity to give without getting back"; men, on the other hand, "are not instinctively motivated to offer their support; they need to be asked."[47]

When men and women experience stress—which is inevitable in all interplanetary relationships—they react differently. When men feel stress, or face a problem, they retreat into their caves to solve their problems by themselves. There, they prioritize and focus on solving the most urgent problem first. They project their blame outward and try to change the world. Women, on the other hand, get together with other women to talk about their problems. They "think out loud, sharing their process of inner discovery with an interested listener," and become aware of the variety of problems. They blame themselves, and therefore try to change their own behaviors.[48]

Communication problems are inevitable. Men "silently 'mull over' or think about what they have heard or experienced"; women gab about it with everyone in sight. Or, from a Venusian perspective, she knows to sensibly talk things through while he becomes an uncommunicative rock.[49]

Happily, these personalities are perfectly complementary and perfectly equivalent—it's only when we pretend there are no differences that real relationship problems occur. But everything is supposed to fit together, like—well, you know.

But the reason they don't fit together anymore is that women changed things. They changed their views of themselves and their views of men. And now they're critical—they want him to change. Men didn't change at all—they're still exactly the same as they have been for millennia. They're just fine, thank you very much. So stop pushing!

So the only solution is for women to stop trying to change men, and for men to stop . . . well, nothing really. OK, sure, send her a card or some flowers sometime.

Look at men's behaviors around the house. Women want more than couch potatoes—they want involved fathers, communicative husbands, and partners who share housework and child care. Give it up, girls! "For thousands of years a man went out on his hunt, patiently waited and then with a burst of energy ran after the animal he was pursuing," he writes.[50] Nowadays, the qualities that once made him look like a good hunter—waiting, watching, conserving energy— now look like hanging out, loafing, laziness. Pass me the remote control and go get me a beer, honey—I'm fulfilling my evolutionary duty!

Gray's view of men seems to be benevolent, but looks can deceive. For example, Gray claims that war and violence happen only on Mars. When a man gets hurt, you see, he "feels a compulsion to release his hurt by inflicting it on someone else." Thus violence "is generally the compulsion of the male psyche to release its pain and feel better." "War and violence are the expressions of man's inability to heal his hurt."[51]

Women are, on the other hand, "essentially nonviolent"; violence is "not her first reaction."[52] So, if we really were serious about peace, the only sensible solution would be to immediately replace all men in politics and the military with women. Wars would stop instantly. Diplomacy would no longer be war carried out by different means.

"But wait a minute," you might be saying. "Women can be violent. What about Golda Meir? Indira Gandhi? Margaret Thatcher?" Don't ask John Gray about that. In his mind, they're just women with overdeveloped masculine sides. And men who oppose war and violence are too indulgent of their feminine sides. (In such cases, Gray prescribes that he "do more things with men, hang out with men, see action movies, or participate in some competitive sport."[53])

What the examples of those rather bellicose female leaders point out is that often it's not the gender of the person holding a position that matters—but the gendered logic of the position itself. Gray's tidy homilies ring true to us because we rarely see women in powerful positions and men in subservient ones. So differences that may be about position *appear* to be about gender.

Take, for example, differences in communication patterns. We read that women and men use the languages of their respective planets—men employ the competitive language of hierarchy and domination to get ahead; women create webs of inclusion with softer, more embracing language that ensures that everyone feels O.K. At home, men are the strong silent types, grunting monosyllabically to their wives, who want to use conversation to create intimacy.

But it turns out that those very same monosyllabic men are very verbal at work, where they are in positions of dependency and powerlessness, and need to use conversation to maintain a relationship with their superiors; and their wives are just as capable of using language competitively to maximize the position in a corporate hierarchy. Gray should have written that "bosses are from

Mars, employees are from Venus" or "landlords are from Mars, tenants are from Venus." Bosses and landlords don't have to share their thought processes; they lay down the law. Employees and tenants smile, keep the conversation alive, and try to make the person with power feel better.

What about Mars and Venus in the workplace? Men are competitive social climbers who seek advancement at every opportunity; women are cooperative team-builders who shun competition and may even suffer from a "fear of success." But the research is clear that when women had the same opportunities, networks, mentors, and possibilities for advancement as men, they behaved the same as the men. Similarly, when men lacked opportunities, they behaved in stereotypically "feminine" ways.

Even in the family, those gender differences turn out to be less about gender and more about position. Gray claims that women are nurturing and maternal, men are strong and silent, relatively emotionally inexpressive arbiters of justice—that is, we assume that women do the work of "mothering" because it is in their nature. But recent research on single fathers found them perfectly capable of "mothering." Single fathers do not hire female workers to do the laundry, cooking, and chauffeuring. And there were no differences between single fathers and mothers (single or married) when it came to what they did around the house, how they acted with their children, or even in their children's emotional and intellectual development. Men's parenting styles were virtually indistinguishable from women's.

What does all this mean? It means that gender differences may simply be power differences—and when men are in the powerless position they behave as Venusians and when women are in the powerful position they act like Martians.

Gray pretends that male and female are equivalent—equal and different, sort of like matching "his" and "hers" bathrobes or coffee mugs. But he and she live in an unequal world, a world that's labeled "his." "Men" and "women" may really be synonyms for "powerful" and "powerless."

This false equivalence leads Gray to dispense advice that discourages women's ambition or men's nurturing, that would set back the cause of gender equality about a century, to the Victorian parlor where separate spheres were rigidly enforced. Who is listening to this?

At the seminars and lectures I've attended, I've noticed that the men were significantly older than the women—old enough, perhaps, to be their fathers. Gray's message seems to appeal to younger women, between twenty and thirty-five, trying to initiate and sustain romantic relationships with men as they're pulled between family and career. His message also appeals to somewhat older men, in their late forties and early fifties, trying to make their second marriage work better than the first.

These "post-feminist" women and "pre-feminist" men get the same basic message. Women must abandon any idea of changing men. "The secret of empowering a man is never to try to change or improve him." You should "give up trying to improve him in any way." When he retreats into his cave, ladies, you should go shopping. "Venusians love to shop."[54]

If all Gray's books, lectures, videotapes, CDs, and calendars could be summed up in one cardinal rule, it would be that if women want to have relationships with men they pretty much have to accept them as they are. "Do not try and change him." (Men learn they are pretty much just fine the way they are.) The four magic words to support a man are "It's not your fault."[55]

And if there's a loser here, it's the vision of gender equality that both opened doors for women and demanded changes from men. Women could become empowered to be ambitious, competent, and dynamic; men had to share housework and child care, and put an end to violence and harassment of women.

Gray and Schlessinger thus provide a pseudo-psychological alternative to the social, economic, and political changes that would ensure true gender equality. It's a soothing elixir for women, telling them that they can and will be able to have a good relationship, if they learn to stop trying to change their men. If they're unhappy, they have no one to blame but themselves.

That message has become staple fodder of women's magazines, and reaches its apotheosis in *The Rules*,[56] a step-by-step guide that promises to help women land a husband through a retreat past the 1950s and back to the 1840s, when Catharine Ward Beecher, Sarah Hale, and others articulated the need for separate spheres and for women to be "the angel in the house," in Virginia Woolf's memorable phrase.

Women's problem is that they can't find husbands, and the reason for that is that women have been too busy being men's equal to connive to trap men in the time-tested ways that our grandmothers did—by holding out through manipulative coquetry. The most successful rule: "treat the men we *wanted* like the men we *didn't* want."[57]

(One would also be remiss not to point out the irony of two Jewish writers, Ellen Fein and Sherrie Schneider, who basically instruct women to stop being loud, pushy, ambitious, and sexual—in other words, to act more like stereotypical WASPs than like dynamic ethnic women. Be "quiet and mysterious, act ladylike, cross your legs and smile. Don't talk so much." Such obvious self-hatred makes the vigorous self-affirmations of their self-help therapeutic writing style ring that much tinnier.)[58]

Women have to bury their competence, their ambition, their drive—and why? Because men are such pathetic creatures, completely preoccupied by surface appearances: "Don't leave the house without wearing makeup. Put lipstick on even when you go jogging!" "Men like women who wear fashionable, sexy clothes in bright colors." We "want as much as [we] can get on the first date," and we "very often want something more just because [we] can't have it."[59]

We're devoted to the chase and conquest, but not the simpler pleasures of domestic life. If your man is a couch potato, here's what *The Rules* would counsel:

> When he watches the ballgame on TV all afternoon instead of helping you clean the house, don't zap the tube off in a moment of anger. Nicely tell him you need his help. If he still insists on watching the game, leave him alone. Tell yourself, "No big deal."[60]

Whew, I thought we were going to have to share that housework and child care! Pass the remote. Actually, domestic equality is the sure sign of a loser in this strange antebellum—that would be before the Civil War!—world: "men who insist that their dates meet them halfway or (worse) on their own turf, turn out to be turds—inconsiderate, uncompromising, and even miserly."[61]

Though the book is intended to be read by women, it's an important book for men to read as well—especially since it tells us what conniving, manipulative women those "Rules" gals are being counseled to be! but also because of what such behavior by women actually says about us. We're "born to respond to challenge," biologically "the aggressor" who "must pursue the woman." We love to be treated badly—treated as though we were not wanted—because that will only prime that testosterone to pump up our competitive hunting urges and really go after our prey. We're overgrown babies, who want everything our own way, want "constant attention and companionship" as well as someone to clean up after us. Peter Pan as the icon for an entire gender: we won't grow up! And if you treat us like adults, we will run away and hide in our cave with John Gray.[62]

So the message here is simple: women, your unhappiness is your own fault. Happiness lies in your own hands—all you have to do is return to those old homilies. Play hard to get—and you'll get "got."

For men, on the other hand, the message is far more insidious. We're fine just as we are; we don't have to change at all. "Don't try to change him because men never really change" write Fein and Schneider.[63] We're incapable of real change, and so fragile that we must be constantly coddled with kid gloves. But we're also destined to be unemotional grunters, at home nowhere in the world except our individually constructed caves. For these man-haters, the best a woman can hope for is to come home, play by the rules, land a man of her very own, and hope he treats her well. Now *that's* insulting to men.

Ultimately, what binds together these vile slanders on my sex is the fact that all the writers are really more lathered about feminism, and the possibilities of gender equality, than they are about actually doing anything that would promote healthy, vibrant masculinity. It requires an Orwellian twist to make feminism—which, after all, believes that men are capable of doing a whole lot better than we are—into men's enemy, and make these real man-haters sound like they are supporting men.

Me, I'll side with Shakespeare. The fault lies "not in our stars, but in our selves"—both collectively and individually. Feminism is more than a strategy for social change; it's therapy for failing relationships. When women and men are seen as equally competent, equally loving, and equally nurturing, we'll have the kinds of relationships we say we want, and for which we are forking over so much money. And more than that, we'll recognize that we're from neither Mars nor Venus. We're Earthlings, and here on Earth it is equality that will endow our relationships with the richness, excitement, and complexity that we crave.

NOTES

1. Lionel Tiger most recently repeats this false claim in *The Decline of Males* (New York: Golden Book, 1999), 63 (footnote on 274), where he cites only a book, but no page. This is because no such claim is made on any page of Dworkin's work.

2. Andrea Dworkin, *Intercourse* (New York: Free Press, 2000), ix–x; "Fighting Talk" (interview with Andrea Dworkin by Michael Moorcock) in *New Statesman and Society*, April 21, 1995; Andrea Dworkin, *Pornography: Men Possessing Women* (New York: Plume, 1981).

3. Robert Wright, "Feminists, Meet Mr. Darwin," *The New Republic*, November 28, 1994, 34–36.

4. Cited in Randy Thornhill and Craig T. Palmer, "Why Men Rape," *The Sciences*, January 2000, 33.

5. Richard Dawkins, *The Selfish Gene* (New York: Oxford University Press, 1976), 153, 162.

6. Natalie Angier, *Woman: An Intimate Geography* (New York: Houghton Mifflin, 1999), 337.

7. Richard Wright, *The Moral Animal* (New York: Vintage, 1995), 71.

8. Randy Thornhill and Craig T. Palmer, *A Natural History of Rape: Biological Bases of Sexual Coercion* (Cambridge: The MIT Press, 1999).

9. Thornhill and Palmer, "Why Men Rape," 30.

10. Thornhill and Palmer, *A Natural History of Rape*, 53.

11. Ibid., 142.

12. Ibid., 134.

13. Thornhill and Palmer, "Why Men Rape," 32, 34.

14. Barbara Ehrenreich, "The Mystery of Misogyny," *The Progressive*, December 2001, 88.

15. George Gilder, *Men and Marriage* (Gretna, LA: Pelican, 1993). The current edition comes with a ringing endorsement from Rush Limbaugh.

16. Ibid., 30, 5.

17. Ibid., 11, 45.

18. Ibid., 39.

19. Ibid., 39, 62.

20. Ibid., 5.

21. Ibid., 118.

22. Ibid., 73.

23. Ibid., 176.

24. Charles Murray, *The Emerging British Underclass* (London: IEA Health and Welfare Unit, 1990), 23; cited in Richard Collier, *Masculinities, Crime, and Criminology* (London: Sage Publications, 1998), 129; Christina Hoff Summers, comment at Symposium on "Reconnecting Males to Liberal Education" (Morehouse College, April 4–5, 2001); David Popenoe, *Life Without Father* (New York: Free Press, 1996), 12.

25. Popenoe, *Life Without Father*, 4.

26. David Blankenhorn, *Fatherless America* (New York: Basic Books, 1995).

27. Ibid., 96.

28. Ibid., 102.

29. Ibid., 225, 122

30. Ibid., 122.

31. Tiger, *The Decline of Males*, 260.

32. Harvey Mansfield, "Why a Woman Can't Be More Like a Man," *Wall Street Journal*, November 3, 1997, A22.

33. Camille Paglia, *Sex, Art, and American Culture* (New York: Vintage, 1992), 51.

34. Tiger, *The Decline of Males*, 95.

35. Lionel Tiger, *Men in Groups* (New York: Vintage, 1969), 262; see also 262–265.

36. Tiger, *The Decline of Males*, 90.

37. To be fair, Farrell does not hold such an anti-male view of men, but he does seem to think that feminist women do.

38. See *San Francisco Chronicle*, March 14, 2001.

39. Laura Schlessinger, *Ten Stupid Things Women Do to Mess Up Their Lives* (New York: HarperCollins, 1995); *Ten Stupid Things Men do to Mess Up Their Lives* (New York: HarperCollins, 1998); and *Ten Stupid Things Couples Do to Mess Up Their Relationships* (New York: HarperCollins, 2001).

40. Schlessinger, *Ten Stupid Things Men Do*, 194, 273.

41. Ibid., 216.

42. Susan Goodman, "Dr. No," *Modern Maturity*, September–October 1999, 68.

43. John Gray, *Men Are from Mars, Women Are from Venus* (New York: HarperCollins, 1992), 5.

44. John Gray, *Men, Women, and Relationships* (New York: HarperCollins, 1993), 53.

45. Ibid., 52, 84.

46. Ibid., 95.

47. Ibid., 27, 246.

48. John Gray, *Men Are from Mars . . .* , 67.

49. Ibid., 68.

50. John Gray, *Men, Women, and Relationships*, xiii.

51. Ibid., 163, 164, 172.

52. Ibid., 170, 169.

53. Ibid., 78.

54. John Gray, *Men Are from Mars . . .* , 146, 148, 78.

55. Ibid., 88.

56. Ellen Fein and Sherrie Schneider, *The Rules: Time-Tested Secrets for Capturing the Heart of Mr. Right* (New York: Warner Books, 1995).

57. Ibid., 14.

58. Ibid., 19. If your therapist—with whom you are supposed to struggle honestly towards even the most painful feelings—disapproves of your reading *The Rules*, the authors counsel concealing it from him or her. Dishonesty is a cardinal rule.

59. Ibid., 19, 17, 78, 110.

60. Ibid., 167.

61. Ibid., 37.

62. Ibid., 7, 9, 28, 127, 157.

63. Ibid., 90.

5

A War against Boys?

By now, you've probably heard there's a "war against boys" in America. The latest heavily hyped right-wing fusillade against feminism, led by Christina Hoff Sommers's book of that title, claims that men have become "the second sex" and that boys—not girls—are the ones who are in serious trouble, the "victims" of "misguided" feminist efforts to protect and promote girls' development. At the same time, best-selling books by therapists, like William Pollack's *Real Boys* and Dan Kindlon and Michael Thompson's *Raising Cain*, also sound the same tocsin, warning of alarming levels of depression and suicide, and describing boys' interior lives as an emotionally barren landscape, with all affect suppressed beneath postures of false bravado. They counsel anguished parents to "rescue" or "protect" boys—not from feminists but from a definition of masculinity that is harmful to boys, girls, and other living things.

In part, they're both right. There *is* a crisis among boys. But the right-wing jeremiads misdiagnose the cause of the crisis and thus their proposed reforms would take us even further away from enabling young boys to negotiate the difficult path to a manhood of integrity, ethical commitment, and compassion. At least the therapists get that part right. But, in part, both sides are also wrong: on most measures boys—at least the middle-class white boys everyone seems concerned about—are doing just fine, taking the places in an unequal society to which they have always felt entitled.

The Boy Crisis

Let's begin with the evidence of crisis. The signs are everywhere. Boys drop out of school, are diagnosed as emotionally disturbed, and commit suicide four

Originally published in *Dissent*, Fall 2006.

times more often than girls; they get into fights twice as often; they murder ten times more frequently and are fifteen times more likely to be the victims of a violent crime. Boys are six times more likely to be diagnosed with Attention Deficit Disorder. Boys get lower grades on standardized tests of reading and writing, and have lower class rank and fewer honors than girls.[1]

On college campuses women constitute the majority of students, passing men in 1982, so that in eight years women will earn 58 percent of bachelor's degrees in U.S. colleges. Doomsayers lament that women now outnumber men in the social and behavioral sciences by about three to one, and they've "invaded" such traditionally male bastions as engineering (where they now make up 20 percent) and biology and business (virtually par).

Elementary schools, we hear, are "anti-boy," emphasizing reading and restricting the movements of young boys. They "feminize" boys, forcing active, healthy, and naturally rambunctious boys to conform to a regime of obedience, "pathologizing what is simply normal for boys," as one psychologist put it. Michael Gurian argues in *The Wonder of Boys*, with testosterone surging through their little limbs, we demand that they sit still, raise their hands, and take naps. We're giving them the message, he says, "boyhood is defective."[2]

According to Christina Hoff Sommers, it's been "misguided feminism" that's been spreading such calumnies about boys. It's boys, not girls, who face the much-discussed "chilly classroom climate," according to Sommers. Schools are an "inhospitable," hostile environment for boys, where their natural propensities for rough and tumble play, competition, aggression, and rambunctious violence are cast as social problems in the making.[3]

"Misguided" feminists have ignored the natural biological differences between boys and girls, and, in their fear and loathing of all things masculine, have demeaned an entire sex. Sommers quotes a line from a speech by Gloria Steinem that "we need to raise boys like we raise girls." (In fact, she quotes that line three times in her short, but repetitive book.) She vilifies William Pollack, author of *Real Boys*, and others (including myself) for our efforts to "save the males"—to rescue boys from the dangerous myths of masculinity. Boys, she argues, are simply different from girls, and efforts to transform time-tested and beneficial definitions of masculinity will run counter to nature's plan. Categorical differences are "natural, healthy, and, by implication, best left alone."[4]

On the other hand, Sommers reserves her fiercest animus for Carol Gilligan, whose work on girls' development suggested that there was more than one moral voice which guided people in their ethical decision-making, and also who has explored the ways in which girls lose their voice as they approach adolescence. In fact, Sommers is so filled with misplaced rage at Gilligan that one is tempted to speculate about her motives, accusing Gilligan of ethical impropriety in her research, duplicity, intellectual fraud, and deceptive cover-ups. (This because Gilligan wouldn't show her raw field notes and interview transcripts to an undergraduate who did not identify himself as working for Sommers.)

But Sommers goes after Gilligan precisely because Sommers believes (based on a misreading of the work) that Gilligan posits categorically different moral voices for boys and girls. Here, Sommers offers evidence that the differences between boys and girls are minimal. When she discusses boys' aggression, those same testosterone-propelled, hard-wired, natural sex differences magically disappear. "[S]chool problems have very little to do with misogyny, patriarchy, or sex discrimination," she writes. They have everything to do with "*children's* propensity to bully and be cruel."[5]

So which is it? She attacks the therapists for failing to recognize the hard-wired differences between the sexes, but then excoriates Gilligan for crediting those same differences, since now she says they do not exist.

Misguided Anti-feminism as Misdiagnosis

As anyone who has kids in school today knows, some of this appears true: some boys seem defensive, morose, unfocused, taciturn, and withdrawn, while the girls in their classes seem to be sailing on toward bright and multifaceted futures, performing science experiments, playing soccer, and delivering vale-dictory addresses. So, what's wrong with Sommers's picture?

In addition to its internal contradictions, Sommers and the boys-as-victims crowd make several key errors. For one thing, though obsessed with numbers, their figures rarely add up. Sommers, Gurian, and others never factor in, for example, the number zero—as in dollars for new public school programs, the dearth of school bond issues that have passed, money from which might have developed remedial programs, intervention strategies, teacher training. Money which might have prevented cutting school sports programs and after-school extracurricular activities. Money which might have enabled teachers and admin-istrators to do more than "store" problem students in separate classes. Far larger portions of those school budgets go toward programming for boys (special education, school sports) than for girls. So much for feminization. Nor do they mention managed care health insurance, which virtually demands that school psychologists diagnose problem behavior as a treatable medical condition so that drugs may be substituted for costly, "unnecessary" therapy.

And what about numbers of students and those test scores? Well, for one thing, more *people* are going to college than ever before. In 1960, 54 percent of boys and 38 percent of girls went directly to college; today the numbers are 64 percent of boys and 70 percent of girls. And while some college presidents fret that to increase male enrollments they'll be forced to lower standards (which is, incidentally, exactly the opposite of what they worried about twenty-five years ago when they all went coeducational) no one seems to find gender disparities going the other way all that upsetting. Among the top colleges and universities in the nation, only Stanford sports a 50–50 gender balance. Amherst enrolls 56 percent men, Princeton and Chicago 54 percent men, Duke and Berkeley 52 percent, and Yale 51 percent. (Harvard was, until 2006, predominantly male.) And that doesn't even begin to approach the gender disparities at Cal Tech (65 percent male, 35 percent female) or MIT (62 percent male, 38 percent female). Nor does anyone seem driven to distraction about the gender disparities in nursing, social work, or education. Did somebody say "what about the girls?" Should we lower standards to make sure they're gender balanced?

Much of the gender difference offered is actually what sociologist Cynthia Fuchs Epstein calls a "deceptive distinction," a difference that appears to be about gender but is actually about something else—in this case, class or race. Girls' vocational opportunities are far more restricted than boys' are. Their opportunities are from the service sector, with limited openings in manufacturing or construction. A college-educated woman earns about the same as a high-school-educated man, $35,000 to $31,000. And the shortage of male college students is also actually a shortage of *non-white* males. Actually, the gender gap between college-age white males and white females is rather small, 51 percent women to 49 percent men. But only 37 percent of black college students are male, and 63 percent female, and 45 percent of Hispanic students are male, compared with 55 percent female.

These differences among boys—by race, or class, for example—do not typically fall within the radar of the cultural critics who would rescue boys. These differences are incidental because, in their eyes, all boys are the same, and that "same" is aggressive, competitive, rambunctious little devils. And this is perhaps the most central problem and contradiction in the work of those who would save boys. They argue that it's testosterone that makes boys into boys, and a society that paid attention to boys would have to acknowledge testosterone. We're making it impossible for boys to be boys.

Now, personally, I find those words, "boys will be boys," which, incidentally are the final four words of Sommers's book, to be four of the most depressing words in policy circles today, because they suggest resignation, a hopeless throwing up of the hands. If boys will be boys, then there is simply nothing we can do about it.

"Masculinity is aggressive, unstable, combustible," writes Camille Paglia—whom Sommers quotes approvingly—in one of the most insulting definitions available. Are we hard-wired only for aggression and competition? Are we not also hard-wired for compassion, nurturance, love?

By contrast, the therapists (Pollack, Kindlon, and Thompson) understand that what lies beneath boys' problems (apparent or real) is an outdated ideology of masculinity to which boys are struggling desperately to adhere, and which is applied ruthlessly and coercively by other boys.

For example, the reason it appears that boys are lagging behind in reading and languages is not because of feminist efforts to improve the lives of girls, nor even because testosterone inhibits the memorization of French syntax. It's about an ideology of masculinity.

Consider the parallel for girls. Gilligan's often moving work on adolescent girls describes how these assertive, confident, and proud young girls "lose their voices" when they hit adolescence. At the same moment, Pollack notes, boys become *more* confident, even beyond their abilities. You might even say that boys *find* their voices, but it is the inauthentic voice of bravado, of constant posturing, of foolish risk-taking and gratuitous violence. The Boy Code teaches them that they are supposed to be in power, and thus they begin to act like it. They "ruffle in a manly pose," as William Butler Yeats once put it, "for all their timid heart."

What's the cause of all this posturing and posing? It's not testosterone, but privilege. In adolescence both boys and girls get their first real dose of gender inequality: girls suppress ambition, boys inflate it.

Recent research on the gender gap in school achievement bears this out. Girls are more likely to undervalue their abilities, especially in the more traditionally "masculine" educational arenas such as math and science. Only the most able and most secure girls take such courses. Thus, their numbers tend to be few, and their grades high. Boys, however, possessed of this false voice of bravado (and many facing strong family pressure), are likely to *over-value* their abilities, to remain in programs though they are less qualified and capable of succeeding.

This difference, and not some putative discrimination against boys, is the reason that girls' mean test scores in math and science are now, on average, approaching that of boys. Too many boys who over-value their abilities remain in difficult math and science courses longer than they should; they pull the boys' mean scores down. By contrast, a few girls, whose abilities and self-esteem are sufficient to enable them to "trespass" into a male domain, skew female data upward.

A parallel process is at work in the humanities and social sciences. Girls' test scores in English and foreign languages outpace those of boys not because of some "reverse discrimination," but because the boys bump up against the norms of masculinity. Boys regard English as a "feminine" subject. Pioneering research in Australia by Wayne Martino found that boys are uninterested in English because of what it might say about their (inauthentic) masculine pose.[6] "Reading is lame, sitting down and looking at words is pathetic," commented one boy. "Most guys who like English are faggots." The traditional liberal arts curriculum is seen as feminizing; as Catharine Stimpson put it sarcastically, "real men don't speak French."[7]

Boys tend to hate English and foreign languages for the same reasons that girls love it. In English, they observe, there are no hard and fast rules, but rather one expresses one's opinion about the topic and everyone's opinion is equally valued. "The answer can be a variety of things, you're never really wrong," observed one boy. "It's not like maths and science where there is one set answer to everything." Another boy noted:

> I find English hard. It's because there are no set rules for reading texts. . . . English isn't like maths where you have rules on how to do things and where there are right and wrong answers. In English you have to write down how you feel and that's what I don't like.

Compare this to the comments of girls in the same study:

> I feel motivated to study English because . . . you have freedom in English—unlike subjects such as maths and science—and your view isn't necessarily wrong. There is no definite right or wrong answer and you have the freedom to say what you feel is right without it being rejected as a wrong answer.

It is not the school experience that "feminizes" boys, but rather the ideology of traditional masculinity that keeps boys from wanting to succeed. "The work you do here is girls' work," one boy commented to a British researcher. "It's not real work."

Ideologies of masculinity are reinforced ruthlessly on playgrounds and in classrooms all across the country. Boys who do like school, or who don't like sports, or who dress or act "different" are often subject to a constant barrage of insults, harassment, beatings. School may become an interminable torment. Students at Columbine High School described how the jocks beat up Eric Harris every day. This isn't playful, rambunctious, rough-and-tumble play: it's harassment, and is actionable under the law. And if masculinity is so "natural" and hard-wired, why does it have to be enforced with so much constant coercion?

Efforts to improve boys' lives in school will either adequately address the cultural—not natural—equation of masculinity and anti-intellectualism or they will fail.

And that leads to the final and most telling problem with these works: They assert a false opposition between girls and boys, pretending that the educational reforms undertaken to enable girls to perform better actually hindered boys' educational development. But these reforms—new initiatives, classroom configurations, teacher training, increased attentiveness to students' processes and individual learning styles—actually enable larger numbers of boys to get a better education. As Susan McGee Bailey and Patricia Campbell point out, "gender stereotypes, particularly those related to education, hurt both girls and boys." The challenging of those stereotypes, decreased tolerance for school violence and bullying, and increased attention to violence at home actually enable *both* girls *and* boys to feel safer at school.

Since Sommers quotes Gloria Steinem's statement no less than three times, out of context, it might be interesting to conclude with what Steinem actually did say:

> We've begun to raise our daughters more like sons—so now women are whole people. But fewer of us have the courage to raise our sons more like daughters. Yet until men raise children as much as women do—and are raised to raise children, whether or not they become fathers—they will have a far harder time developing in themselves those human qualities that are wrongly called "feminine" . . .

Hardly a call for androgyny—she seeks to degender traits, not people—Steinem reminds us of the most vital connection between parents and children, the centrality of caring, nurturing parenting as the fulfillment of our ethical responsibilities, and suggests that the signal successes of feminism has been to raise girls to become competent, confident, and strong-minded. Would that our boys could achieve those traits.

NOTES

1. See Judith Kleinfeld, "Student Performance: Males versus Females," *The Public Interest* (Winter 1999); Brad Knickerbocker, "Young and Male in America: It's Hard Being a Boy," *Christian Science Monitor*, April 29, 1999. For a summary of the problem, see Peg Tyre, *The Trouble with Boys* (New York: Crown, 2008).

2. Quoted in G. Pascal Zachary, "Boys Used to Be Boys, But Do Some Now See Boyhood as a Malady?" *Wall Street Journal*, May 2, 1997.

3. Christina Hoff Sommers, *The War against Boys* (New York: Simon and Schuster, 2000).

4. Ibid., 75.

5. Ibid., 65, my italics.

6. Wayne Martino, "Gendered Learning Practices: Exploring the Costs of Hegemonic Masculinity for Girls and Boys in Schools," in *Gender Equity: A Framework for Australian Schools* (Canberra: ACT Department of Employment, Education, and Training, 1997); Wayne Martino, "'Cool Boys,' 'Party Animals,' 'Squids,' and 'Poofters': Interrogating the Dynamics and Politics of Adolescent Masculinities in School," *British Journal of Sociology of Education* 20(2) (1999). In general, serious academic research provides a startling empirical riposte to the doomsayer-pundits who fret about putative abandonment of boys. See, for example, Lyn Yates, "Gender Equity and the Boys Debate: What Sort of Challenge Is It?" *British Journal of Sociology of Education* 18(3) (1997); and Yates, "The 'What about the Boys?' Debate as a Public Policy Issue," in *Masculinities and Schools*, ed. N. Lesko (Newbury Park, CA: Sage Publications, 2000); Martin Mills, "Disrupting the 'What about the Boys?' Discourse: Stories from Australia" (Paper presented at the Men's Studies Conference, SUNY at Stony Brook, August 6, 1998); Martin Mills and Bob Lingard, "Masculinity Politics, Myths, and Boys' Schooling: A Review Essay," *British Journal of Educational Studies* 45(3) (September 1997). A superb summary can be found in Bob Lingard, Wayne Martino, and Martin Mills, *Boys and Schooling: Beyond Structural Reform* (London: Palgrave, 2009).

7. Cited in Tamar Lewin, "American Colleges Begin to Ask, Where Have All the Men Gone?" *New York Times*, December 6, 1998, A16.

6

"Gender Symmetry" in Domestic Violence

Domestic violence has emerged as one of the world's most pressing problems. The United Nations estimates that between 20 percent and 50 percent of all women worldwide have experienced physical violence at the hands of an intimate partner or family member. In the United States, more than one million cases of "intimate partner violence" are reported to police each year, according to the U.S. Department of Justice. One of the major platforms for action adopted at the World Conference on Women in Beijing in 1995 was "the prevention and elimination of violence against women and girls."

Efforts to prevent domestic violence and to facilitate the successful prosecution of batterers have followed research and advocacy on behalf of its victims. New laws, police procedures, medical and forensic efforts to collect and preserve evidence have all encouraged prosecution; at the same time, refuges and shelters for battered women, and education and therapy groups for men who are violent toward their partners, have sought to transform the conditions that have traditionally supported and sustained domestic violence.

In recent years, a serious debate has erupted among activists, activist organizations, and individuals about the nature of domestic violence, and especially the gender of the perpetrators. Decades after first bringing the problem to public awareness, feminist activists now confront a growing chorus of researchers and political activists who claim that women and men are victimized by domestic violence in roughly equal numbers.[1]

Despite numerous studies that report the preponderance of domestic violence to be perpetrated by males against females, there are also now more than 100 empirical studies or reports that suggest that rates of domestic violence are equivalent. In the United States, numerous studies have found that women and

Originally published in *Violence against Women* 8 (11) November 2002.

men are equally likely to report to researchers of having hit their partner during the preceding twelve months. In Great Britain also, 4.2 percent of women *and* men said that had been physically assaulted by a partner during the previous twelve months.[2]

Thus, activists for "men's rights" have suggested that policy-oriented efforts for women have been misplaced, because they focus entirely on women as the victims of domestic violence. Instead of the picture painted by feminist researchers and activists, these activists argue that, as one writer put it, "men are the victims of domestic violence at least as often as women."[3] Domestic violence, they argue, exhibits *gender symmetry*—an equal number of women and men are its victims.

While such activists draw our attention to the often-ignored problem of men as victims of domestic violence, their efforts are also often motivated by a desire to undermine or dismantle those initiatives that administer to women victims. To many of these advocates of gender symmetry, compassion is a zero-sum game, and when we show any compassion for women who are the victims of domestic violence, we will never address the male victims.

These apparent discrepancies between claims of gender symmetry and claims of dramatic asymmetry have led to significant confusion among policy-makers and the general public. Is domestic violence a "women's" issue, or do equivalent rates indicate that the "problem" of domestic violence is a problem shared by women and men equally, or even not a problem at all? In this essay, I examine the claims of *gender symmetry* in domestic violence. I review existing sources of data on domestic violence and suggest why the rates of domestic violence appear so varied. I offer some ways to understand and reconcile these discordant data, so that both scholars and policymakers alike may acknowledge the male victims of domestic violence within the larger context of domestic violence. In particular, I argue that claims about "gender symmetry" exclude a thorough analysis of *gender* and how gender identity and ideology—the cultural definitions of masculinity and femininity—may help to clarify these seemingly discordant claims.

The Idea of Gender Symmetry

Reports of gender symmetry have come to play a significant role in public and media discussions of domestic violence. Since these reports run counter to existing stereotypes of male-female relationships, they often have the headline-grabbing value of a "man bites dog" story. One review of the literature by psychologist Martin Fiebert found seventy-nine empirical studies and sixteen reviews of literature that demonstrated gender symmetry among couples. In a more recent meta-analytic review of this literature, John Archer looked at eighty-two studies that found gender symmetry.[4]

These empirical studies raise troubling questions about what the public is thought to "know" to be true of domestic violence—that it is something that men overwhelmingly "do" to women and not the other way around; that domestic violence is among the leading causes of serious injury to women every year; and that worldwide, men's violence against women is one of the most widespread public health issues.

The questions these studies raise are indeed troubling—but the questions they themselves *ask* are far from clear. For example, does gender symmetry mean that women hit women *as often* as men hit women? Or does it mean that an equal *number* of men and women hit each other? Or does symmetry refer to men's and women's *motivations* for such violence, or does it mean that the *consequences* of it are symmetrical? These questions are often lumped together in reviews of literature and "meta-analyses" which review existing data sets.

The two large-scale reviews of literature that demonstrate gender symmetry are useful indicators of the types of evidence offered and the arguments made by their proponents. Of the seventy-nine empirical articles that Fiebert reviews, fifty-five used the same empirical measure of "family conflict," the Conflict Tactics Scale, as the sole measure of domestic violence. This scale was also used in seventy-six out of the eighty-two studies that Archer examined. In addition, twenty-eight of those studies noted by Fiebert discussed samples composed entirely of young people—college students, high school students, or dating couples under thirty—and not married couples. (These two groups overlap somewhat, as thirteen of those studies of young, dating couples also used the CTS.) I will discuss the CTS at some length below, and also examine some of the reasons that studies of college-age and dating couples yield different rates of violence and aggression than studies of somewhat older married couples.

Of the remaining nine studies in Fiebert's 1997 survey that neither used the CTS nor sampled only young, dating, unmarried couples, two were based on people's perceptions of violence, but offered no data about violence itself, while another was based on reports of witnessing violence that contained no useful data. Another was a study of spousal homicide that did not include homicides by ex-spouses (to which I shall also give some attention). One was a study of young people that had no comparisons by gender. And one was based on violence in American comic strips in 1950.

Of the three remaining studies, two were based on clinical samples undertaken by my colleagues at Stony Brook working with psychologist Dan O'Leary. While these studies suggest that couples that seek clinical therapeutic help have high rates of mutual aggression, O'Leary has insisted that the age of the individuals dramatically changes the data, and that clinical samples cannot necessarily be generalized to a national population. Even so, as Fiebert notes, the study by Tyree and Malone (1991) found that women's violence was a result of a "desire to improve contact with partners," by which they meant that the women tended to slap or push their partner in order to get him to pay attention, but not to hurt him.[5]

It would appear, therefore, that Gonzalez's unpublished master's thesis, written apparently under Fiebert's supervision, is the only quantitative survey that purports to find gender symmetry without relying on the CTS. While it may be of interest that most of the women said their violence was a "spontaneous reaction to frustration," Gonzalez did not survey males nor administer to a sample of males the same questionnaire, and thus, one can make *no inferences whatever* about gender symmetry.

Are we clear here? Fiebert's scholarly-sounding annotated bibliography thus turns out to be far more of an ideological polemic than a serious scholarly undertaking. But since it has become a touchstone for those who support a gender symmetry analysis, it is important to consider the studies on which it is based. Despite the vituperative ideological debates, there are serious and credible social science researchers who have used reliable social science and found gender symmetry. Below, I examine (1) the Conflict Tactics Scale, and especially what it measures and what it does not measure; and (2) the effects of age and marital status on domestic violence.

Those who insist on gender symmetry must also account for two statistical anomalies. First, there is the dramatic disproportion of women in shelters and hospital emergency care facilities. Why is it that when we begin our analysis at the end point of the domestic violence experience—when we examine the serious injuries that often are its consequence—the rates are so dramatically asymmetrical? Second, claims of gender symmetry in marital violence must be squared with the empirical certainty that in every single other arena of social life, men are far more disproportionately likely to use violence than women. Why are women so much more violent in the home that their rates approach, or even exceed, those of men, while in every other non-domestic arena men's rates of violence are about nine times those of women?

How Do We Know What We Know: Types of Data

Our understanding of domestic violence has relied on a wide variety of evidence, from clinical observations to narrative accounts of victims and batterers, and the experiences of advocates, and qualitative data gleaned from police and medical sources. Large-scale surveys have fallen into two distinct types. These are "crime victimization studies," which rely on large-scale aggregate data on crime victimization, and "family conflict studies," which measure the prevalence of aggression between married or cohabiting couples. These two sources of data find very different rates of domestic violence—in part because they are measuring two different things.

Crime Victimization Studies

Data about crime victimization are gathered from a variety of sources. Some are obtained from household surveys, such as the National Violence against Women in America Survey (NVAW), sponsored by the National Institute of Justice and the Centers for Disease Control and Prevention. This nationally representative sample surveyed 8,000 women and 8,000 men representing 16,000 households in the United States. Other crime studies are compiled from police statistics, the National Crime Survey (NCS), and the National Crime Victimization Study (NCVS), in which 60,000 households are surveyed annually. Police data typically relies on calls to domestic violence hotlines or calls to police departments.[6]

Crime victimization studies have large sample sizes, in part because they are funded by national, state, and local government agencies. Crime victimization studies include a wide range of assaults, including sexual assault, in their samples. They ask not only about assaults by a current partner (spouse or cohabiting partner) but also by an ex-spouse or ex-partner. But they ask only about those events that the person experiences—or even reports to municipal authorities—as a crime, and therefore miss those events that are neither perceived as nor reported as crimes. They also find significantly lower rates of domestic violence than family conflict studies—ranging from significantly less than 1 percent to about 1.1 percent of all couples. Some reasons that they find lower rates of violence are that crime victimization studies include all individuals in a household over age twelve, even though rates of domestic assault are far lower for women over age sixty-five and between twelve and eighteen. All family members are interviewed, which also may prevent some respondents from disclosing incidents of violence out of fear of retaliation.[7]

These studies uniformly find dramatic gender asymmetry in rates of domestic violence. The National Crime Victimization Survey found females reported six times as many incidents of violence by an intimate as men did in 1992 and 1993. The NVAW found that, in 1998, men physically assaulted their partners at three times the rate at which women assaulted their partners. Crime victimization studies further find that domestic violence increases in severity over time, so that earlier "moderate" violence is likely to be followed by more severe violence later. This emerges also in discussions of spousal homicide, where significant numbers of women killed by their spouses or ex-spouses were also earlier victims of violence. In sum, crime victimization studies typically find that domestic violence is rare, is serious, escalates over time, and is primarily perpetrated by men.

Family Conflict Studies

By contrast, family conflict studies are based on smaller-scale nationally representative household surveys such as the National Family Violence Survey or the

National Survey of Families and Households, and the British and Canadian national surveys. These surveys interview respondents once and ask only one partner of a cohabiting couple (over eighteen) about their experiences with various methods of expressing conflict in the family. Other survey evidence comes from smaller-scale surveys of college students or dating couples, and some draw from clinical samples of couples seeking marital therapy. Still other data are drawn from convenience samples of people who responded to advertisements for subjects placed in newspapers and magazines. According to Fiebert, the total number of respondents for *all* studies that find gender symmetry is slightly more than 66,000—that is, slightly more than the single annual number of one of the crime victimization studies in any one year.[8]

These surveys both expand and contract the types of questions asked of the respondents compared to crime victimization studies. On the one hand, they ask about all the possible experiences of physical violence, including those that are not especially serious or severe and that do not result in injury—that is, those that might not be reported, or even considered a crime. On the other hand, they ask questions only about cohabiting couples (and therefore exclude assaults by ex-spouses or ex-partners) and exclude sexual assault, embedding domestic violence within a context of "family conflict." So, for example, the Conflict Tactics Scale asks respondents about what happens "when they disagree, get annoyed with the other person, or just have spats or fights because they're in a bad mood or tired or for some other reason."[9]

Family conflict studies tend to find much higher general rates of domestic violence than crime victimization studies—typically about 16 percent of all couples report some form of domestic violence. One summary of 21 of the approximately 120 studies that have explored family conflict found that about one-third of men and two-fifths of women indicated using violence in their marriages. As surprising as it may be to see high levels of violence, the most surprising finding has been the gender symmetry in the use of violence to try to resolve family conflicts; as Fiebert writes, "women are as physically aggressive, or more aggressive, than men in their relationships."[10]

These studies also find much lower rates of injury from domestic violence, typically about 3 percent. When "minor" forms of injury (such as slapping, pushing, and grabbing) are excluded from the data, the yearly incidence falls significantly, from 16 percent noted above to around 6 percent of all couples. They also find that violence is unlikely to escalate over time. In sum, then, family conflict studies tend to find high rates of domestic violence, stable levels of severity, and low rates of injury, and find it perpetrated equally by women and men.

How are such different conclusions to be reconciled? A first step is to make the sources of data similar and make sure they are asking similar questions and comparing the same sorts of events. Crime victimization studies rely on two types of data—surveys of national probability samples that are representative of the population at large, and "clinical" samples—calls to police and shelters and visits to emergency rooms. Family conflict studies are based on three sources of data: nationally representative probability samples, clinical samples, and convenience samples based on responses to advertisements.

Nationally representative probability samples are the only sources of data that are consistently reliable and generalizable. While clinical samples may have important therapeutic utility, especially in treatment modalities, they are relatively easy to dismiss as adequate empirical surveys since they do not offer control groups from the non-clinical population and therefore offer no grounds whatever for generalizability. Therefore, I shall omit from further discussion both types of clinical data—police, shelter, and emergency room data, and data drawn from marital therapy cases.

Recruitment via ads in newspapers and magazines offers related problems of the representativeness of the sample and, therefore, undermines efforts at generalizability. Often people who respond to such ads respond because they have a "stake" in the issue, and feel that they want to contribute to it somehow. The representativeness of such people to the general population is unclear at best.[11]

Virtually all the "family conflict" surveys rely on the "Conflict Tactics Scales" (CTS and CTS2), a survey measure developed by New Hampshire sociologist Murray Straus and his collaborators, so we must examine that scale a bit further.

The Conflict Tactics Scale

Developed by Murray Straus and his colleagues over the past two decades, the Conflict Tactics Scale is enormously useful, especially for eliciting the quotidian, commonplace acceptance of violence as a means to "communicate." Let's begin our discussion where the CTS begins. Here is the opening paragraph to the survey as administered:

> No matter how well a couple gets along, there are times when they disagree, get annoyed with the other person, or just have spats or fights because they're in a bad mood or tired or for some other reason. They also use many different ways of trying to settle their differences. I'm going to read some things that you and your (spouse/partner) might do when you have an argument. I would like you to tell me how many times . . . in the past 12 months you . . .

Such a framing assumes that domestic violence is the result of an argument, that it has more to do with being tired or in a bad mood than it does with an effort to control another person.[12]

The CTS asks about frequency, although only for one year. Asking how often in the past year either spouse or partner hit the other may capture some version of reality, but does not capture an ongoing systematic pattern of abuse and violence over many years. This is akin to the difference between watching a single frame of a movie and the movie itself.

Context

The CTS simply counts acts of violence, but takes no account of the circumstances under which these acts occur. Who initiates the violence, the relative size and strength of the people involved, and the nature of the relationship all will surely shape the experience of the violence, but not the scores on the CTS. Thus, if she pushes him back after being severely beaten, it would be scored one "conflict tactic" for each. And if she punches him to get him to stop beating their children, or pushes him away after he has sexually assaulted her, it would count as one for her, none for him.

In response, Straus and his colleagues acknowledge that the context is important, but believe that it is preferable to explore the context separately from the incidence. This response is unpersuasive. Imagine simply observing that death rates soared for males between nineteen and thirty during a few-year period without explaining that a country has declared war. Context matters.

Initiation

Some critics have argued that simply asking how many times a person or his/her spouse used a series of conflict tactics is inadequate to measure the initiation of the violence. Straus argues that, according to the CTS, initiation is about even, and that self-defense is not the motivation for most women. Straus finds that women initiated in 53 percent of the cases; in 42 percent they reported that their husbands initiated the aggression; and about 3 percent said they could not tell who initiated it. Data from other studies, however, indicated that women were far more likely to use violence defensively against the aggression of their partner. With such discordant findings, the CTS's value is limited unless there are a variety of measures incorporated to adequately ascertain the motivation for violence.

Intention and Motivation

Asking people how often they used various conflict tactics during an argument assumes that people use violence *expressively*—that is, in the heat of anger, as a way to settle an argument, to get one's point across, or to get the spouse or partner to listen or pay attention. It misses the way violence might be used *instrumentally*—to control or subdue, to reproduce subordination. Such an absence would be analogous to discussing rape, and only focusing on those date and acquaintance rapes in which there had been some sexual foreplay and the boundaries were less than fully clear, while ignoring, for example, rapes that ended in homicides; rape as a systematic policy of militarily subduing a population; rape in prison; and rape of strangers that has nothing to do with sexual ardor. In short, motivation for violence matters.

Does Location Matter?: The Public/Private Split

In general, men are more aggressive than women. In fact, violence is the only behavioral variable for which there are intractable and overwhelmingly skewed results showing gender differences. While gender differences on a host of other variables—such as spatial orientation and visual perception, academic achievement and ability—have been demonstrated, these differences are typically quite small. Rates of violence based on gender, however, are large and consistent. In their path-breaking work, *The Psychology of Sex Differences*, Eleanor Maccoby and Carol Jacklin found that violence exhibits the greatest gender variation; twenty years later, an analysis by Baron and Richardson found the same thing.[13] So we would have to ask why women would hit men inside the house in roughly equal numbers but almost never commit violence toward men—or women—outside the home.

Studies that propose gender symmetry must explain this apparent paradox. Some, like Fiebert, argue that women assume that their violence towards their male partners is harmless. Straus believes that slapping a man might actually be considered appropriately feminine behavior. It is likely that each of these has some validity, but neither addresses the motivation of the women's violence nor the context in which it occurs. Actually, most empirical research on female aggression points in a very different direction. For example, Bjorkqvist and Niemela found that females are as aggressive as males—but *only* when they are in no danger of being recognized; i.e., when the target is not a family member and there is no danger of retaliation. When parties know each other, women's violence tends to be defensive and men take the initiative. Obviously, domestic violence cannot fit the pattern of women retaining their anonymity.[14]

TWO FINAL CRITICISMS of the CTS—one methodological and one substantive—deserve somewhat fuller elaboration: (1) The methodological problem of memory; and (2) retrospective analysis and reporting bias. The CTS relies on retrospection, asking people to accurately remember what happened during the past year. (It shares this method with crime victimization studies, and these biases may well extend to those studies as well.) Retrospection may not be completely reliable, because memory often serves our current interests, but is unlikely to provide an accurate rendition of what actually happened. There is some evidence that the gender symmetry of domestic violence breaks down when retrospective studies are used alone. Why?

One argument commonly made is that men would be likely to underestimate how often they were victimized because being hit by a woman is so emasculating that they would be too ashamed to admit it, while women would tend to overestimate how often they were hit because it might serve their interests to make false allegations of domestic assault in divorce or custody proceedings.

Both of these assumptions turn out to be empirically groundless; in fact, the evidence points decidedly in the other direction.

What is missing, oddly, from these claims of gender symmetry is an analysis of gender. By this I mean more than simply a tallying up of which biological sex is more likely to be perpetrator or victim, and an analysis that explicitly underscores the ways in which gender identities and gender ideologies are embodied and enacted by women and men. Examining domestic violence through a gender lens helps clarify several issues.

For example, both women and men tend to see their use of violence as gender *non*conforming, but the consequences of this nonconformity might lead women and men to estimate their use of violence and their victimization quite differently. Women are socialized *not* to use violence and, as a result, they would tend to remember every transgression. As Dobash, Dobash, Cavanagh, and Lewis write:

> [W]omen may be more likely to remember their own aggression because it is deemed less appropriate and less acceptable for women than for men and thus takes on the more memorable quality of a forbidden act or one that is out of character.[15]

Men, however, might find it emasculating to reveal that their assumed control over "their women" is so tenuous that they are forced to use violence to "keep her in line." They may find it difficult to admit that they cannot "handle their wives." *Thus, men might underestimate their violence and women might tend to overestimate theirs.*

What's more, in addition to overestimating their own violence, women may also tend to *underestimate* their partners' violence given the norms of domestic life, which frequently find women discounting, downplaying, or normalizing their partners' violent behavior, or even excusing it since they "deserved" it. By the same token, in addition to underestimating their own violence, men may *overestimate* their partners' violence, for the same norms of masculinity. American men, at least, believe violence is legitimate if used as retaliation for violence already committed. The expression "having a chip on one's shoulder" actually has its literal origin among young southern white boys after the Civil War, placing a piece of wood on their shoulder and daring someone to knock it off, so that they might legitimately fight and prove their manhood. Initiating violence is never legitimate according to the norms of traditional masculinity in America; retaliating against a perceived injustice with violence is always legitimate. *As a result, men will tend to overestimate their victimization and women will tend to underestimate theirs.*

In response to the notion that men would be too ashamed or humiliated to call the police or go to the hospital if they were beaten by their wives, available empirical evidence suggests a very different picture: that men who are assaulted by intimates are actually *more* likely to call the police, more likely to press charges, and less likely to drop them. This makes sense in the terms outlined above, as women would be more likely to forgive being hit, or to normalize it with statements about how he really does love her. Another study found that men under-report the violence they perpetrate against women by 50 percent. Dobash et al. found a useful measure of the gender asymmetry in reporting—the women's narrative descriptions of the events of their experiences are far longer and more richly detailed, entering the narrative at a much earlier point in the unfolding drama, and extending the narrative to include injuries and other consequences.[16]

If men underestimate their own violence and overestimate their victimization, while women overestimate their own violence and underestimate their victimization, this would have enormous consequences in a survey that asks only one partner to recall accurately how much they and their spouse used various "conflict-resolution" techniques.

The Causes and Consequences of Violence: Severity and Injury

A final substantive critique of the CTS is that it does not measure the consequences of physical assault (such as physical or emotional injury) or the causes of the assault (such as the desire to dominate). Straus responds that assessing causes and consequences may be interesting, but it is not a necessary part of the picture. He scolds his critics, saying that to fault his research on this question "is akin to thinking that a spelling test is inadequate because it does not measure why a child spells badly, or does not measure possible consequences of poor spelling, such as low self-esteem or low evaluations by employers."[17]

Were Straus not a credible social scientist, one might suspect the reply to be disingenuous. As such, it is simply inadequate. It is more akin to a teacher who doesn't look at how far off the spelling mistakes are or whether there is a pattern in the mistakes that might point to a physiological problem like dyslexia or some other learning disability, as compared to academic laziness, and thus leaves the learning problems untouched and misdirects funds away from remediation towards punitive after-school programs for lazy students. And even that analogy is imperfect because, unlike spelling, domestic violence is not about what happens to the perpetrator (the poor speller) but to someone else. Can one imagine any other issue in which causes and consequences are thought to be irrelevant?

The consequences of violence raise perhaps the most telling criticism of the CTS—a criticism, not incidentally, that Straus and his more thoughtful collaborators share, as I will discuss below. The CTS lumps together many different forms of violence, so that a single slap may be equated with a more intensive assault. In the National Violence against Women Survey, for example, lifetime percentages of persons physically assaulted by an intimate partner found dramatic differences in some types of assault, but not others. For example, just under 1 percent of men and women (0.9 percent of women and 0.8 percent of men) said their attacker used a knife in the attack, but 3.5 percent of women and only 0.4 percent of men said their partner threatened to use a gun; and 0.7 percent of women and 0.1 percent of men said their spouse actually did use a gun. (It is interesting to note that these differences inside the home are actually slightly smaller than the differences outside the home, where men are overwhelmingly more likely to use weapons in an attack.)[18]

Even more telling are the gender disparities in serious physical injuries without weapons. For example, in a British study that found equal rates of reporting victimization of violence, there were no injuries at all reported in the 59 percent of incidents that involved pushing, shoving, and grabbing (these are the behaviors more typically reported being committed by women than by men). In the National Violence against Women study (a crime victimization–type study), half as many men as women (4.4 percent of men and 8.1 percent of women) said their partner threw something at them, and three times as many women (18.1 percent of women and 5.4 percent of men) said their partner pushed or grabbed or shoved them, or that their partner slapped or hit them (16.0 percent of women and 5.5 percent of men). But over ten times as many women (8.5 percent of women and 0.6 percent of men) reported that their partner "beat them up."[19]

The consequences of violence range from minor to fatal, and these are significant in understanding domestic violence in general and its gendered patterns. Far more men than women kill their spouses (and, of course, "couples" in which one spouse killed the other could not participate in the CTS studies since both partners must be cohabiting at the time of the study). And rates of homicides of ex-spouses are even more gender asymmetrical. According to the FBI, female victims represent about 70 percent of all intimate homicide victims. About one-third of all female homicide victims in the United States were killed by an intimate, compared with 4 percent of male homicide victims. (What this suggests, of course, is that both women *and* men are more likely to be killed by a man; efforts to end all types of violence ought properly to focus on the association of masculinity and violence; the legitimacy of violence to men; and men's sense of entitlement to use violence.) In the United States, the number of men killed by intimates has dropped by 69 percent since 1976. The number of women killed by intimates was relatively stable until 1993, when it too began to drop, but only by about 15 percent.

Gender symmetry tends to be clustered entirely at the lower end of violence. According to some data, women are six times more likely to require medical care for injuries sustained by family violence. Straus also reports that in family conflict studies the injury rate for assaults by men is about seven times greater than the injury rate for assaults by women. This dramatic difference in rates of injury, found in both types of studies, leads Straus, the creator of the CTS and the researcher who is most often cited by those claiming gender symmetry, to write that:

> [a]lthough women may assault their partners at approximately the same rate as men, because of the greater physical, financial, and emotional injury suffered by women, they are the predominant victims. Consequently, the first priority in services for victims and in prevention and control must continue to be directed toward assaults by husbands.[20]

Straus also understands that women, on average, suffer much more frequent and more severe injury (physical, economic, and psychological) than men.

These different rates of injury are so pronounced that when injury data has been obtained in studies using the CTS, the rate of violence drops to that predicted by the crime victimization studies, and the gender asymmetry of such studies is also revealed. This leads another researcher to conclude that both husbands and wives may be said to be "aggressive" but many more husbands are "violent."

Age and Aggression

The CTS measures family conflict in intact partnerships, either cohabiting or married couples. However, as I've previously mentioned, more than one-third of the studies noted by Fiebert that found gender symmetry were surveys of college-age, dating couples who were not cohabiting. About one-half of Archer's samples in his meta-analytic review involved high school or college students. Therefore, it is important to examine the way age exerts an effect on domestic violence.

According to all available research, age—especially being under thirty—is a strong predictor of partner violence. O'Leary and his associates have consistently found that age is a significant variable in the distribution of partner violence. Rates of violence rise significantly between age ten (less than 2 percent violent) and age twenty-five, where levels peak at 35 percent of all couples. But after twenty-five, rates begin to drop and keep dropping to return to about 5 percent by age seventy-five. This suggests that younger couples are most likely to have the highest rates of violence. The National Survey of Adolescents in the United States found that of 22.3 million adolescents (age 12–17), 1.8 million had been victims of what researchers label "serious sexual assault," and 3.9 million had been victims of a serious physical assault. Females were four times more likely to have been sexually assaulted (13 percent compared to 3.4 percent of males), and young males were significantly more likely to have been physically assaulted (21.3 percent compared to 13.4 percent of young females). This is because violence means different things to younger dating couples than to married couples at midlife, when violence is usually associated with significant marital discord. The two populations—young, unmarried dating couples and older married couples at midlife—are so dissimilar that results from one population cannot be generalized to the other.[21]

Younger people also report using only a few of the various forms of conflict—pushing and slapping. These are not typically associated with injury or with fear of the partner. Stets' work on the centrality of control in dating violence also helps explain the relationship of age and gender on non-spousal violence. It is possible that men's rates of violence drop after marriage because they establish their control over the relationship (financial, physical, emotional) and that therefore overt acts of violence are less necessary as long as the threat of violence is present.

What the CTS Leaves Out

It is important not only to understand what the CTS measures, but to make explicit what it does not measure. First, the CTS does not include sexual assault in its definition of family conflict. This is crucial, because a significant number of spousal assaults are sexual assaults. The National Violence against Women Survey found that 7.7 percent of all female respondents had been raped by an intimate partner at some point in their lifetime; this translates into approximately 201,394 U.S. women who are raped by an intimate partner each year. Yet, Straus and Gelles do not include rape as a category in the index.

Second, the CTS only includes violence by a *current* spouse or cohabiting partner. It does not include violence by an ex-spouse or partner. Crime victimization studies do include these. This is important because crimes by former spouses comprise a significant number of domestic assaults. It may be that when women exit a relationship, they have no "need" for violence, while men tend to continue, or even escalate, their use of violence when women leave. The NCVS found that rates of intimate-perpetrated violence for separated women are over eight times higher than rates for married women. It may be true that these might be somewhat overrepresented in crime victimization studies because people who are assaulted by a former spouse would be more likely to report that as a crime, since the former spouse clearly had no "right" to aggress against the victim and so, it would clearly be seen as a crime and more likely to be reported. But to ignore these data would so skew any study as to make it unreliable. For example, in one Australian study, only 1 percent of all violent victimization of men involved an ex-spouse or ex-partner, but it involved fully one-third of all female incidents. Failure to include ex-spouses may fail to capture up to one-third of all cases.

Failure to include sexual assault and assaults by ex-spouses or ex-partners compounds the problem that the CTS does not adequately measure rates of serious injury from domestic violence. The National Violence against Women Survey (1998) found that 72.6 percent of rape victims and 66.6 percent of physical assault victims sustained injuries such as a scratch, bruise, or welt, and that 14.1 percent of rape victims and 12.2 percent of physical assault victims sustained a broken bone or dislocated joint. Rape victims were far more likely to sustain an internal injury (5.8 percent to 0.8 percent), or a chipped or broken tooth (3.3 percent to 1.8 percent). On the other hand, physical assault victims were more likely to sustain a laceration or knife wound (16.9 percent to 6.2 percent), a head or spinal cord injury (10.1 percent to 6.6 percent), and burns and bullet wounds (0.7 percent and 1.8 percent respectively; rape rates too low to estimate).[22]

Violence by ex-husbands also tends to be more serious. For example, the risk of spousal homicide goes up by about 50 percent for women who leave abusive husbands. (This may also help explain the "rationality" in the decision by women to stay in abusive relationships.) Men may kill their ex-wives because their ex-wives left them; women may kill their ex-husbands because they believe that their ex-husband will otherwise kill them for leaving. In both cases, then, the larger context for *both* women's and men's violence is men's violence. One study of spousal homicide found that over half of all defendants were separated from their victims at the time at which they were accused of committing the murder.

In sum, the gender symmetry found by CTS-based studies results from the omission of severity of injury, sexual assault, and assaults by former spouses. Some fail to adequately account for marital status and age. Including these would certainly make the gender *asymmetry* of domestic violence more clear.

How Can We Understand the Use of Aggression in Domestic Life?

These two different types of studies—crime victimization studies and family conflict studies—rely on two different theoretical perspectives and two different sources of data. They measure two different phenomena based on different conceptualizations of aggression in families. But they can be reconciled conceptually and methodologically.

If one is interested in the level of aggression in family conflict—i.e., the likelihood of any type of aggression occurring when a couple has an argument—then the CTS scale may be somewhat useful. I say "somewhat" because, among other problems that I have outlined above, the utility of the CTS is limited by the fact that it fails to take into account sexual assault and also assault by an ex-spouse. But it does enable us to see the overall amount of a particular kind of violence in families, what we might call *expressive* violence—the way a person might express anger, frustration, or loss of control. If, however, one were interested in the ways in which one partner uses violence not expressively but *instrumentally*, to achieve some end of control, injury, or terror, then the CTS would be a poor measure. Then, crime victimization surveys will be more valuable because these measure serious injury, and include sexual assault and assaults by ex-spouses in their purview. These surveys may capture those family conflicts where the level of violence escalates beyond a mere "conflict tactic" to something far more ominous and perhaps lethal.

Some violence by men against women is motivated not by the desire to express anger, frustration, or some other immediate emotion during a family conflict, but may be more instrumentally motivated by the desire to control. However, the use of violence may indicate not the experience of control but the experience of loss of control. "Violence is a part of a system of domination," writes R. W. Connell, "but it is at the same time a measure of its imperfection."[23]

In that sense, we might say that many men who assault their partners or ex-partners indicate using violence when they fear that their control is breaking down, that their ability to control their partners by the implicit threat of violence is compromised, and the men feel compelled to use explicit violence to "restore" their control. Thus men see their violence as restorative and retaliatory. For example, in an earlier study, Dobash and Dobash found three antecedents of men's use of violence: his sexual jealousy; his perception that she failed to perform a household task such as cleaning or preparing a hot meal; and her challenging his authority on financial matters—all of these are indicators of a breakdown of his expected dominance and control.[24]

This understanding of control-motivated, instrumental violence is particularly important in our understanding of claims of gender symmetry. For one thing, men's control over women has clearly broken down when their spouses have left them; thus, measures of physical assault that do not include assaults by ex-spouses will entirely miss these events. Second, breakdowns of men's control over women may be revealed not by physical assault, but by the woman's withholding or refusing of sexual intimacy. She may exert what limited power she may have by attempting to refuse his sexual advances. Thus, measures that do not include sexual assaults among acts of aggression will be equally inadequate to measure the problem.

Control-motivated instrumental violence is experienced by men not as an expression of their power but as an instance of its collapse. The men may feel entitled to experience that control over women, but at the moments when they become violent, they do not feel that control. Masculinity, in that sense, has already been compromised; violence is a method to restore one's manhood and domestic inequality at the same time. Such control-motivated, instrumental violence is more likely to escalate over time, less likely to be mutual, and more likely to involve serious injury. This difference between expressive and instrumental violence is a difference not simply in purpose, but also in frequency, severity, and initiation. It addresses whether the violence is part of a systematic pattern of control and fear, or an isolated expression of frustration or anger. These two types of violence are so different that Johnson has come to call instrumental violence "intimate terrorism" (IT) and the types of expressive violence measured by the CTS as "common couple violence" (CCV).[25]

Social control–motivated abuse can be illustrated in another form of domestic violence: stalking. Control-motivated abuse refers to intentionally inflicted physically or psychologically painful or hurtful acts (or threats) by one partner as a means of compelling or constraining the conduct, dress, or demeanor of the other. Rates of stalking by an intimate, more prevalent than previously thought, can best be understood as an effort to restore control or dominance after the partner has left. Stalking exhibits dramatic gender asymmetry: nearly 5 percent of American women and about one-half of one percent (0.6 percent) of men report being stalked by a current or former intimate partner at some time in their lives.

Claims about the gender symmetry of "conflict-motivated" expressive violence must be complemented with claims about the dramatic gender *asymmetry* in "control-motivated" instrumental violence. When these two are factored together, it is clear that women and men may express their anger or frustration during an argument more equally than we earlier thought. This, however, is by no means fully symmetrical, because even the CTS leaves out two of the dominant forms of expressive "conflict-motivated" aggression—sexual assault and assault by an ex-spouse. And when "control-motivated" instrumental violence is added—the violence that more typically results in serious injury, is more systematic, and is independent of specific "conflict" situations—the gender asymmetry is clear.

Why We Should Be Concerned about Women's Violence toward Men

Despite the evidence that gender symmetry is largely a myth, we should nonetheless be concerned about women's violence for a variety of reasons. For one thing, compassion for the victims of violence is not a zero-sum game—reasonable people would naturally want to extend compassion, support, and interventions to all victims of violence. (It is an indication of the political intentions of those who argue for gender symmetry that they never question the levels of violence against women, only that the level of violence against men is equivalent. Their solution, though, is not *more* funding for domestic violence research and intervention, but to *decrease* the amount of funding that women receive—even though they never challenge the levels of violence against women.)

Second, acknowledging women's capacity for intimate violence will illuminate the *gender symmetry* in intimate violence among gay male and lesbian couples. According to the National Violence against Women Survey, slightly more than 11 percent of women living with a same sex partner report being raped, physically assaulted, or stalked by a female cohabitant (compared with 30.4 percent of women with a live-in male partner). About 15 percent of men living with a male live-in partner report having experienced violence (compared with 7.7 percent of men with female live-in partners).

Third, perhaps ironically, examining women's violence can better illuminate the dynamics of men's aggression against women. Since women's violence is often retaliatory or committed in self-defense, it may help to expose some of the ways men use violence to control women, and women's perceived lack of options except "fighting back."

Fourth, acknowledging assaults by women is important, Straus writes, because they "put women in danger of much more severe retaliation by men." In an interview, Straus elaborated that since women generally suffer greater fear and more injuries, "when she slaps, she sets the stage for him to hit her. The safety of women alone demands we make a big deal of women hitting men."[26]

Finally, men actually benefit from efforts to reduce men's violence against women. It turns out that efforts to protect women in the United States have had the effect of reducing the homicide rate of men by their partners by almost 70 percent over the past 24 years. According to James Alan Fox, Professor of Criminal Justice at Northeastern University, homicides by women of their spouses, ex-spouses, or boyfriends have steadily declined from 1,357 in 1976 to 424 in 1999. Fox attributes this decline to the availability of alternatives for battered women. "We have given women alternatives, including hotlines, shelters, counseling and restraining orders. Because more battered women have escape routes, fewer wife batterers are being killed," Fox told reporters. A 1999 study by the National Consortium on Violence Research found that the greater availability of hotlines and other resources for battered women, the greater the decline in homicide of their male partners. (The study found that 80 percent of these male domestic homicide victims had abused their partners and that nearly two-thirds of female murder victims had been abused before they were killed.) It turns out that those very initiatives that have greatly benefited women—shelters, hotlines, and the like—save *men's* lives as well.

Toward an Inclusive Explanation of Domestic Violence

It is certainly possible and politically necessary to acknowledge that some women use violence as a tactic in family conflict while also understanding that men tend to use violence more instrumentally to control women's lives. Further, these two types of aggression must also be embedded within the larger framework of gender inequality. Women's violence toward male partners certainly does exist, but it tends to be very different from that of men toward their female partners: it is far less injurious and less likely to be motivated by attempts to dominate or terrorize the partner.

The different types of data sources, family violence studies and crime vic-timization studies, each point to different problems and each is useful to develop intervention strategies. As Straus writes, "research using a broad defi-nition [of violence] and emphasizing injury may be most useful for informing programs designed to treat offenders or help victims of repeated severe assault." On the other hand, "research focusing on the act of assault, most of which does not involve injury but does involve millions of couples, may be most useful in informing programs of 'primary prevention' i.e. steps that will prevent physical assaults from ever happening." And he concludes:

> I believe humanity needs research inspired by the moral agenda and per-spective of those who focus on the *oppression of women*, regardless of whether the oppression is physical, sexual, psychological, or economic; and also research inspired by the moral agenda of those who focus on *physical assault*, regardless of whether the assault is by a man, woman, or child.[27]

Coupled with studies of parental violence toward children—which routinely find that more than 90 percent of parents aggress against their children—family conflict studies are useful in pointing out the ubiquity and the casualness with which violence structures our daily lives. Coupled with data about intimate partner homicide, rape, and other forms of sexual assault, crime victimization data are useful in pointing out the ways in which men's domination over women requires the implicit threat, and often the explicit instrumental use, of violence to maintain that power.

Claims of gender symmetry are often made by those who do not understand the data: what the various studies measure and what they omit. Others make claims of gender symmetry based on disingenuous political motives, attempting to discredit women's suffering by offering abstract statistical equivalences that turn out to be chimerical. Gelles and Straus understand the political misuses to which their work has been put, and strongly disavow those political efforts. In a summary of their work, they write:

> Perhaps the most controversial finding from our 1975 National Family Violence Survey was the report that a substantial number of women hit and beat their husbands. Since 1975 at least ten additional investigations have confirmed the fact that women hit and beat their husbands. *Unfortunately the data on wife-to-husband violence has been misreported, mis-interpreted, and misunderstood.* Research uniformly shows that about as many women hit men as men hit women. However, those who report that husband abuse is as common as wife abuse overlook two important facts. First, the greater average size and strength of men and their greater aggressiveness means that a man's punch will probably produce more

pain, injury, and harm than a punch by a woman. Second, nearly three-fourths of the violence committed by women is done in self-defense. While violence by women should not be dismissed, neither should it be overlooked or hidden. On occasion, legislators and spokespersons . . . have used the data on violence by wives to minimize the need for services for battered women. *Such arguments do a great injustice to the victimization of women.*[28]

And Gelles underscores this disingenuous political use of their work with this clear and unequivocal statement that "it is categorically false to imply that there are the same number of 'battered' men as battered women." (Note how he even puts the word "battered" in quotations when describing men.) It is not surprising that credible researchers disavow the political ends to which their work is often put.

Despite the dramatic differences in frequency, severity, and purpose of the violence, we should be compassionate towards *all* victims of domestic violence. There are some men who are battered by their female partners, and these men are no less deserving of compassion, understanding, and intervention than are women who are battered. And male domestic violence victims deserve access to services and funding, just as female domestic violence victims do. They do not need to be half of all victims in order to deserve either sympathy or services.

But just as surely, compassion and adequate intervention strategies must explore the full range of domestic violence—the different rates of injury, the different types of violence, including sexual assault, and the likelihood of violence by an ex-spouse. Such strategies must also understand the differences between violence that is an expression of family conflict and violence that is instrumental to the control of one partner over the other.

With all the caveats and modifications I have suggested to the Family Conflict model, and especially the CTS as the standard of measurement, I would therefore argue that violence as an expression of family conflict is somewhat less than symmetrical, but would include a significant percentage of women. I would hypothesize that, including assaults and homicides by ex-spouses, spousal homicide, and sexual assault, the gendered ratio of male-perpetrated violence to female-perpetrated violence would be closer to 4:1. On the other hand, violence that is instrumental in the maintenance of control—the more systematic, persistent, and injurious type of violence—is overwhelmingly perpetrated by men, with rates captured best by crime victimization studies. Over 90 percent of this violence is perpetrated by men.

When sexual violence and violence by an ex-spouse are considered, the evidence is overwhelming that gender *asymmetry* in domestic violence remains in full effect. Men *are* more violent than women—both inside the home and in the public sphere. The home is not a refuge from violence, nor is it a site where gender differences in the public sphere are somehow magically reversed. As concerned citizens, we need to be concerned about all victims of violence. And we must also be aware that the perpetrators of that violence—both in public and in private, at home or on the street, and whether the victim is male or female—are overwhelmingly men.

NOTES

This chapter is based on my article in *Violence against Women*. I have compressed the citations into these few endnotes. Readers requiring further documentation are encouraged to see the original articles.

1. See, for example, S. Steinmetz, "The Battered Husband Syndrome," *Victimology* 2 (1978): 499–509; E. Pleck, J. Pleck, M. Grossman, and P. Bart, "The Battered Data Syndrome: A Comment on Steinmetz's Article," *Victimology* 2 (1978): 680–684. M. D. Schwartz and W. S. DeKeseredy, "The Return of the 'Battered Husband Syndrome' through the Typification of Women as Violent," *Crime, Law, and Social Change* 20 (1993): 249–265; J. Straton, "The Myth of the 'Battered Husband Syndrome,'" *Masculinities* 2 (1994): 79–82.

2. J. Archer, ed., *Male Violence* (London: Routledge, 1994); J. Archer, "Sex Differences in Aggression between Heterosexual Partners: A Meta-analytic Review," *Psychological Bulletin* 126 (2000): 651–680; M. Fiebert, "Annotated Bibliography: References Examining Assaults by Women on Their Spouses/Partners," *Sexuality and Culture* 1 (1997): 273–286.

3. Armin Brott, "Men: The Secret Victims of Domestic Violence," *Washington Post*, December 28, 1993.

4. Martin Fiebert, "Annotated Bibliography: References Examining Assaults by Women on Their Spouses," *Sexuality and Culture* 1 (1997): 273–286; John Archer, "Sex Differences in Aggression between Heterosexual Partners: A Meta-analytic Review," *Psychological Bulletin* 126 (2000): 651–680.

5. K. D. O'Leary, "Are Women Really More Aggressive Than Men in Intimate Relationships?" *Psychological Bulletin* 126 (2000): 685–689. K. D. O'Leary, J. Barling, I. Arias, A. Rosenblum, J. Malone, and A. Tyree, "Prevalence and Stability of Physical Aggression between Spouses: A Longitudinal Analysis," *Journal of Consulting and Clinical Psychology* 57 (1989): 263–268; A. Tyree and J. Malone, "How Can It Be That Wives Hit Husbands As Much As Husbands Hit Wives and None of Us Knew It?" (Paper presented at the annual meeting of the American Sociological Association, August 1991, Cincinnati, OH).

6. P. Tjaden and N. Thoennes, *Prevalence, Incidence, and Consequences of Violence against Women: Findings from the National Violence against Women Survey* (Washington, DC: National Institute of Justice and Centers for Disease Control and Prevention, 1998). Retrieved May 7, 2002, from http://www.ncjrs.org/pdffiles/172837.html; P. Tjaden and N. Thoennes, *Extent, Nature, and Consequences of Intimate Partner Violence* (Washington, DC: National Institute of Justice and Centers for Disease Control and Prevention, 2000); P. Tjaden and N. Thoennes, "Prevalence and Consequences of Male-to-Female and Female-to-Male Intimate Partner Violence as Measured by the National Violence against Women Survey," *Violence against Women* 6 (2000): 142–161; P. Tjaden and N. Thoennes, *Full Report of the Prevalence, Incidence, and Consequences of Violence against*

Women: Findings from the National Violence against Women Survey (Washington, DC: National Institute of Justice and Centers for Disease Control and Prevention, 2000).

7. For a summary of these findings, see W. S. DeKeseredy, "Current Controversies on Defining Nonlethal Violence against Women in Intimate Heterosexual Relationships: Empirical Implications," *Violence against Women* 6 (2000): 728–746; M. Straus, "The Controversy over Domestic Violence by Women: A Methodological, Theoretical, and Sociology of Science Analysis," in *Violence in Intimate Relationships*, ed. X. B. Arriaga and S. Oskamp (Thousand Oaks, CA: Sage Publications, 1999), 17–44; R. Gelles, "Domestic Violence: Not an Even Playing Field," *The Safety Zone*. Retrieved October 12, 2000, from http://www.serve.com/zone/everyone/Gelles/html.

8. The family conflict study is represented by the work of Murray Straus and his colleagues. See, for example, M. A. Straus, "Measuring Intrafamily Conflict and Violence: The Conflict Tactic (CT) Scales," in *Physical Violence in American Families*, ed. M. A. Straus and R. J. Gelles (New Brunswick, NJ: Transaction Publishers, 1990), 29–47; M. A. Straus, "Identifying Offenders in Criminal Justice Research on Domestic Assault," *American Behavioral Scientist* 36 (1993): 587–600; M. Straus, "Physical Assaults by Women Partners: A Major Social Problem," in *Gender: Ongoing Debates*, ed. M. R. Walsh (New Haven, CT: Yale University Press, 1997), 204–221; Straus, "The Controversy over Domestic Violence by Women"; M. Straus and R. Gelles, "Societal Change and Family Violence from 1975 to 1985 as Revealed by Two National Surveys," *Journal of Marriage and the Family* 48 (1986): 445–479; M. Straus and R. Gelles, *Physical Violence in American Families: Risk Factors and Adaptations to Violence in 8,145 Families* (New Brunswick, NJ: Transaction Publishers, 1990); M. Straus, R. Gelles, and S. Steinmetz, *Behind Closed Doors: Violence in the American Family* (Newbury Park, CA: Sage Publications, 1980).

9. Straus, "Physical Assaults by Women Partners: A Major Social Problem," 217.

10. Fiebert, "Annotated Bibliography," 273.

11. In the best of these studies, O'Leary and his colleagues have found that about 31 percent of the men and 44 percent of the women indicated that they had engaged in some aggression to their partners in the year before they were married. A year after the marriage, rates had dropped for both groups and 27 percent of the men and 36 percent of the women indicated they had aggressed, and thirty months into the marriage the rates for the previous year were 25 percent of the men and 32 percent of the women (O'Leary et al., "Prevalence and Stability of Physical Aggression between Spouses," 264).

12. For critiques of the CTS and CTS2 generally, see W. S. DeKeseredy and M. D. Schwartz, *Measuring the Extent of Woman Abuse in Intimate Heterosexual Relationships: A Critique of the Conflict Tactics Scales* (1989). Retrieved May 7, 2002, from http://www.vawnet .org/vnl/library/general/AR_ctscrit.html; W. S. DeKeseredy and M. D. Schwartz, *Woman Abuse on Campus: Results from the Canadian National Survey* (Thousand Oaks, CA: Sage Publications, 1998); W. S. DeKeseredy and M. D. Schwartz, eds., *Rethinking Violence against Women* (Thousand Oaks, CA: Sage Publications, 1998); R. E. Dobash and R. P. Dobash, *Violence against Wives: A Case against the Patriarchy* (New York: Free Press, 1979). R. P. Dobash, R. E. Dobash, M. Wilson, and M. Daly, "The Myth of Sexual Symmetry in Marital Violence," *Social Problems* 39 (1992): 71–91; L. D. Brush, "Violent Acts and Injurious Outcomes in Married Couples: Methodological Issues in the National Survey of Families and Households," in *Violence against Women: The Bloody Footprints*, ed. P. B. Bart (Newbury Park, CA: Sage Publications, 1993), 240–251; L. Okun, *Women Abuse: Facts Replacing Myths* (Albany: State University of New York Press, 1986);

D. Kurz, "Physical Assaults by Husbands: A Major Social Problem," in *Current Controversies on Family Violence*, ed. R. J. Gelles and D. R. Loseke (Thousand Oaks, CA: Sage Publications, 1993), 88–103.

13 Eleanor Maccoby and Carol Jacklin, *The Psychology of Sex Differences* (Stanford: Stanford University Press, 1974); R. A. Baron and D. Richardson, *Human Aggression* (New York: Plenum, 1994).

14. K. Bjorkqvist and P. Niemela, eds., *Of Mice and Women: Aspects of Female Aggression* (San Diego, CA: Academic Publishers, 1992).

15. R. P. Dobash, R. E. Dobash, K. Cavanagh, and R. Lewis, "Separate and Intersecting Realities: A Comparison of Men's and Women's Accounts of Violence against Women," *Violence against Women* 4 (1998): 382–414.

16. This turns out to be true; see A. Ferrante, F. Morgan, D. Indermaur, and R. Harding, *Measuring the Extent of Domestic Violence* (Perth, Australia: Hawkins Press, 1996); L. Rouse, R. Breen, and M. Howell, "Abuse in Intimate Relationships: A Comparison of Married and Dating College Students," *Journal of Interpersonal Violence* 3 (1988): 414–419; M. Schwartz, "Gender and Injury in Spousal Assault," *Sociological Focus* 20 (1987): 61–75.

17. Straus, "Physical Assaults by Women Partners: A Major Social Problem," 218.

18. Tjaden and Thoennes, *Prevalence, Incidence, and Consequences of Violence against Women*, 7.

19. Ibid.

20. Straus, "Physical Assaults by Women Partners: A Major Social Problem," 219.

21. See K. D. O'Leary "Are Women Really More Aggressive Than Men in Intimate Relationships?" *Psychological Bulletin* 126 (2000): 685–689.

22. The CTS2 does include a measure of sexual coercion, which seems to me a pretty cogent acknowledgement that it must be included in all understandings of gender symmetry.

23. R. W. Connell, *Masculinities* (Berkeley: University of California Press, 1995), 230.

24. It must be noted, of course, that the "retaliation" is more often for a *perceived* injury or slight than any real injury. See, for example, T. Beneke, *Men on Rape* (New York: St. Martin's Press, 1982).

25. See M. P. Johnson, "Patriarchal Terrorism and Common Couple Violence: Two Forms of Violence against Women," *Journal of Marriage and the Family* 57 (1995): 283–294; M. P. Johnson, "Conflict and Control: Images of Symmetry and Asymmetry in Domestic Violence," in *Couples in Conflict*, ed. A. Booth, A. Crouter, and M. Clements (Hillsdale, NJ: Lawrence Erlbaum, 2000), 178–204.

26. Straus, "Physical Assaults by Women Partners: A Major Social Problem," 210.

27. Straus, "The Controversy over Domestic Violence by Women," 39–40.

28. Straus and Gelles, "Societal Change and Family Violence from 1975 to 1985 as Revealed by Two National Surveys," 450; M. Straus and R. Gelles, *Physical Violence in American Families: Risk Factors and Adaptations to Violence in 8,145 Families* (New Brunswick, NJ: Transaction Publishers, 1990).

PART THREE

Restorations

In his book *Columbine* (2009), published on the tenth anniversary of that tragic day, journalist Dave Cullen jettisons a bird's-eye view of that school shooting in favor of an extreme close-up psychological portrait of Eric Harris and Dylan Klebold. As in a pointillist painting, each dot of color is rendered in excruciating detail, as we read about Harris's deep-seated psychopathologies and Klebold's pathetic eagerness to be accepted by his sociopathic friend and mentor.

He's right, of course, as right as any analyst of those tiny dots of color can be. I suppose that any event, looked at closely enough, ceases to resemble any other, as the existential uniqueness of the individuals involved makes comparison with other events impossible. It's no doubt true that Harris externalized his rage at the world and his contempt for those he considered inferior, and that Klebold, depressed and suicidal, followed like a lost puppy. (That such a decidedly disturbed kid managed to fool everyone who ever came into contact with him, as he glided under the radar of every parent, teacher, administrator, and guidance counselor, offers a seemingly unintentional vilification of our entire school system and mental health system—not to mention our parenting styles.)

So, in this sense, Cullen is right. He also misses the point.

A more sociological approach of the school shooters stands further back from that pointillist painting, where the microdots of juxtaposed color actually form discernible patterns, where the minimalist details form recognizable shapes that make such individual psychologies comprehensible. That's why humans invented such concepts as categories in the first place, as heuristic devices that enable us to see such social patterns.

Humans are born comparers. We comparison shop, and we develop comparisons to make sense of the particular as well as to discern larger patterns. Each specific instance may be as unique as a snowflake, but try telling that to someone stuck in a snowdrift.

The sociology of these school shootings need not ignore the individual pathologies of Eric Harris and Dylan Klebold. It neither diminishes the horror of their crime, nor elevates them to some status as sublimely martyred victims, to acknowledge that these two boys had some similarities—and some differences—with Michael Carneal, Barry Loukatis, Evan Ramsey, Gary Scott Pennington, Luke Woodham, Andy Williams, Kip Kinkel, and all the rest of the young suburban white boys who opened fire on their classmates and teachers.

To ignore these "categories"—all were boys, all but one were white, all but two were suburban or rural—is to have no sense of the forest in which these boys were lost, but a very good idea of the feel of the twig. Race, region, religion—all these and more shape the social context in which school shootings take place.

There are discernible patterns among all the school shooters, and a group sociological profile of those young boys sheds a different sort of light on the problems of these tragic events—more diffuse, perhaps, but one also misses the entire room if one only points a laser at one tiny point on a wall. Not to belabor the art history metaphor, but we must examine more than those two lonely and psychologically disturbed dots on the canvas. We need to look at the entire picture, from a significant enough distance, to observe the patterns.

Nor does it diminish the specificity of that tragedy to also note that all the *schools* in which random school shooters committed their crimes also exhibited certain similarities. The schools themselves share characteristics that make random school shootings more likely in some places than in others. Had Harris and Klebold attended Denver's East High School, would they have so easily slipped between the cracks—especially if they were as maniacally crazy as Cullen thinks? Had the certifiably crazy Seung-Hui Cho attended William and Mary and not Virginia Tech, would all the murderous chips have still fallen into place? Any public policy designed to make our schools safer will need to address both the commonalities among the shooters, their specific psychological differences, and the cultural and social environments in which some of those individual psychopathologies come to frightening fruition.

The truth is we need *all* these levels of analysis—and then some. School shootings are a psychiatric issue, but also a community issue if no responsible adult even bothers to notice the psychopaths in their midst. It's a sociological issue, given the eerie similarities among the shooters. And it's a cultural issue, an issue of how we educate our children and what sorts of differences we tolerate—and which ones we don't.

And a fuller picture also requires that we pay attention to gender. They aren't just misguided "kids" or "youth" or "troubled teens"—they're boys. All of them. They are a group of boys, deeply aggrieved by a system that they may feel is cruel or demeaning, or, in the case of Eric Harris's fraudulent reversal, beneath him. Feeling aggrieved, wronged by the world—these are boilerplate adolescent feelings, common to many boys and girls. What transforms the aggrieved into mass murderers is also a sense of entitlement, a sense of using violence against others, making others hurt as you, yourself, might hurt. Aggrieved entitlement inspires revenge against those who have wronged you; it is the compensation for humiliation. Humiliation is emasculation: humiliate someone and you take away his manhood. For many men, humiliation must be avenged, or you cease to be a man. Aggrieved entitlement is a gendered emotion, a fusion of that humiliating loss of manhood and the moral obligation and entitlement to get it back. And its gender is masculine.

That sense of masculinity as something that must be retrieved, restored, is the theme that unites the essays in this section. Following the two essays about the school shooters, I turn my attention to the extreme right, where the restoration of masculinity is a dominant theme. Based on my interviews with neo-Nazis, white supremacists, and other Aryan groups in both the United States and Scandinavia, I've come to understand these groups as using masculinity both as a lens (one of several) through which they can view and understand their situation and also as a prime recruiting device to appeal to young white men.

And that sense of the restoration of manhood has a sinister global component. A group profile of the terrorists of 9/11 reveals some surprising similarities with our own homegrown domestic terrorists; indeed Mohammed Atta and Timothy McVeigh might have had a lot to talk about had they found themselves in prison together. (Indeed, many of McVeigh's [com]patriot pals might have been the extreme right-wingers who cheered, on 9/11, that those "towel heads" had the "testicular fortitude" to attack the global headquarters of the Zionist Occupied Government. Others on the extreme right thought it was the beginning of the end-time holy race war.)

Many of the movements to restore, rescue, or retrieve masculinity from the feminist deluge focused less on political, economic (let alone military) challenges and more on men's inner lives, their souls. In the early 1990s, what became known as the "mythopoetic" men's movement offered a critique of contemporary masculinity as spiritually empty, a masculinity of disconnection and isolation, with no emotional resonance and little sense of fulfillment. Distracted by consumerism, detached from meaning, driven by material acquisition, we had become a new generation of T. S. Eliot's "hollow men."

Largely associated with the poet Robert Bly, the mythopoetic movement echoed other critiques of consumer culture, like those of Benjamin Barber or Jedediah Purdy, and exposés of American hyperindividualism from Robert Bellah to Robert Putnam. Bly and his followers offered "bellowing together" as the alternative to "bowling alone."

The deeper critique of a shallowed-out sense of manhood rippled through other communities in the late 1990s. Black men took up a spiritual calling for the Million Man March, and evangelical white men flocked to sports stadiums to hear the manly gospel offered by the Promise Keepers.

Such mediagenic spectacles momentarily enraptured the nation. I went, observed, participated, and tried to make some sense of them. I was touched by the earnestness of many of the participants, but felt uncomfortable by the faux-religious or seriously evangelical tenor of the ideologies. I felt I shared a kinship in searching for a deeper, more resonant, more emotionally fulfilling notion of masculinity, but I could not relate to the means by which these groups hoped to achieve it. I embraced many of the searchers, shared their search, but thought they were looking in all the wrong places.

And it seemed to me then, as it does now, to entirely miss the point if we think we're going to be able to realize this vision of a new manhood in some homosocial arena away from women—which brings up the core contradiction at the heart of each of these expressions of masculine malaise and spiritual searching. They were very insistent that men needed to be only among other men, away from women, to experience the resonant depth of emotion and spirituality that the movements promised. Although they claimed to be *for* men, they were also movements *about* women—that is, they were movements of men afraid of women's increased equality.

Each of these movements was a movement of retreat from women, from women's increased presence in the public arenas in which men had felt entitled to be for generations. When the going got tough, the tough got going—away.

Achieving a new, deeper, and more resonant manhood is a project that should be undertaken within the context of our actual relationships—with women, with our children, and with other men. The spiritual resonance for which men may yearn is to be found in those daily activities with our families, friends, and communities. Involved fatherhood, nurturing husbanding, and deeply felt friendships are not to be found by running away from the very relationships we need to embrace. Nurturing is not some mystical state of being that one must drum and chant in order to experience. Nurturing, caring, loving—these are what we sociologists call a set of practices, things people actually *do*. We will only be the kinds of fathers, husbands, partners, and friends we run off to the woods or the sports arena to experience when we come home and rejoin those we love in daily life—which is why I argued then that what was needed was more Ironing Johns and fewer Iron Johns.

Eventually, the moment passed, their media-spotlit fifteen minutes elapsed. The Promise Keepers returned to their local churches, starting Christian men's groups within their local communities. The Million Man March generated no local movements in part because it was never a social movement but an event, designed to generate media attention to a problem, but not to provide the organizational infrastructure to solve it. Many of the marchers simply went home, where they rededicated themselves to being responsible fathers and mentors to a generation of black boys who desperately need guidance—in part because they've been so utterly abandoned by national public policy during the Bush-Cheney years.

And the drum-beating, poetry-chanting, tree-hugging mythopoets? My contacts from those years tell me that the men did, indeed, return to their families, and often established second marriages (the overwhelming majority had been divorced) that were more egalitarian and more emotionally sustaining than their first. Many reconnected with their grown children (mythopoets tended to range from their late forties to their mid-sixties in age) and refounded a relationship that was more open and emotionally rewarding than it had been.

Quieter now, away from the woods and the glare of the media flashbulbs, maybe the mythopoets learned the most important lesson of all: not that you can come home again, as Thomas Wolfe might have said had he hung out with Robert Bly, but that you must.

Finally, I turn to two essays about VMI and the Citadel and their effort to "save the males."

On June 26, 1996, the Supreme Court declared the Virginia Military Institute's all-male admissions policy to be unconstitutional, ending a tradition that had stood for over 150 years. By a vote of 7-1, the Court held that exclusion of women from this state-supported institution of higher learning violated women's constitutional rights to equal protection under the Fourteenth Amendment. Within a week, the Citadel, the all-male military college of South Carolina, declared its readiness to become coeducational, thus clearing the way for four young women to join its Corps of Cadets in the fall. By Thanksgiving, two had withdrawn from the school, charging systematic and excruciating sexual harassment by upperclassmen.

Those four had followed in the footsteps of another South Carolina woman, Shannon Faulkner. Three years earlier, Faulkner had sought to challenge the Citadel's policy by erasing any indication of her gender on her Citadel application, and had been admitted. She was rejected when the college found out she was a woman, and thus began her three-year court battle. Her case was approached piecemeal, as it was adjudicated in tandem with the VMI case (both were argued to the Circuit Court of Appeals for the Fourth Circuit). At first, Faulkner had been allowed to attend classes while her suit was adjudicated, and was finally admitted into the Corps of Cadets in 1995. Isolated, humiliated, and alone, she left the Citadel less than a week later, broken and in tears.

Shannon Faulkner's pyrrhic victory, and the Supreme Court decision in VMI, written by newly appointed Justice Ruth Bader Ginsburg, were both widely hailed as victories for women's rights. And that they were.

After all, VMI and the Citadel had used the same arguments that had been used for centuries to exclude women from entry into the public arena—higher education, the labor force, the professions, the voting booth, the military. Finally, and seemingly forever, those arguments—that women's biological constitution makes them unfit or incapable of performing adequately, that women do not seek those opportunities, and, if presented, would not take them—were laid to rest, and women's entry into all facets of public life were secured.

But underneath those issues lay unexamined and deeply held assumptions about the meaning of masculinity and the efforts that young men must make to successfully prove their manhood. It was indicative of this deeper, unexamined level that the slogan adopted by Citadel supporters—worn on buttons at the trial and seen on car bumpers all across the South—was the phrase "Save the Males."

Why did the males need to be saved? And from what? How could the entry of women into the Citadel or VMI precipitate such a profound crisis among men?

One of the arguments made by the Citadel was that the entry of women would so significantly dilute the experience that it would be irrevocably transformed. Women were a "toxic kind of virus" according to Major General Josiah Bunting III, VMI graduate and former head of Lawrenceville School, who testified in both trials, and then became president of VMI.

Others believed that women would be a distraction for the male cadets. "Adolescent males benefit from being able to focus exclusively on the task at hand, without the intrusion of any sexual tension," commented another expert for the Citadel. (Research that suggests that women are not a distraction to males only when they occupy equal positions, and not when the women are in subordinate roles, did not seem to break the surface of consciousness in this case.)

VMI and the Citadel employed an educationally discredited and historically tarnished methodology, which they called the "adversative method," claiming that such a method of breaking down the individual and rebuilding him into a corporate-defined version of a man was necessary to produce men of honor and valor, "citizen soldiers" (VMI) and "whole men" (Citadel). This adversative method includes a deliberate introduction of stress into the young man's life, especially in his first year–a highly regimented brutality that prepares him for leadership and responsibility in his chosen field. (Fewer than 15 percent of all VMI and Citadel graduates actually earn commissions in the armed forces; most go into business and to law school.) Hazing is not only tolerated; it is virtually mandatory.

What kind of vision of masculinity do we have that boys must be brutalized into becoming honorable and virtuous? What does it mean to be a man to the cadets at the Citadel? To men in general? Why do men develop such elaborate and barbaric rituals of initiation–in premodern societies, in fraternities, on athletic teams, and in the military? It seems that in every all-male enclave these rituals occur, whether well organized and administered by older men, or developed entirely by the younger men, without adult supervision. And in virtually every case, the goal of such rituals is to separate the boy from the world of women, to prove himself worthy as a man to other men.

To say that the presence of women would dilute the experience, though, is of course to miss the point. Women are *everywhere* at VMI and the Citadel. Symbolically. Rhetorically. There are constant references to women. Boys who seem slower, weaker, or less aggressive are taunted unmercifully about how they must be "pussies," "skirts," or "women." (Of course, the rhetorical presence of gay men as symbolic "other" parallels both institutions' assertions that there are no gay cadets at either school.)

What the VMI and Citadel cases were about was the desperate efforts and the exorbitant lengths to which men will go to prove their manhood. It meant restoring not only masculinity, but also the pristine homosocial arenas in which men have tested and proved their manhood for centuries. Women's "entry" was experienced as an "invasion" against which the troops must be mobilized–an invasion facilitated by the "New York-based ACLU" and its "New York-based lawyers," according to pamphlets distributed by Citadel supporters. It's again about that sense of aggrieved entitlement–to those homosocial Edens, which are challenged by gender equality.

At VMI and the Citadel, that arena is now, as they might say in Dixie, gone with the wind.

7

Profiling School Shooters and Shooters' Schools

The Cultural Contexts of Aggrieved Entitlement and Restorative Masculinity

In the aftermath of Seung-Hui Cho's horrific massacre of thirty-two of his classmates and professors at Virginia Tech on April 16, 2007, pundits from all over the political spectrum weighed into the national grief and confusion over what could have led this young man to commit such a vicious, murderous act.

When I watched the redacted portions of the enraged tirade that Cho left as his Last Will and Testament, I kept hearing the words of those other two, now infamous, school shooters, Dylan Klebold and Eric Harris at Columbine High School in Littleton, Colorado. As they began their shooting spree, a group of girls asked Harris and Klebold, "Why are you doing this?"

They replied: "We've always wanted to do this. This is payback. We've dreamed of doing this for years. This is for all the shit you put us through. This is what you deserve."[1]

How and why do these boys get to such a place where they could murder their classmates and take their own lives in a paroxysm of violence?

In the aftermath of Cho's rampage at Virginia Tech, three sorts of explanations were offered. Most frequently, we heard hyper-individualized psychological profiles of a certifiably mentally ill young man, diagnosed but largely untreated, with ready, legal, access to guns despite his diagnosis. To some it was mental illness, to others pure evil, but these explanations stopped short of any social analysis.

A second, pernicious, if predictable, response was entirely social, based on grandiose ethnic stereotyping. Finally, after two decades of school shootings by white kids in which race was never once mentioned as a variable, suddenly the entire explanation centered on the fact that Cho was Asian American. "Whatever

Originally published in *There Is a Gunman on Campus: Tragedy and Terror at Virginia Tech*, edited by Ben Agger and Timothy Luke. Lanham, MD: Rowman and Littlefield, 2008.

happened to the model minority?" some asked. Perhaps being an Asian American came with so much pressure to perform, to be that model minority that it was simply too much. Perhaps he simply cracked under the strain.

Such an explanation can, of course, either be anti-racist—those poor Asians have such racialized expectations that it's a wonder they can perform at all—or racist, echoing the claims about the Chinese during the cold war and/or the Vietnamese during that war, claiming that Asians just don't have the respect for human life that "we enlightened Americans" have.

A third type of explanation tried to steer through middle-range variables that might have prompted Cho to explode as he did. The usual suspects— violent video games, access to guns—were trotted out as the intervening variable that inspired a deranged young man to embark on such a deadly rampage.

Of course, in the past, we've heard, for example, that Columbine was caused by Goth music, Marilyn Manson, and violent video games. Then-President Bill Clinton argued that it might be the Internet; Newt Gingrich credited the hippie embrace of freedom of the sixties, while Thomas Sowell argued that the sixties exonerated individuals from responsibility (it was "society's fault") that led to rampage violence. Tom DeLay just blamed daycare, the teaching of evolution, and "working mothers who take birth control pills."[2]

All of these pretty much missed the point. Or, better put, missed one point to make another. As with all rampage school shootings, the rush to develop a psychological profile of school shooters left us without a sociological profile of the "shooters' school."

It is surely the case that some "students" are more likely to explode in a murderous rage than others. But it is equally true that some schools are more susceptible to such rampages than others. If we are really going to understand "school shooters" we have to look at each word separately, and then look at the phrase as the synthesis of the two different elements. In this essay, I will con- sider these three levels of analysis—shooters, schools, and school shootings— suggesting that there is a profile of the type of school that is more likely to witness rampage school shootings, and that, in such schools, only some stu- dents are the likely perpetrators.

But first, a few caveats. Random school shootings are extremely rare. More than 99 percent of public high schools have never had a homicide—and never will. In the 1992–93 school year there were fifty-four violent deaths on high school campuses; in 2000 there were sixteen. And yet students report that they are increasingly afraid to go to school; among young people twelve to twenty- four, three in ten say violence has increased in their schools in the past year and nearly two-fifths have worried that a classmate was potentially violent. Nearly two-thirds (63 percent) of parents believe a school shooting is somewhat or very likely to occur in their communities.[3]

That's just not true. School shootings are extremely rare, and will remain so. But that doesn't mean that some schools are not more prone than others. Or that some students aren't more likely to open fire than others.

Profiling Shooters

Government-supported investigations—such as the FBI report, the Surgeon General's report on *Youth Violence*, and the Bureau of Justice Statistics' "Indicators of School Crime and Safety 2000," as well as a major study of bullying—all concentrated on identifying potential antecedents of school violence, for example media influence, drugs and alcohol behavior, Internet usage, father absence, parental neglect.[4] Such models assume that these causal influences spread evenly over every child like the old advertisement for Sherman-Williams paints covering the globe.

But these variables would apply equally to boys and to girls. And so it is that we worry about "teen violence," "youth violence," "gang violence," "suburban violence," "violence in the schools." Just who are these teens, youths, gangs— girls? Imagine if the killers in schools in Littleton, Pearl, Paducah, Springfield, and Jonesboro were all black girls from poor families who lived instead in New Haven, Newark, or Providence. We'd be having a national debate about inner-city poor black girls. The entire focus would be on race, class, and gender. The media would invent a new term for their behavior, as with "wilding" a decade ago. We'd hear about the culture of poverty; about how living in the city breeds crime and violence; about some putative natural tendency among blacks toward violence. Someone would even blame feminism for causing girls to become violent in vain imitation of boys.

Yet the obvious fact that nearly all the school shooters were middle-class white boys barely broke a ripple in the torrent of public discussion. This uniformity cut across all other differences among the shooters: some came from intact families, others from single-parent homes; some boys had acted violently in the past, others were quiet and unsuspected; some boys also expressed rage at their parents (two killed their parents the same morning), and others seemed to live in happy families.

It is no doubt true that several of the boys who committed these terrible acts did have serious psychological problems; but such framing also masks the way race and class play a significant role in school violence. Again, imagine if all the school shooters had been poor African American *boys* in inner-city schools. It is unlikely that our search for causes would have pathologized the boys as much as the culture of poverty or the "normality" of violence among inner-city youth.

So, why is it that only boys open fire on their classmates? And why are the shooters almost exclusively white boys?

First, well, the obvious: it's not just any boys. It's boys who have been targeted, bullied, beat up, gay-baited, and worse—virtually every single day of their lives. They were called every homophobic slur in the books, and then some. They were ridiculed, threatened, attacked, and tortured. Nearly all have stories of being mercilessly and constantly teased, picked on, and threatened. And, most strikingly, it was *not* because they were gay (none of them was gay as far as I can tell), but because they were *different* from the other boys—shy, bookish, an honor student, artistic, musical, theatrical, non-athletic, a "geek," or weird. Theirs are stories of "cultural marginalization" based on criteria for adequate gender performance—specifically the enactment of codes of masculinity.

And so they did what *any* self-respecting man would do in a situation like that—or so they thought. They retaliated. In his insightful book on violence, James Gilligan suggests that violence has its origins in "the fear of shame and ridicule, and the overbearing need to prevent others from laughing at oneself by making them weep instead." Shame, inadequacy, vulnerability—all threaten the self. Violence is restorative, compensatory.[5]

Boys who are bullied are supposed to be real men, supposed to be able to embody independence, invulnerability, manly stoicism. (In fact, the very search for such collective rhetorics might be seen as an indication of weakness.) The cultural marginalization of the boys who committed school shootings extended to feelings that they had no other recourse: they felt they had no other friends to validate their fragile and threatened identities; they felt that school authorities and parents would be unresponsive to their plight; and they had no access to other methods of self-affirmation. It was not because they were deviants, but rather because they were over-conformists to a particular normative construction of masculinity, a construction that defines violence as a legitimate response to a perceived humiliation.

Profiling Schools

Bullying and gay-baiting take place in every school. But rampages have taken place at only a small number. Is there something that distinguishes the schools as well as the shooters? What makes a violence-prone school different from a violence-free school? Look at the distribution of school shootings: School shootings are *not* a national trend. Of twenty-eight school shootings between 1982 and 2001, all but one were in rural or suburban schools (one was in Chicago). New York, Boston, Minneapolis, San Francisco, LA—nothing. All but two (Chicago again, and Virginia Beach) were committed by a white boy or boys. The Los Angeles school district has had no school shootings since 1984; in 1999, San Francisco, which has several programs to identify potentially violent students, had only two kids bring guns to school.

What's more, if one uses the "red" and "blue" state coding that has become so common since the 2000 presidential election, you'd see that of the twenty-eight school shootings that took place prior to Virginia Tech, twenty took place in red states. Of those in the blue states, one was in suburban Oregon; one was in rural (eastern) Washington; two were in Southern California; one was in rural and another in suburban Pennsylvania; and one was in rural New Mexico. Of those eight from "blue states," half of the counties in those blue states (Santee, CA: Red Hill, PA; Moses Lake, WA; and Deming, NM) voted Republican in the last election.

What this suggests is that school violence is unevenly distributed. Of course, I'm not suggesting that Republicans are more prone than Democrats to random school shootings. But I am suggesting that different political cultures develop in different parts of the country, and that those political cultures have certain features in common. Some of those features are "gun culture" (what percentage of homes have firearms, gun registrations, NRA memberships), local gender culture, and local school cultures (which include attitudes about gender nonconformity, tolerance of bullying, teacher attitudes).

Here's one element of local culture that directly affects whether or not the psychological profile would show up on anyone's radar. Since local school districts are funded by local property taxes, some "violence-prone schools" may have been subject to a significant decline in school funding over the past two decades. Coupled with the curricular demands of the No Child Left Behind Act, which mandates performance outcomes that require increased attention to a set curriculum, schools have cut back significantly on after-school programs, sports, extracurricular activities, teacher training, remedial programs, and, most importantly, counseling.

One in five adolescents have serious behavioral and emotional problems and about two-thirds of these are getting no help at all. In the average school district in the United States, the school psychologist must see ten students each day just to see every student once a year. In California, there is one counselor (let alone a psychologist) for every 1,000 students, and 50 percent of schools do not have guidance counselors at all. It is likely that this paucity of funding for psychological services enabled several very troubled students to pass undetected in a way they might not have in past years.

In his exemplary analysis of the shootings at Columbine High School, sociologist Ralph Larkin identified several variables that he believed provided the larger cultural context for the rampage. The larger context—the development of a culture of celebrity, the rise of paramilitary chic—spread unevenly across the United States; some regions are more gun-happy than others. (Larkin credits the West; Cho's rampage implicates the South.) But more than that, he profiles both the boys and the school, and suggests that the sociological and psychological variables created a lethal mixture.

First, he stresses that the school must be characterized by the presence and tolerance of intimidation, harassment, and bullying within the halls of the high school and on the streets of the larger community. One boy described what it was like to be so marginalized:

> Almost on a daily basis, finding death threats in my locker. . . . It was bad. People . . . who I never even met, never had a class with, don't know who they were to this day. I didn't drive at the time I was in high school; I always walked home. And every day when they'd drive by, they'd throw trash out their window at me, glass bottles. I'm sorry, you get hit with a glass bottle that's going forty miles and hour, that hurts pretty bad. Like I said, I never even knew these people, so didn't even know what their motivation was. But this is something I had to put up with nearly every day for four years.[6]

One friend said that "[e]very time someone slammed them against a locker and threw a bottle at them, I think they'd go back to Eric or Dylan's house and plot a little more—at first as a goof, but more and more seriously over time."[7]

It wasn't just that Harris and Klebold—and other eventual rampage shooters—were bullied and harassed and intimidated every day; it was that the administration, teachers, and community colluded with it. At Columbine, whenever one boy tried to tell teachers and administrators "the way those who were 'different' were crushed . . . what it was like to live in constant fear of other kids who'd gone out of control," the teachers and administrators invariably would turn a blind eye. "After all," he says, "those kids were their favorites. We were the troublemakers." Thus, Larkin concludes that "[b]y allowing the predators free reign in the hallways and public spaces and by bending the rules so that bad behavior did not interfere too much with sports participation, the faculty and administration inadvertently created a climate that was rife with discrimination, intimidation, and humiliation."[8]

And sanctimony. Larkin also argues that religious intolerance and chauvinism directly contributed to the cultural marginalization of the boys. Jefferson County, where Columbine High School is located, is more than 90 percent white, 97 percent native-born, and almost entirely Christian with nearly 40 percent evangelical Protestants. (Indeed, it has one of the largest concentrations of Christian evangelicals in the country.)[9] And while local preachers saw in Klebold and Harris the presence of the devil, Larkin believes that evangelical intolerance of others is more cause than consequence. "Evangelicals were characterized," he writes, "as arrogant and intolerant of the beliefs of others." Evangelical students were intolerantly holier than thou—they would "accost their peers and tell them that if they were not born-again, they would burn in hell." In most cases, Larkin writes, this would be "merely annoying." But "in combination with the brutalization and harassment dished out on a regular basis by the student athletes, it only added to the toxicity of the student climate at Columbine HS."[10]

That toxic climate combined brutal harassment, sanctimonious superiority, traditional gender norms, and a belief in violence as restorative. It's a long-standing masculine trope. Cho and the others were, according to *New York Times* columnist Bob Herbert, "young men riddled with shame and humiliation, often bitterly misogynistic and homophobic, who have decided that the way to assert their faltering sense of manhood and get the respect they have been denied is to go out and shoot somebody."[11] In a 1994 study, Felson and his colleagues found that regardless of a boy's personal values, boys are much more likely to engage in violence if the local cultural expectations are that boys retaliate when provoked. And their local gender culture certainly encouraged that.

Klebold and Harris and Seung-Hui Cho experienced what I call "aggrieved entitlement"—a gendered sense that they were entitled—indeed, even expected—to exact their revenge on all who had hurt them. It wasn't enough to have been harmed; they also had to believe that they were justified, that their murderous rampage was legitimate.

Once they did, they followed the time-honored script of the American western: the lone gunman (or gang) retaliates far beyond the initial provocation and destroys others to restore the self. It is historian Richard Slotkin's thesis on American history—a "gunfighter nation" pursuing "regeneration through violence." It's Margaret Mead's indictment of the culture of revenge, *And Keep Your Powder Dry.* American men don't get mad; they get even. It's *GTA* and hundreds of other violent video games. It's not just some westerns or action movies—it's virtually *every* western or action movie.

The Aggrieved Entitlement of Seung-Hui Cho

The profile of Seung-Hui Cho suggests less overt bullying, but certainly some. He was teased and dismissed as a nonentity. Perhaps he was less overtly bullied, but he was no less marginalized. Awkward socially, Cho never seemed to feel that he fit in. He had no friends, rarely if ever spoke with his dorm mates, and maintained a near-invisibility on campus. His web screen name was a question mark—he toyed with his invisibility. No one seems to have actually known him—although his teachers in the English department said they thought he was strange and possibly dangerous.

His marginalization also appeared to be cultural, and class-based, not entirely the result of his obvious underlying psychiatric problems. His videotape raged against the "brats," and "snobs" at Virginia Tech, who weren't even satisfied with their "gold necklaces" and "Mercedes." And, apparently, some of it had a racist component. The few times he had mustered the courage to actually speak in class, his tormentors told him to "go back to China." (Remember, Cho was Korean American; his parents owned and operated a dry cleaner, and he felt his marginalization had a class and race basis.)

And his marginalization also seems to have been a deep alienation from campus culture as well. Few campuses are as awash in school spirit as Virginia Tech: the campus is festooned with maroon and orange everywhere, and the branding of the campus is a collegiate consumerist orgy of paraphernalia.

But what if one doesn't feel him- or herself to be much of a citizen in "Hokie Nation"? What if one isn't much interested in football, or in sports-themed, beer-soaked weekend party extravaganzas? It's possible that to the marginalized, "Hokie Nation" doesn't feel inclusive and embracing, but alien and coercive. If one is not a citizen in Hokie Nation, one does not exist. And perhaps, for some, if *I* don't exist, then *you* have no right to exist either.

Of course, as Ben Agger notes, "[n]ot everyone who is bullied in school, or marginalized, picks up the gun."[12] There has to be something more. Cho's video-taped testament shows a young man enthralled with fantasies of revenge, in full-bore aggrieved entitlement, externalizing his inner torment on everyone around him. "You have vandalized my heart, raped my soul, and torched my conscience," he declared on his videotape. "You thought it was one pathetic boy's life you were extinguishing. Thanks to you, I die like Jesus Christ to inspire generations of the weak and the defenseless people." He was a time-bomb, and he exploded.

But did he have to? Many have commented that no one in authority seemed to pay any attention to Cho, despite warnings from teachers and female students that they felt unsafe around him, that his fantasies expressed in class papers were disturbing enough to warrant attention. Nikki Giovanni, the celebrated feminist poet, refused to teach him because she said he was "mean." Diagnosed with mental problems, he was able to buy guns, attend classes, fantasize revenge, and eat in the dining halls—all, apparently, just like anyone else.

There are so many Seung-Hui Chos out there, so many victims of incessant bullying, of having their distress go unnoticed. So many teen suicides have this same profile: they turn their rage on themselves. So many teenagers who fit this profile self-medicate, taking drugs, drinking, cutting themselves. So many others revel in their marginalization as a coping strategy, the way Erving Goffman described "minstrelizing" in the face of experiencing the shock of a stigmatized identity. There are so many of them, and virtually all fly just beneath the radar of teachers, parents, and administrators. (And, as I have suggested, the level of distress has to rise to heightened radar levels, since the paucity of funding has so raised that bar.)

But they don't all explode. Is it possible that the environment in which Cho lived had anything to do with it? Is it possible that the elements of a rampage school shooting include access to firepower, an explosive young man who is utterly marginalized, humiliated, and drenched in what he feels is righteous rage—as well as an environment that sees such treatment of its weakest and most marginalized as justified, as "reasonable"?

They also need a fertile culture like Columbine, where one of the predators openly and proudly recalled the relentless torment he and his fellow wrestlers and football teammates unleashed on Klebold and Harris:

> Sure we teased them. But what do you expect with kids who come to school with weird hairdos and horns on their hats? It's not just jocks; the whole school's disgusted with them. They're a bunch of homos. . . . If you want to get rid of someone, usually you tease 'em. So the whole school would call them homos, and when they did something sick, we'd tell them, "You're sick and that's wrong."[13]

Consider, for a moment, the case of a young woman named Christy Brzonkala. In the first semester of her freshman year in college in 1994, Brzonkala was viciously gang-raped by two football players at her school. Traumatized by the event, she sought assistance from the campus psychiatrist, who treated her with antidepressants. Neither the campus psychiatrist nor any other "employee or official made more than a cursory inquiry into the cause of [her] distress." Brzonkala eventually recovered enough to bring charges against her attackers, and, to her surprise, was successful in prosecuting the case through campus judicial channels. The fact that everyone testified that she repeatedly said no seemed to count! One of the players was suspended for a year. However, the judicial board soon reversed her decision, largely, it appeared, because the football coach pressured the administration to make the problem go away. The university restored his scholarship and postponed his suspension until after he graduated.

Shocked, humiliated, and outraged, Brzonkala never returned to school, but eventually brought a Title IX suit against the university for creating a hostile environment. The 4th Circuit Court found that the university had "permitted, indeed fostered, an environment in which male student athletes could gang rape a female student without any significant punishment to the male attackers, nor any real assistance to the female victim."[14]

What sort of university could have been so in thrall of its football players that it would trample over an innocent young woman, and create such a hostile environment, you might ask?[15]

Or take another example. I lecture about issues such as sexual assault, violence against women, date rape, and, more generally, about why men should support gender equality. In fifteen years, lecturing at about twenty to twenty-five colleges and universities every year, I have been physically harassed after a lecture at only one. There, members of some on-campus fraternities had been required to attend, after reports of some potentially actionable incidents on campus. As I walked to my hotel room, in the hotel located on campus, a bunch of guys hanging off the back of a moving pickup truck threw a glass beer bottle at me, missing me by inches. The truck had decals from both the fraternity and the university on its rear window.

At what kind of university are the men so threatened by such a message, and so emboldened to assault a visiting lecturer?

Virginia Tech.

Let me be clear: I am not in any way saying that Virginia Tech was itself to blame for Cho's enraged madness, or even that one might have predicted his horrifying explosion from the callous indifference of the administration to a young first-year student a decade earlier. Indeed, Virginia Tech is in no way unique: it embodies, as Tim Luke explains, a heritage of violence: in the coercive coherence of the community of Hokie Nation, the nexus of campus and regional cultures with the jockocratic dominance of football (what Luke called "gridiron gemeinschaft")—and the sanctimoniously sadistic exclusion of anyone who doesn't fit into that narrowly circumscribed community. Community is always about membership and belonging—and about exclusion and isolation.[16]

I am saying, however, that one of the things that seems to have bound all the school shooters together in their murderous madness was their perception that their school was a jockocracy, a place where difference was not valued, a place where, in fact, it was punished. There are students hovering on the precipice of murderous madness everywhere, young boys who "feel so weak [they] just want to explode . . . and tear this whole town apart," as Bruce Springsteen famously sang in a song that showed how he believed in a "Promised Land."

But as we learned with Klebold and Harris, the boys also had to feel that no one was paying attention, that no one in authority noticed, that no one gave a damn at all.

Social science is a tricky predictive science, and one would have to go way out on a limb to hypothesize that despite there being plenty of disturbed young men at other schools—say, for example, at Vassar or Princeton or NYU or Williams or UC Santa Barbara—that those schools would be less likely to experience a rampage school shooting.

Such an argument would be tendentious: it's a virtual certainly that none of them will—but because such rampage school shootings are so unbelievably rare in the first place. Yet, on the other hand, those schools also do not extract such universal allegiance to campus culture, nor are they ruled by one, impenetrable, entitled, jockocratic clique. Nor is the administration under relentless alumni pressure to maintain and build the sports programs at the expense of every other program—especially the campus counseling program that might identify and treat such deeply troubled, indeed maniacally insane, students a bit sooner.

Rampage school shooters may be mad, but their madness must pass unseen, their marginalization be perceived as justified. And those dynamics have less to do with crazy individuals and more to do with campus cultures.

But. The emphasis on local school cultures must also be placed alongside the possibility that global media cultures exert such an important countervailing impact as to virtually guarantee the possible globalization of rampage school shootings. When, for example, Pekka-Eric Auvinen opened fire at his Tuusula, Finland, high school in November 2007, he claimed access to the same global media culture as the Americans. His framing of his distress, his growing rage, drew from the same narrative repertoire as Harris and Klebold, and from Cho. And before his massacre of eight of his classmates, and himself, Auvinen posted his intentions on YouTube.[17]

That narrative has become a globalized rhetoric of aggrieved entitlement, and teenagers all over the world have access to the same story. And yet it is still an utterly gendered story, and that suicidal explosion remains a distinctly masculine trope.

So, it may be necessary to shift our frame slightly, to implicate the more local cultures of schools and regions, the political economy of psychological intervention, the institutional complicity with bullying and harassment (as long as it's "our guys" who are doing it). And yet alongside these local iterations lies the possibility of an overarching global master narrative in which an increasing number of young boys might find murderous solace.

At the local level, schools that want to prevent such rampage school shootings in the future might do well to profile the shooters—identify those students whose marginalization might become entangled with such aggrieved entitlement—as well as conduct a profile of their school, to mediate the effects of that marginalization on all its marginalized students (including those who are suicidal, self-medicating, and self-harming).

Local school culture and this globalized media culture form two of the three legs of a triangulated explanation of rampage school shootings; only placed in this glocal context will any psychological profiling make sense. "Good wombs" may have "borne bad sons," as Dylan Klebold said, quoting *The Tempest*. But there are bad seeds everywhere. They also need fertile ground in which their roots can take firm hold.

NOTES

1. Ralph Larkin, *Comprehending Columbine* (Philadelphia: Temple University Press, 2007), 6.

2. Thomas Sowell, "Are Today's Mass Shootings a Consequence of '60s Collective Guilt?" *Baltimore Sun*, April 26, 2007, 19A; "News of the Weak in Review," *The Nation*, November 15, 1999, 5.

3. J. Cloud, "The Legacy of Columbine," *Time*, March 19, 2001, 32; "Fear of Classmates," *USA Today*, April 22, 1999, A1; D. Carlson and W. Simmons, "Majority of Parents Think a School Shooting Could Occur in Their Community," Gallup Poll Release, March 6, 2001. http://www.gallup.com/poll/releases/pr010306.asp, retrieved March 6, 2001.

4. T. Nansel, M. Overpeck, R. Pilla, J. Rune, B. Simmons-Morton, and P. Scheidt, "Bullying Behaviors among U.S. Youth: Prevalence and Association with Psychosocial Adjustment," *Journal of the American Medical Association* 285 (16) (2001): 2094–2100.

5. James Gilligan, *Violence* (New York: Vintage, 1998), 77.

6. Larkin, *Comprehending Columbine*, 91

7. Eric Pooley, "Portrait of a Deadly Bond," *Time*, May 10, 1999, 26–27.

8. Larkin, *Comprehending Columbine*, 107, 121.

9. Ibid., 17, 119.

10. Ibid., 53, 61.

11. Bob Herbert, "A Volatile Young Man, Humiliation, and a Gun," *New York Times*, April 19, 2007.

12. Ben Agger, "Cho, Not Che?: Positioning Blacksburg in the Political," *Fast Capitalism* 3 (1) (2007); available at: http://www.uta.edu/huma/agger/fastcapitalism/3_1/agger.html.

13. Cited in *Time*, December 20, 1999, 50–51.

14. The case against the state of Virginia was eventually settled out of court, and the Supreme Court eventually ruled that Congress had overreached its authority by basing the Violence Against Women Act on the commerce clause of the U.S. Constitution, thus rendering moot Brzonkala's federal case against the university.

15. *Brzonkala v VPI State University*, 4th Ct 96–1814, 1997.

16. See Timothy Luke, "April 16, 2007, at Virginia Tech—To: Multiple Recipients: 'A Gunman Is Loose on Campus' . . . ," in *There Is a Gunman on Campus*, ed. Ben Agger and Timothy Luke (Lanham, MD: Rowman and Littlefield, 2008).

17. I'm grateful to Tim Luke for raising this, which reframes these issues as truly "glocal."

8

Globalization and
Its Mal(e)contents

Masculinity on the Extreme Right

Globalization changes masculinities—reshaping the arena in which national and local masculinities are articulated, and transforming the shape of men's lives. Globalization disrupts and reconfigures traditional, neocolonial, or other national, regional, or local economic, political, and cultural arrangements. In so doing, globalization transforms both domestic and public patriarchy (see Connell 1998). Globalization includes the gradual proletarianization of local peasantries, as market criteria replace subsistence and survival. Local small craft producers, small farmers, and independent peasants traditionally stake their notions of masculinity in ownership of land and economic autonomy in their work; these are increasingly transferred upward in the class hierarchy and outward to transnational corporations. Proletarianization also leads to massive labor migrations—typically migrations of *male* workers—who leave their homes and populate migrant enclaves, squatter camps, and labor camps.

Globalization thus presents another level at which hegemonic and local masculinities are constructed. Globalization was always a gendered process. As Andre Gunder Frank pointed out in his studies of economic development, there was no single continuum along which individual nations might be positioned, and underdevelopment was not simply a "stage" through which all countries pass. Rather, he argued, there was a relationship between development and underdevelopment, that, in fact, the development of some countries implied the specific and deliberate underdevelopment of others. The creation of the metropole was simultaneous and coordinated with the creation of the periphery.

As with economic development, so too with gender, with the historical constructions of the meanings of masculinity. As the hegemonic ideal was being

Originally published in *International Sociology* 18 (3) September 2003.

created, it was created against a screen of "others" whose masculinity was thus problematized and devalued. Hegemonic and subaltern emerged in mutual, but unequal interaction in a gendered social and economic order. Colonial administrations often problematized the masculinity of the colonized. For example, in British India, Bengali men were perceived as weak and effeminate, though Pathas and Sikhs were perceived as hypermasculine—violent and uncontrolled (see Sinha 1995). Similar distinctions were made in South Africa between Hottentots and Zulus, and in North America between Navaho or Algonquin on the one hand, Sioux, Apache, and Cheyenne on the other (see Connell 1998: 14). In many colonial situations, the colonized men were called "boys" by the colonizers.

Today, although they appear to be gender-neutral, the institutional arrangements of global society are equally gendered. The marketplace, multinational corporations, and transnational geopolitical institutions (World Court, United Nations, European Union) and their attendant ideological principles (economic rationality, liberal individualism) express a gendered logic. The "increasingly unregulated power of transnational corporations places strategic power in the hands of particular groups of men," while the language of globalization remains gender-neutral so that "the 'individual' of neoliberal theory has in general the attributes and interests of a male entrepreneur" (Connell 1998: 15).

As a result, the impact of global economic and political restructuring is greater on women. At the national and global level, the world gender order privileges men in a variety of ways, such as unequal wages, unequal labor force participation, unequal structures of ownership and control of property, unequal control over one's body, as well as cultural and sexual privileges. What's more, in the economic South, for example, aid programs disproportionately affect women, while in the metropole, the attack on the welfare state generally weakens the position of women, domestically and publicly. These effects, however, are less the result of bad policies or even less the results of bad—inept or evil—policymakers, and more the results of the gendered logic of these institutions and processes themselves (Connell 1998).

Hegemonic Masculinity and Its Discontents

In addition, the patterns of masculinity embedded within these gendered institutions are rapidly becoming the dominant global hegemonic model of masculinity, against which all local, regional, and national masculinities are played out and to which they increasingly refer. The emergent global hegemonic version of masculinity is readily identifiable: He sits in first-class waiting rooms or in elegant business hotels the world over in a designer business suit, speaking English, eating "continental" cuisine, talking on his cell phone, his laptop computer plugged into any electrical outlet, while he watches CNN International on television. Temperamentally, he is increasingly cosmopolitan, with liberal tastes in consumption (and sexuality) and conservative political ideas of limited government control of the economy. This has the effect of increasing the power of the hegemonic countries within the global political and economic arena, since everyone, no matter where they are from, talks and acts as they do.

The processes of globalization and the emergence of a global hegemonic masculinity have the ironic effect of increasingly "gendering" local, regional, and national resistance to incorporation into the global arena as subordinated entities. Scholars have pointed out the ways in which religious fundamentalism and ethnic nationalism use local cultural symbols to express regional resistance to incorporation (see especially Juergensmeyer 1993, 2000; Barber 1992). However, these religious and ethnic expressions are often manifest as gender revolts, and include a virulent resurgence of domestic patriarchy (as in the militant misogyny of Iran or Afghanistan); the problematization of global masculinities or neighboring masculinities (as in the former Yugoslavia); and the overt symbolic efforts to claim a distinct "manhood" along religious or ethnic lines to which others do not have access and which will restore manhood to the formerly privileged (white militias in the United States and skinhead racists in Europe).

Thus gender becomes one of the chief organizing principles of local, regional, and national resistance to globalization, whether expressed in religious or secular, ethnic, or national terms. These processes involve flattening or eliminating local or regional distinctions, cultural homogenization as citizens, and social heterogenization as new ethnic groups move to new countries in labor migration efforts. Movements thus tap racialist and nativist sentiments at the same time as they can tap local and regional protectionism and isolationism. They become gendered as oppositional movements also tap into a vague masculine resentment of economic displacement, loss of autonomy, and collapse of domestic patriarchy that accompany further integration into the global economy. Efforts to reclaim economic autonomy, to reassert political control, and to revive traditional domestic dominance thus take on the veneer of restoring manhood.

To illustrate these themes, one could consider several political movements of men, in North America or elsewhere. Indeed, Promise Keepers, men's rights, and fathers' rights groups all respond to the perceived erosion of public patriarchy with an attempted restoration of some version of domestic patriarchy. The "mythopoetic" men's movement responds instead to a perceived erosion of domestic patriarchy with assertions of separate mythic or natural space for men to experience their power—since they can no longer experience it in either the public or private spheres. (For more on the movements of men, see Kimmel 1996a, 1996b; and Messner 1998).

In this chapter, I will examine the ways in which masculinities and globalization are embedded in the emergence of extremist groups on the far right and also in the Islamic world. Specifically I will discuss the ways in which global political and economic processes affect lower-middle-class men in both the economic North and the Islamic world, and describe several of their political reactions, especially their efforts to restore public and domestic patriarchy. It is the lower middle class—that strata of independent farmers, small shopkeepers, craft and highly skilled workers, and small-scale entrepreneurs—who have been hardest hit by the processes of globalization. "Western industry has displaced traditional crafts—female as well as male—and large-scale multinational-controlled agriculture has downgraded the independent farmer to the status of hired hand" (Ehrenreich 2001). This has resulted in massive male displacement—migration, downward mobility. And it has been felt the most not by the adult men who were the tradesmen, shopkeepers, and skilled workers, but by their sons, by the young men whose inheritance has been seemingly stolen from them. They feel entitled and deprived—and furious. These angry young men are the foot soldiers of the armies of rage that have sprung up around the world. In this essay, I will discuss white supremacists and Aryan youth in both the United States and Scandinavia, and compare them with the gendered backgrounds of Iranian fundamentalists in the Revolution of 1979, and the terrorists of Al Qaeda who were responsible for the heinous acts of September 11. All these groups, I argue, use a variety of ideological and political resources to reestablish and reassert domestic and public patriarchies. They are movements not of revolution, but of restoration.

Types of Patriarchies

In this essay, I describe the transformation of two forms of patriarchy. It is important to note that patriarchy is both a system of domination by which men dominate women, and also a system by which some men (older men, fathers, in the classic definition of the term) dominate other men.

Public patriarchy refers to the institutional arrangements of a society, the predominance of males in all power positions within the economy and polity, both locally and nationally, as well as the "gendering" of those institutions themselves (by which the criteria for promotion, for example, appear to be gender-neutral, but actually reproduce the gender order).

Domestic patriarchy refers to the emotional and familial arrangements in a society, the ways in which men's power in the public arena is reproduced at the level of private life. This includes male-female relationships as well as family life, child socialization, and the like.

Both public patriarchy and domestic patriarchy are held together by the threat, implicit or explicit, of violence. Public patriarchy, of course, includes the military and police apparatus of society, which are also explicitly gendered institutions (revealed in their increased opposition to women's entry into the public sphere). In the aggregate, rape and domestic violence help sustain domestic patriarchy.

These two expressions of men's power over women and other men are neither uniform nor monolithic; they vary enormously, and are constantly in flux. Equally, they are not coincident, so that increases or decreases in one invariably produce increases or decreases in the other. Nor are they so directly linked that a decrease in one automatically produces an increase in the other, although there will be pressures in that direction. Thus women's entry into the work force or increased representation in legislatures undermine public patriarchy and are likely to produce both backlash efforts to reinforce domestic patriarchy (covenant marriage, tightening divorce laws to restrain women's exit from the home, increased domestic assault) or even a virulent resurgence of domestic patriarchy (the Taliban). At the same time, increased public presence will also undermine domestic patriarchy (shared parenting and housework).

All of these movements exhibit what Connell (1995: 109–112) calls "protest masculinity"—a combination of stereotypical male norms with often unconventional attitudes about women. Exaggerated claims of potency are accompanied by violent resistance to authority, school, and work, and engagement with crime and heavy drinking. In such a model, the "growing boy puts together a tense, freaky façade, making a claim to power where there are no real resources for power," Connell writes (1995: 109). "There is a lot of concern with face, a lot of work keeping up a front." However, those groups in the economic North claim to support women's equality (in varying degrees) while those in the Islamic world have made women's complete re-subordination a central pillar of the edifice of their rule.

By examining far right Aryan white supremacists in the United States, and their counterparts in Scandinavia, we can see the ways in which masculinity politics may be mobilized among some groups of men in the economic North, while looking at the Iranian Revolution of 1979 and the social origins of the Taliban and Al Qaeda terrorists, we can see how they might work out in Islamic countries. Although such a comparison in no way effaces the many differences that exist among these movements, and especially between the movements in the economic South and North, a comparison of their similarities enables us to explore the political mobilization of masculinities, and map the ways in which masculinities are likely to be put into political play in the coming decades.

Right-Wing Militias: Racism, Sexism, and Anti-Semitism as Masculine Reassertion

In an illustration in *WAR*, the magazine of the White Aryan Resistance, for 1987, a working-class white man, in hard hat and flak jacket, stands proudly before a suspension bridge while a jet plane soars overhead. "White Men *Built* This Nation!!" reads the text, "White Men *Are* This Nation!!!"[1]

Most observers immediately see its racist intent. But rarely do we see the deeply gendered meaning of the statement. Here is a moment of fusion of racial and gendered discourses, when both race and gender are made visible. "This nation," we now understand, "is" neither white women, nor non-white.

The White Aryan Resistance that produced this illustration is situated on a continuum of the far right that runs from older organizations, such as the John Birch Society, the Ku Klux Klan, and the American Nazi Party, to Holocaust deniers, neo-Nazi or racist skinheads, White Power groups like Posse Comitatus and White Aryan Resistance, and radical militias, like the Wisconsin Militia or the Militia of Montana. This last set of organizations, the rural militias, appeared in the 1990s in the farm belt (and Rust Belt), and became especially visible in the aftermath of standoffs in Ruby Ridge, Idaho, and the bombing of the federal building in Oklahoma City.

Like other fringe groups on the far right, these rural-based militias are composed of young white men, the sons of independent farmers and small shopkeepers. Buffeted by the global political and economic forces that have produced global hegemonic masculinities, they have responded to the erosion of public patriarchy (displacement in the political arena) and domestic patriarchy (their wives now work away from the farm) with a renewal of their sense of masculine entitlement to restore patriarchy in both arenas. Ideologically, what characterizes these scions of small-town rural America—both the fathers and the sons—is (1) their ideological vision of producerism, threatened by economic transformation; (2) their sense of small-town democratic community, an inclusive community that was based on the exclusion of broad segments of the population; and (3) a sense of entitlement to economic, social, and political, and even military power.

To cast the middle-class straight white man as the hegemonic holder of power in America would be to fully miss the daily experience of these straight white men. They believed themselves to be *entitled* to power—by a combination of historical legacy, religious fiat, biological destiny, and moral legitimacy— but they believe they do not have power. That power has been both surrendered by white men—their fathers—and stolen from them by a federal government controlled and staffed by legions of the newly enfranchised minorities, women, and immigrants, all in service to the omnipotent Jews who control international economic and political life. "Heaven help the God-fearing, law-abiding Caucasian middle class," explained Charlton Heston to a 1998 Christian Coalition convention, especially

> Protestant or even worse evangelical Christian, Midwest or Southern or even worse rural, apparently straight or even worse admittedly [heterosexual], gun-owning or even worse NRA card-carrying average working stiff, or even worst of all, male working stiff. Because not only don't you

count, you're a downright obstacle to social progress. (quoted in Citizens Project: 3; available at: http://citizensproject.org/wp-content/uploads/ 2009/07/freedom-watch-july-1999.pdf, accessed October 6, 2009)

Downwardly mobile rural white men—those who lost the family farms and those who expected to take them over—are squeezed between the omnivorous jaws of capital concentration and a federal bureaucracy which is at best indifferent to their plight, and at worse, facilitates their further demise. What they want, says one, is to "take back what is rightfully ours" (quoted in Dobratz and Shanks-Meile 2001: 10).

In many respects, the militias' ideology reflects the ideologies of other fringe groups on the far right, from whom they typically recruit, especially racism, homophobia, nativism, sexism, and anti-Semitism. These discourses of hate provide an explanation for the feelings of entitlement thwarted, fixing the blame squarely on "others" whom the state must now serve at the expense of white men. The unifying theme of these discourses, which have traditionally formed the rhetorical package Richard Hofstadter labeled "paranoid politics," is *gender*. Specifically, it is by framing state policies as emasculating and problematizing the masculinity of these various "others" that rural white militia members seek to restore their own masculinity.

Contemporary American white supremacists tap into a general malaise among American men who seek some explanations for the contemporary "crisis" of masculinity. Like the Sons of Liberty who threw off the British yoke of tyranny in 1776, these contemporary Sons of Liberty see "R-2," the Second American Revolution, as restorative—to retrieve and refound traditional masculinity on the exclusion of others. The entire rhetorical apparatus that serves this purpose is saturated with gendered readings—of the problematized masculinity of the "others," of the emasculating policies of the state, and of the rightful masculine entitlement of white men. As sociologist Lillian Rubin puts it:

> It's this confluence of forces—the racial and cultural diversity of our new immigrant population; the claims on the resources of the nation now being made by those minorities who, for generations, have called America their home; the failure of some of our basic institutions to serve the needs of our people; the contracting economy, which threatens the mobility aspirations of working-class families—all these have come together to leave white workers feeling as if everyone else is getting a piece of the action while they get nothing. (Rubin 1994: 186)

One issue of an extreme-right magazine, *The Truth at Last*, put it this way:

> Immigrants are flooding into our nation willing to work for the minimum wage (or less). Super-rich corporate executives are flying all over the

world in search of cheaper and cheaper labor so that they can "lay off" their American employees. . . . Many young White families have no future! They are not going to receive any appreciable wage increases due to job competition from immigrants. (cited in Dobratz and Shanks-Meile 2001: 115)

White supremacists see themselves as squeezed between global capital and an emasculated state that supports voracious global profiteering. In a song, "No Crime Being White," Day of the Sword, a popular racist skinhead band, confronts the greedy class:

The birthplace is the death of our race.
Our brothers being laid off is a truth we have to face.
Take my job, it's equal opportunity
The least I can do, you were so oppressed by me
I've only put in twenty years now.
Suddenly my country favors gooks and spicks and queers.
Fuck you, then, boy I hope you're happy when your new employees
    are the reason why your business ends. (cited in Dobratz and
    Shanks-Meile 2001: 271)

NAFTA took away American jobs; what they see as the "Burger King" economy leaves no room at the top so "many youngsters see themselves as being forced to compete with nonwhites for the available minimum wage, service economy jobs that have replaced their parents' unionized industry opportunities" (Coplon 1989: 84).

That such ardent patriots as militia members are so passionately antigovernment might strike the observer as contradictory. After all, are these not the same men who served their country in Vietnam or in the Gulf War? Are these not the same men who believe so passionately in the American dream? Are they not the backbone of the Reagan Revolution? Indeed they are. Militia members face the difficult theoretical task of maintaining their faith in America and in capitalism, and simultaneously providing an analysis of an indifferent state, at best, or an actively interventionist one, at worst, coupled with a contemporary articulation of corporate capitalist logic that leaves them, often literally, out in the cold—homeless, jobless, hopeless.

It is through a decidedly gendered and sexualized rhetoric of masculinity that this contradiction between loving America and hating its government, loving capitalism and hating its corporate iterations, is resolved. First, like others on the far right, militia members believe that the state has been captured by evil, even Satanic forces; the original virtue of the American political regime deeply and irretrievably corrupted. "The enemy is the system—the system of international world dominance" according to the Florida Interklan Report (cited in Dobratz and Shanks-Meile 2001: 160). Environmental regulations, state policies dictated by urban and northern interests, the Internal Revenue Service, are the outcomes of a state now utterly controlled by feminists, environmentalists, blacks, and Jews.

In their foreboding futuristic vision, communalism, feminism, multiculturalism, homosexuality, and Christian-bashing are all tied together, part and parcel of the New World Order. Multicultural textbooks, women in government, and legalized abortion can individually be taken as signs of the impending New World Order. Increased opportunities for women can only lead to the oppression of men. Tex Marrs proclaims, "In the New Order, woman is finally on top. She is not a mere equal. *She is Goddess*" (Marrs 1993: 28). In fact, she has ceased to be a "real" woman—the feminist now represents the confusion of gender boundaries and the demasculinization of men, symbolizing a future where men are not allowed to be real men.

The "Nanny State" no longer acts in the interests of "true" American men, but is, instead, an engine of gender inversion, feminizing men, while feminism masculinizes women. White men not involved in the movement are often referred to as "sheeple" while feminist women, it turns out, are more masculine than men are. Not only does this call the masculinity of white men into question, but it uses gender as the rhetorical vehicle for criticizing "other" men. Typically, problematizing the masculinity of these others takes two forms simultaneously: other men are both "too masculine" and "not masculine enough," both hypermasculine—violent rapacious beasts incapable of self-control—and hypomasculine—weak, helpless, effete, incapable of supporting a family.

Thus in the logic of militias and other white supremacist organizations, gay men are both promiscuously carnal and sexually voracious, and effete fops who do to men what men should only have done to them by women. Black men are both violent hypersexual beasts, possessed of an "irresponsible sexuality," seeking white women to rape (*WAR* 8[2], 1989: 11) and less-than fully manly, "weak, stupid, lazy" (*NS Mobilizer*, cited in Ferber 1998: 81). In *The Turner Diaries*, the apocalyptic novel which served as the blueprint for the Oklahoma City bombing and is widely read and peddled by militias, author William Pierce depicts a nightmarish world where white women and girls are constantly threatened and raped by "gangs of Black thugs" (Pierce 1978: 58). Blacks are primal nature—untamed, cannibalistic, uncontrolled, but also stupid and lazy—and whites are the driving force of civilization. "America and all civilized society are the exclusive products of White man's mind and muscle," is how *The Thunderbolt* put it (cited in Ferber 1998: 76). "[T]he White race is the Master race of the earth . . . the Master Builders, the Master Minds, and the Master warriors of civilization." What can a black man do but "clumsily [shuffle] off, scratching his wooley head, to search for shoebrush and mop" (in *New Order*, cited in Ferber 1998: 91)?

Most interesting is the portrait of the Jew. One the one hand, the Jew is a greedy, cunning, conniving, omnivorous predator; on the other, the Jew is small, beady-eyed, and incapable of masculine virtue. By asserting the hyper-masculine power of the Jew, the far right can support capitalism as a system while decrying the actions of capitalists and their corporations. According to militia logic, it's not the capitalist corporations that have turned the govern-ment against them, but the international cartel of Jewish bankers and finan-ciers, media moguls, and intellectuals who have already taken over the U.S. state and turned it into ZOG (Zionist Occupation Government). The United States is called the "Jewnited States," and Jews are blamed for orchestrating the demise of the once-proud Aryan man.

In white supremacist ideology, the Jew is the archetypal villain, both hypermasculine—greedy, omnivorous, sexually predatory, capable of the destruction of the Aryan way of life—and hypomasculine, small, effete, homo-sexual, pernicious, weasely.

In lieu of brawn power, Jewish men have harnessed their brain power in their quest for world domination. Jews are seen as the masterminds behind the other social groups who are seen as dispossessing rural American men of their birthright. And toward that end, they have co-opted blacks, women, gays, and brainwashed and cowardly white men to do their bidding. In a remarkable passage, white supremacists cast the economic plight of white workers as being squeezed between non-white workers and Jewish owners:

> It is our RACE we must preserve, not just one class. . . . White Power means a permanent end to unemployment because with the non-Whites gone, the labor market will no longer be over-crowded with unproduc-tive niggers, spics, and other racial low-life. It means an end to inflation eating up a man's paycheck faster than he can raise it because OUR econ-omy will not be run by a criminal pack of international Jewish bankers, bent on using the White worker's tax money in selfish and even destruc-tive schemes. (cited in Ferber 1998: 140)

Since Jews are incapable of acting like real men—strong, hardy, virtuous manual workers and farmers—a central axiom of the international Jewish conspiracy for world domination is their plan to "feminize White men and to masculinize White women" (*Racial Loyalty* [72] 1991: 3). *The Turner Diaries* describes the "Jewish-liberal-democratic-equalitarian" perspective as "an essentially femi-nine, submissive worldview" (Pierce 1978: 42). *WAR* echoes this theme: "One of the characteristics of nations which are controlled by the Jews is the gradual eradication of masculine influence and power and the transfer of influence into feminine forms" (cited in Ferber 1998: 125–126).

Embedded in this anti-Semitic slander is a critique of white American manhood as soft, feminized, weakened—indeed, emasculated. Article after article decries "the whimpering collapse of the blond male," as if white men have surrendered to the plot (in Ferber 1998: 127). According to *The Turner Diaries*, American men have lost the right to be free; slavery "is the just and proper state for a people who have gown soft" (Pierce 1978: 33). Yet it is there that the militias simultaneously offer white men an analysis of their present situation and a political strategy for retrieving their manhood. As *National Vanguard* puts it:

> As Northern males have continued to become more wimpish, the result of the media-created image of the "new male"—more pacifist, less authoritarian, more "sensitive," less competitive, more androgynous, less possessive—the controlled media, the homosexual lobby and the feminist movement have cheered . . . the number of effeminate males has increased greatly . . . legions of sissies and weaklings, of flabby, limp-wristed, non-aggressive, non-physical, indecisive, slack-jawed, fearful males who, while still heterosexual in theory and practice, have not even a vestige of the old macho spirit, so deprecated today, left in them. (cited in Ferber 1998: 136)

It is through the militias that American manhood can be restored and revived—a manhood in which individual white men control the fruits of their own labor, and are not subject to the emasculation of Jewish-owned finance capital, or a black- and feminist-controlled welfare state. It is a militarized manhood of the heroic John Rambo—a manhood that celebrates their God-sanctioned right to band together in armed militias if anyone—or any governmental agency—tries to take it away from them. If the state and capital emasculate them, and if the masculinity of the "others" is problematic, then only real white men can rescue this American Eden from a feminized, multicultural, androgynous melting pot. "The world is in trouble now only because the White man is divided, confused, and misled," we read in *New Order*. "Once he is united, inspired by a great ideal and led by real men, his world will again become livable, safe, and happy" (in Ferber 1998: 139). The militias seek to reclaim their manhood gloriously, violently.

Perhaps this is best illustrated with another cartoon from *WAR*. In this deliberate parody of countless Charles Atlas advertisements, the timid white ninety-seven-pound weakling finds his power, his strength as a man, through racial hatred. In the ideology of the white supremacist movement, and their organized militia allies, it is racism that will again enable white men to reclaim their manhood. The amorphous groups of white supremacists, skinheads, and neo-Nazis may be the symbolic shock troops of this movement, but the rural militias are their well-organized and highly regimented infantry.

White Supremacists in Scandinavia

While significantly fewer in number than their American counterparts, white supremacists in the Nordic countries have also made a significant impact on those normally tolerant social democracies. Norwegian groups such as Bootboys, NUNS 88, the Norsk Arisk Ungdomsfron (NAUF), Varg, and the Vikings, the Green Jacket Movement (Gronjakkerne) in Denmark, and the Vitt Ariskt Motstand (VAM, or White Aryan Resistance), Kreatrivistens Kyrka (Church of the Creator, COTC), and Riksfronten (National Front) in Sweden have exerted an impact beyond their modest numbers. Norwegian groups number a few hundred, while Swedish groups may barely top one thousand adherents, and perhaps double that number are supporters and general sympathizers.

Their opposition seems to come precisely from the relative prosperity of their homelands, a prosperity that has made the Nordic countries attractive to ethnic immigrants from the economic South. Most come from lower-middle-class families; their fathers are painters, carpenters, tillers, bricklayers, road maintenance workers. Some come from small family farms. Several fathers own one-man businesses; they are small capitalists or self-employed tradesmen (Fangen 1999c: 36). In her life-history analysis of young Norwegian participants, Katrine Fangen (1999b: 359–363) found that only one claimed a working-class identity, and his father owned his own business; another's father owned a small printing company, another was a carpenter, and the fourth came from a family of independent fishermen.

All the sons are downwardly mobile; they work sporadically, they have little or no control over their own labor or workplace, and none owns his own business. Almost all members are between sixteen and twenty (Fangen 1999b: 84). Youth unemployment has spiked, especially in Sweden, just as the numbers of asylum seekers has spiked, and with it attacks on centers for asylum seekers. They struggle, Fangen notes, to recover a class identity "that no longer has a material basis" (1999a: 2). Danish Aryans have few assets and "few prospects for a better future" (Bjorgo 1997: 104).

This downward mobility marks these racist skinheads from their British counterparts, who are embedded within working-class culture. These young Nordic lower-middle class boys do not participate in a violent, racist counter-culture as preparation for their working lives on the shop floor. Rather, like their American counterparts, they see *no* future in the labor market. They do not yearn nostalgically for the collective solidarity of the shop floor; for them that life was already gone.

Like the American white supremacists, Scandinavian Aryans understand their plight in terms of masculine entitlement, which is eroded by state immigration policies, international Zionist power, and globalization. All desire a return to a racially and ethnically homogenous society, seeing themselves, as one put it, as a "front against alienation, and the mixing of cultures" (Fangen 1998a: 214).

Antigay sentiments also unite these white supremacists. "Words are no use; only action will help in the fight against homosexuals," says a Swedish magazine, *Siege*. "With violence and terror as our weapons we must beat back the wave of homosexual terror and stinking perversion whose stench is washing over our country" (cited in Bjorgo 1997: 127). And almost all have embraced anti-Semitism, casting the Jews as the culprits for immigration and homosexuality. According to the Vitt Ariskt Motstand, the Jew represents a corrupt society that "poisons the white race through the immigration of racially inferior elements, homosexuality, and moral disorder" (in Loow 1998a: 86). As *Storm*, the magazine of the Swedish White Aryan Resistance, put it:

> In our resistance struggle for . . . the survival of the white race . . . we must wield the battle axe against our common enemy—the Zionist Occupation Government (ZOG) and the liberal race traitors, the keen servants of the hook noses who are demolishing our country piece by piece. (cited in Bjorgo 1997: 219)[2]

A startling cartoon suggests the ways that Jews can be seen as both hypermasculine and hypomasculine. While they were traditionally cast as effete, bookish, and unmanly, one cartoon in *Vigrid* recounts Menachim Begin's career as a mass murderer and terrorist—trained by the Polish Liberation Army, a leader of the terrorist group the Irgun, responsible for hanging and torturing two British soldiers, bombing the King David Hotel, and massacring 250 Palestinians in the village of Deir Yassin—although he is, in the end, embraced by the West.[3] In the last frame, he is hailed as a "great statesman" as blood drips from between his teeth and he says, "Blood, more blood!"

The anti-Semitism, however, also has inhibited alliances across the various national groups in Scandinavia. Danish and Norwegian Aryans recall the resistance against the Nazis, and often cast themselves as heirs to the resistance struggle against foreign invasion. Some Swedish groups, on the other hand, openly embrace Nazism and Nazi symbols. In order to maintain harmony among these different national factions of the Nordic Aryan movement, the Danish groups have begun to use Confederate flags and other symbols of the racist U.S. South, which all sides can agree signifies the Ku Klux Klan and the "struggle against Negroes, communists, homosexuals and Jews" (in Bjorgo 1997: 99).

Another unifying set of symbols includes constant references to the Vikings. Vikings are admired because they lived in a closed community, were fierce warriors, and were feared and hated by those they conquered (Fangen 1998a: 36). Vikings also represent an untrammeled masculinity, an "armed brotherhood" of heroes and martyrs (Bjorgo 1997: 136).

Masculinity figures heavily in their rhetoric and their recruitment. Young recruits are routinely savagely beaten in a "baptism of fire." Among Danes, status is achieved "by daring to do something others don't. You are a hell of a guy if you go to 'work' at night and come home the next day with 85,000 crowns [about US$10,000]" (cited in Bjorgo 1997: 104). One Norwegian racist recounted in court how his friends had dared him to blow up a store owned by a Pakistani in Brumunddal. He said he felt a lot of pressure, that they were making fun of him, and he wanted to prove to them that he was a man after all. After he blew up the shop, he said, the others slapped his back and cheered him. Finally, he felt accepted (Fangen 1999b: 92). A former Swedish skinhead recounted his experience of masculine transformation as he joined up:

> When I was 14, I had been bullied a lot by classmates and others. By coincidence, I got to know an older guy who was a skinhead. He was really cool, so I decided to become a skinhead myself, cutting off my hair, and donning a black bomber jacket and Doc Martens boots. The next morning, I turned up at school in my new outfit. In the gate, I met one of my worst tormentors. When he saw me, he was stunned, pressing his back against the wall, with fear shining out of his eyes. I was stunned as well— by the powerful effect my new image had on him and others. Being that intimidating—boy, that was a great feeling! (cited in Bjorgo 1997: 234)

Like their American counterparts, Scandinavian white supremacists also exhibit the other side of what Connell calls "protest masculinity"—a combination of stereotypical male norms with often untraditional attitudes respecting women. All these Nordic groups experience significant support from young women, since the males campaign against prostitution, abortion, and pornography—all of which are seen as degrading women (see Durham 1997). On the other hand, many of these women soon become disaffected when they feel mistreated by their brethren, "unjustly subordinated" by them, or just seen as "mattresses."

Often sexualized images of women are used to recruit men. In one comic strip for Vigrid's newspaper, a topless woman, with exaggerated breasts, is hawking the newspaper on the streets. "Norway for Norwegians!" she shouts. She's arrested by the police for "selling material based on race discrimination"; meanwhile caricatures of blacks and Pakistanis burn the city and loot a liquor store.

One significant difference between the American and the Scandinavian Aryan movements concerns their view of the environment. While American Aryans support right-wing and conservative Republican efforts to discard environmental protection in the name of job creation in extractive industries, and are more than likely meat-eating survivalists, Nordic white supremacists are strong supporters of environmentalism. Many are vegetarians, some vegan.

Each group might maintain that their policies flow directly from their political stance. The Nordic groups claim that the modern state is "impure," "perverted," and full of "decay and decadence" and that their environmentalism is a means to cleanse it. As Matti Sundquist, singer in the Swedish skinhead group Svastika, puts it (in Loow 1998a: 134):

> Well, it's the most important thing, almost, because we must have a func-
> tioning environment in order to have a functioning world . . . and it's
> almost too late to save the earth, there just must be some radical changes
> if we are to stand a chance.[4]

The Restoration of Islamic Masculinity
among the Terrorists of 9/11

Although too little is known to develop as full a portrait of the terrorists of Al Qaeda and the Taliban regime in Afghanistan, certain common features warrant brief comment. For one thing, the class origins of the Al Qaeda terrorists appear to be similar to those of these other groups. Virtually all the young men were under twenty-five, well educated, lower middle class, downwardly mobile. As a corollary, Nasra Hassan's study of suicide bombers in the Middle East found that "none of them were uneducated, desperately poor, simple minded, or depressed"—the standard motivations ascribed to those who commit suicide (Hassan 2001: 38).

Other terrorist groups in the Middle East appear to have appealed to similar young men, although they were also organized also by theology professors— whose professions were also threatened by continued secularization and Westernization. For example, Jamiat-I-Islami, formed in 1972, was begun by Burhannudin Rabbani, a lecturer in theology at Kabul University. (Another leader, Ahmed Shah Masoud, was an engineering student at Kabul University.) Hisb-e-Islami, which split off in 1979 from Jamiat, was organized by Gulbuddin Hekmatyar, also an engineering student at Kabul University. This group appealed particularly to relatively well-educated radical students, most of whom were studying engineering. Ittihad-I-Islami was formed by Abdul Rasoul Sayyaf, former theology lecturer at Kabul University (cf. Marsden 2002: 29–31). The Taliban, itself formed in 1994 by disaffected religious students, seems to have drawn from a less fortunate class. Taliban soldiers were uneducated, and recruits were drawn often from refugee camps in Pakistan, where they had been exposed to the relative affluence of the West through aid organizations and television (see Marsden 2002: 70).

Several of the leaders of Al Qaeda were wealthy. Ayman al-Zawahiri, the fifty-year-old doctor who was the closest advisor to Osama bin Laden, was from a fashionable suburb of Cairo; his father was dean of the pharmacy school at the university there. And bin Laden, himself, was a multimillionaire. By contrast, many of the hijackers were engineering students, for whom job opportunities had been dwindling dramatically. (From the information I found, about one-fourth of the hijackers had studied engineering.) Kamel Daoudi studied computer science at a university in Paris; Zacarias Moussaoui, the first man to be formally charged with a crime in the United States for the events of September 11, took a degree at London's South Bank University. Marwan al-Shehhi, a chubby, bespectacled twenty-three-year-old from the United Arab Emirates, was an engineering student, while Ziad Jarrah, a twenty-six-year-old Lebanese, had studied aircraft design.

The politics of all these Islamic radical organizations appear to have been similar. All were opposed to globalization and the spread of Western values; all opposed what they perceived as corrupt regimes in several Arab states (notably Saudi Arabia and Egypt), which were merely puppets of U.S. domination. "The resulting anger is naturally directed first against their rulers, and then against those whom they see as keeping those rulers in power for selfish reasons" (Lewis 2001: 57).

Central to their political ideology is the recovery of manhood from the devastatingly emasculating politics of globalization. Over and over, Nasra Hassan writes, she heard the refrain, "The Israelis humiliate us. They occupy our land, and deny our history" (2001: 38). The Taliban saw the Soviet invasion and Westernization as humiliations. Osama bin Laden's October 7, 2001, videotape describes the "humiliation and disgrace" that Islam has suffered for "more than eighty years."

This fusion of antiglobalization politics, convoluted Islamic theology, and virulent misogyny has been the subject of much speculation. Viewing these through a gender lens, though, enables us to understand the connections better. The collapse of public patriarchal entitlement led to a virulent and violent reassertion of domestic patriarchal power. "This is the class that is most hostile to women," said the scholar Fouad Ajami (Crossette 2001: 1). But why? Journalist Barbara Ehrenreich explains that while "males have lost their traditional status as farmers and breadwinners, women have been entering the market economy and gaining the marginal independence conferred even by a paltry wage." As a result, "the man who can no longer make a living, who has to depend on his wife's earnings, can watch Hollywood sexpots on pirated videos and begin to think the world has been turned upside down" (Ehrenreich 2001).

Taliban policies were designed both to remasculinize men and to refeminize women. "The rigidity of the Taliban gender policies could be seen as a desperate attempt to keep out that other world, and to protect Afghan women from influences that could weaken the society from within" (Marsden 2002: 99). Thus, not only were policies of the Afghani republic that made female education compulsory immediately abandoned, but women were prohibited from appearing in public unescorted by men, from revealing any part of their body, or from going to school or holding a job. Men were required to grow their beards, in accordance with religious images of Mohammed—but also, I believe, because wearing beards has always been associated with men's response to women's increased equality in the public sphere. Beards especially symbolically reaffirm biological natural differences between women and men, even as they are collapsing in the public sphere.

Such policies removed women as competitors and also shored up masculinity, since they enabled men to triumph over the humiliations of globalization, as well as to triumph over their own savage, predatory, and violently sexual urges that would be unleashed in the presence of uncovered women.

Perhaps this can be best seen paradigmatically in the story of Mohammed Atta, apparently the mastermind of the entire operation and the pilot of the first plane to crash into the World Trade Center. The youngest child of an ambitious lawyer father and pampering mother, Atta grew up a shy and polite boy. "He was so gentle," his father said. "I used to tell him 'Toughen up, boy!'" (in the *New York Times Magazine*, October 7). Atta spent his youth in a relatively shoddy Cairo neighborhood. Both his sisters are professionals—one is a professor, the other a doctor.

Atta decided to become an engineer, but his "degree meant little in a country where thousands of college graduates were unable to find good jobs."[5] His father had told him he "needed to hear the word 'doctor' in front of his name. We told him your sisters are doctors and their husbands are doctors and you are the man of the family." After he failed to find employment in Egypt, he went to Hamburg, Germany, to study to become an architect. He was "meticulous, disciplined and highly intelligent," yet an "ordinary student, a quiet friendly guy who was totally focused on his studies," according to another student in Hamburg.

But his ambitions were constantly thwarted. His only hope for a good job in Egypt was to be hired by an international firm. He applied and was constantly rejected. He found work as a draftsman—highly humiliating for someone with engineering and architectural credentials and an imperious and demanding father—for a German firm involved with razing lower-income Cairo neighborhoods to provide more scenic vistas for luxury tourist hotels.

Defeated, humiliated, emasculated, a disappointment to his father and a failed rival to his sisters, Atta retreated into increasingly militant Islamic theology. By the time he assumed the controls of American Airlines flight 11, he evinced a gendered hysteria about women. In the message he left in his abandoned rental car, he made clear what really mattered to him in the end. "I don't want pregnant women or a person who is not clean to come and say good-bye to me," he wrote. "I don't want women to go to my funeral or later to my grave" (on CNN, October 2, 2001).

Masculine Entitlement and the Future of Terrorism

Of course such fantasies are the fevered imagination of hysteria; Atta's body was without doubt instantly incinerated, and no funeral would be likely. But the terrors of emasculation experienced by the lower middle classes globally will no doubt continue to resound for these young men whose world seems to have been turned upside down, their entitlements snatched from them, their rightful position in their world suddenly up for grabs. And they may continue to articulate with a seething resentment against women, "outsiders," or any other "others" perceived as stealing their rightful place at the table.

The common origins and common complaints of the terrorists of 9/11 and their American counterparts were not lost on American white supremacists. In their response to the events of 9/11, American Aryans said they admired the terrorists' courage, and took the opportunity to chastise their own compatriots. "It's a disgrace that in a population of at least 150 million White/Aryan Americans, we provide so few that are willing to do the same," bemoaned Rocky Suhayda, Nazi Party chairman from Eastpointe, Michigan. "A bunch of towel head/sand niggers put our great White Movement to shame" (in Ridgeway 2001: 41).

In his 1978 song, "The Promised Land," Bruce Springsteen, America's poet laureate of the dispossessed white working class, explained how that gendered humiliation can be so easily translated into violent rage, how you can "feel so weak" that you "just want to explode." The last two lines of that song's chorus provide perhaps a poignant epitaph to frame this discussion. "Mister I ain't a boy, no, I'm a man," he sings, defiantly, "And I believe in a promised land."

The assertion of manhood—a homosocial assertion since he assumes the listener is also a man—is followed by a declaration of faith in the promised land. To some men facing global displacement, that promised land is a heavenly garden of virginal delights; to others it's a purified material world. But in both cases, it's a world that will let men be men. And in a globalizing world of cynical consumerism, these men might be last of the true believers.

NOTES

1. This section is based on collaborative work with Abby Ferber, and appears in Kimmel and Ferber (2000).
2. Interestingly, Loow (1994: 21) found that the localities with the highest numbers of attacks on asylum seekers in the early 1990s had the highest concentrations of national socialist or racist organizations in the 1920–1940s.
3. I am grateful to Jorgen Lorentzen for translation from the Norwegian.
4. In that sense, these groups are similar to British groups such as Blood and Soil and the Patriotic Vegetarian and Vegan Society.
5. All unattributed quotes come from a fascinating portrait of Atta (Yardley 2001).

REFERENCES

Barber, B. 1992. *McDonald's and Jihad*. New York: Simon and Schuster.

Bjorgo, Tore. 1997. *Racist and Right-Wing Violence in Scandinavia: Patterns, Perpetrators, and Responses*. Leiden: University of Leiden.

———. 1998. "Entry, Bridge-Burning, and Exit Options: What Happens to Young People Who Join Racist Groups—and Want to Leave?" In *Nation and Race*, ed. J. Kaplan and T. Bjorgo, 231–258. Boston: Northeastern University Press.

Connell, R. W. 1987. *Gender and Power*. Stanford: Stanford University Press.

———. 1995. *Masculinities*. Berkeley: University of California Press.

———. 1998. "Masculinities and Globalization." *Men and Masculinities* 1(1): 3–23.

Coplon, J. 1989. "The Roots of Skinhead Violence: Dim Economic Prospects for Young Men." *Utne Reader*, May/June.

Crossette, B. 2001. "Living in a World without Women." *New York Times*, October 4.

Dobratz, B., and S. Shanks-Meile. 2001. *The White Separatist Movement in the United States: White Power! White Pride!* Baltimore: Johns Hopkins University Press.

Durham, Martin. 1997. "Women and the Extreme Right: A Comment." *Terrorism and Political Violence* 9: 165–168.

Ehrenreich, B. 2001. "Veiled Threat." *Los Angeles Times*, November 4.

Fangen, Katrine. 1998a. "Living Out Our Ethnic Instincts: Ideological Beliefs among Rightist Activists in Norway." In *Nation and Race: The Developing Euro-American Racist Subculture*, ed. Jeffrey Kaplan and Tore Bjorgo, 202–230. Boston: Northeastern University Press.

——— 1998b. "Right-Wing Skinheads: Nostalgia and Binary Oppositions." *Young* 6(2): 33–49.

———. 1999a. "Death Mask of Masculinity." In *Images of Masculinities: Moulding Masculinities*, ed. Soren Ervo, 184–211. London: Ashgate.

———. 1999b. "On the Margins of Life: Life Stories of Radical Nationalists." *Acta Sociologica* 42(4): 357–373.

———. 1999c. "Pride and Power: a Sociological Interpretation of the Norwegian Radical Nationalist Underground Movement." Ph.D. dissertation, Department of Sociology and Human Geography, University of Oslo.

———. 2000. "Skinheads (Norwegian)." In *White Power Encyclopedia*, ed. Jeffrey Kaplan, 281–283. Walnut Creek, CA: AltaMira Press.

Ferber, A. L. 1998. *White Man Falling: Race, Gender, and White Supremacy*. Lanham, MD: Rowman and Littlefield.

Frank, Andre Gunder. 1968. *The Development of Underdevelopment*. New York: Monthly Review Press.

Griffith, V., P. Spiegel, and H. Williamson. 2001. "The Hijackers' Tale: How the Men of September 11 Went Unnoticed." *Financial Times*, November 30.

Hassan, Nasra. 2001. "An Arsenal of Believers." *The New Yorker*, November 19.

Juergensmeyer, Mark. 1993. *The New Cold War? Religious Nationalism Confronts the Secular State*. Berkeley: University of California Press.

———. 2000. *Terror in the Mind of God: The Global Rise of Religious Violence*. Berkeley: University of California Press.

Kaplan, Jeffrey. 1995. "Right Wing Violence in North America." In *Terror from the Extreme Right*, ed. Tore Bjorgo, 44–95. London: Frank Cass.

Kimmel, M. 1989. "'New Prophets' and 'Old Ideals': Charisma and Tradition in the Iranian Revolution." *Social Compass* 36(4): 493–510.

———. 1996a. *Manhood in America: A Cultural History*. New York: The Free Press.

———, ed. 1996b. *The Politics of Manhood*. Philadelphia: Temple University Press.

———, and A. Ferber. 2000. "'White Men Are This Nation': Right-Wing Militias and the Restoration of Rural American Masculinity." *Rural Sociology* 65(4): 605–620.

Lewis, B. 2001. "The Revolt of Islam." *The New Yorker*, November 19.

Loow, Helene. 1994. "'Wir sind wieder da'—From National Socialism to Militant Race Ideology: The Swedish Racist Underground in a Historical Context." Paper presented to the XIII World Congress of Sociology, Bielefeld, July.

———. 1998a. "Racist Youth Culture in Sweden: Ideology, Mythology, and Lifestyle." In *Racism, Ideology, and Political Organisation*, ed. C. Westin, 77–98. Stockholm: CEIFO Publications, University of Stockholm.

———. 1998b. "White Power Rock and Roll: A Growing Industry." In *Nation and Race*, ed. J. Kaplan and T. Bjorgo, 126–147. Boston: Northeastern University Press.

Marrs, T. 1993. *Big Sister Is Watching You: Hillary Clinton and the White House Feminists Who Now Control America—And Tell the President What to Do.* Austin, TX: Living Truth Publishers.

Marsden, P. 2002. *The Taliban: War and Religion in Afghanistan.* London: Zed.

Messner, M. 1998. *Politics of Masculinities: Men and Movements.* Newbury Park, CA: Pine Forge.

Pedersen, W. 1996. "Working-Class Boys at the Margins: Ethnic Prejudice, Cultural Capital, and Gender." *Acta Sociologica* 39: 257–279.

Pierce, W. 1978. *The Turner Diaries.* Hillsboro, VA: National Vanguard Books.

Ridgeway, J. 2001. "Osama's New Recruits." *The Village Voice*, November 6.

Rubin, L. 1994. *Families on the Fault Line.* New York: HarperCollins.

Sinha, M. 1995. *Colonial Masculinity: The Manly Englishman and the Effeminate Bengali in the Late Nineteenth Century.* Manchester: Manchester University Press.

Stern, K. S. 1996. *A Force upon the Plain: The American Militia Movement and the Politics of Hate.* New York: Simon and Schuster.

Tiger, L. 2001. "Osama bin Laden's Man Trouble." *Slate*, September 28.

Westin, Charles, ed. 1998. *Racism, Ideology, and Political Organisation.* Stockholm: CEIFO Publications, University of Stockholm.

Willner, A. 1984. *The Spellbinders: Charismatic Political Leadership.* New Haven: Yale University Press.

Witte, R. 1995. "Racist Violence in Western Europe." *Journal of Ethnic and Migration Studies* 21(4): 489–500.

Yardley, J. 2001. "A Portrait of the Terrorist: From Shy Child to Single-Minded Killer." *New York Times*, October 10.

9

Promise Keepers

Patriarchy's Second Coming as Masculine Renewal

It is Shea Stadium in late September [1996] after all, so a crowd of 35,000 men chanting, whooping, hollering, and high-fiving each other isn't all that unusual. But the Mets attract barely half that number late in their woeful season. And there are no women in the stands. That is unusual. And besides, the Mets are on the road.

On this day Shea is the setting for the latest rally by Promise Keepers, a Christian organization that seeks to revitalize men through a mass-based evangelical ministry. The dramatic growth and continuing appeal of Promise Keepers indicate that the movement of masculine fundamentalism has struck a nerve among American men with its messages of personal responsibility and racial reconciliation: Promise Keepers is arguably the largest "men's movement" in the nation. Its calls to men to be more domestically responsible, socially conscious, and responsive friends, fathers, and husbands make Promise Keepers seem innocuous at worst, and potentially a force for masculine reform. But its ominous ties with fanatic right-wing organizations, as well as their views on women, homosexuals, and non-Christians, suggest that the rest of us had better start paying attention.

Who Are Promise Keepers?

Promise Keepers hasn't been around very long to have caused such a monumental stir. The group was founded in 1990 by former University of Colorado football coach Bill McCartney, who had brought a national title to his school that year. A devout Catholic, McCartney had become, he admits, a workaholic absentee husband who demanded that family life be subordinated to his

Originally published in *Tikkun*, January–February 1997.

professional ambitions. In 1989, his unwed teenage daughter Kristyn had given birth to a child fathered by one of McCartney's players. The following summer, after a religious epiphany, he left the Catholic Church for the more evangelical Protestant Vineyard Christian Fellowship and heeded the call to expand his mission from athletes to men in general.

The move wasn't that uncharacteristic. McCartney had always been pulled toward the charismatic and evangelical. While an assistant coach at Michigan in the 1970s, he had become involved with the right-wing Catholic "Word of God" movement, with its emphasis on biblical literalism. The Vineyard Fellowship's cultish theology uses faith healing, miracles, and other "signs and wonders." With a diagnosis of the nation's moral and spiritual crisis gleaned partly from his family's sexual scandals and partly from the Vineyard Fellowship's ultra-right political agenda, McCartney put out a call to men to come to a rally for masculine Christian renewal. Just over four thousand men turned up in July 1991, at the Colorado basketball arena.

From that modest beginning, the organization's growth has been almost exponential. Twenty-two thousand men half-filled the Colorado football stadium in 1992, and 50,000 filled it the next year. In 1994, 278,600 men attended several stadium events, 700,000 came in 1995, and an estimated 1.2 million met this year at twenty-two sites.

The organizational infrastructure has kept pace, growing from 22 full-time staff with a budget of $4 million in 1993 to more than 400 full-time employees and a budget of more than $100 million by 1998. They publish a slick magazine, *New Man*, which places devotional stories and prayers alongside political debates on questions like home schooling (they're for it), more practical tips like "how to save bucks on your home mortgage" (standard fare like comparing rates, paying more than the monthly premium, and refinancing the home), and advertisements for various Christian consumables. McCartney himself now works for the organization full-time, having resigned from his more secular coaching duties—followers still call him "coach"—in 1994, after Kristyn had given birth to yet another illegitimate child fathered by another of his players, and his wife had threatened to divorce him if he did not pay more attention to his home life.

Although data on the rank-and-file Promise Keepers is scarce, the National Center for Fathering in Shawnee, Kansas, found that, as of 1995, 88 percent of rally attendees were married, 21 percent had been divorced, and about 20 percent had parents who were divorced. Their median age was thirty-eight, and 84 percent were white. Over one-fourth reported becoming Christian after age twenty-four, and one-third had attended Baptist or Southern Baptist churches. Half reported that their own fathers were absent while they were growing up.

Unlike the Fellowship for Christian Athletes, which organizes prayer meetings among athletes in virtually every sport, including those little devotional moments at midfield for religious gridders from both teams, Promise Keepers want more than just jocks. They want all men.

Sports seem to be the way they intend to get them, at least metaphorically. At their stadium rallies, the parade of speakers, dressed in vertically striped polo shirts, khakis, and sneakers, look more like a lineup of sales clerks at Foot Locker than of evangelical stump preachers. Coach McCartney, and the other speakers—who include Ed Cole, organizer of the Christian Men's Network, who had the guys high-fiving for Jesus, and Charles Colson, convicted Watergate conspirator who found God in prison and now runs the Prison Fellowship Ministries—exhort their "worshiping warriors" with manly homilies like "go the distance," snatched from that masculine weepy, *Field of Dreams*, and "break down the walls," the rally's theme, which sounds like a cross between *Home Improvement* and a karate exhibition. The massive tent set up in the parking lot is a virtual messianic mini-mall, hawking books, T-shirts, and souvenirs; but the best-selling items by far are the ubiquitous baseball caps.

Non-Muscular Christianity?

Such a move to bring men back into the church by muscling up is not new in American history. And, after all, athletes are used by advertisers to sell everything from shoes to cologne and flashlight batteries, so why not God? At the turn of the twentieth century, the fleet-footed former Chicago Cub right fielder Billy Sunday quit professional baseball and remade himself as a Bible Belt evangelist, preaching "Muscular Christianity" to throngs of men, and bringing, in the words of one journalist, "bleacher-crazed, frenzied aggression to religion." To Sunday, Protestantism had turned Christ into a henpecked wimp, whose angelic countenance smiled down even on his enemies from the national pulpit. Inveighing against this "dainty, sissified, lily-livered piety" to massive men-only crowds in tents throughout the Midwest and the South—the same states where Promise Keepers today find the majority of their audience—Sunday offered his minions a "hard muscled, pick-axed religion, a religion from the gut, tough and resilient." Jesus, himself, was no "dough-faced lick-spittle proposition," he roared, but "the greatest scrapper who ever lived."

Some Promise Keepers echo Sunday's critique of feminized masculinity. "The demise of our community and culture is the fault of sissified men who have been overly influenced by women," writes Tony Evans, a black Dallas-based evangelist, who is among the Promise Keepers' most popular rally speakers. Men, he admonishes, must "reclaim" their manhood, saying, "I want to be a man again." But in the bright September sun at Shea Stadium one would search in vain for such hypermasculine bravado. Gone also are the virulent misogyny, the homophobia, and the specter of theocracy that has brought most of the criticism of the organization. Instead, one is struck by the immense sincerity of the guys in attendance, the earnestness of their searching, the heartfelt expressions of remorse. Were it not for the exclusion of women and the endless, tacky sports stuff, this could have been any Billy Graham Crusade. And were it not for the Christian fundamentalism, this might have been a mythopoetic men's meeting with Robert Bly and Sam Keen.

While Muscular Christians railed against a feminized Christianity grown soft and indolent, drawing on inspiring oratory about religious combat and righteous rage, most Promise Keepers are virtual SNAGs, "sensitive New Age guys" celebrating Christian sweetness and kindness. They are less Christian soldiers "marching as to war," and more friends, confidants, therapists, and partners, promising to listen carefully to their wives and children, sharing with their friends, healing their wounds and their worlds.

A Kinder, Gentler Patriarchy

The message has certainly resonated for large number of American men, who feel their lives are less deeply fulfilling, less meaningful, less animated by higher purpose than the one to which they believed they were entitled. Without community, a sense of purpose and connection, masculinity can feel hollow; we become ectomorphs—hard-shelled workaholics who are afraid there is nothing of any substance inside, and who deny that fear with drugs, alcohol, or strings of meaningless affairs. The marketplace is a perilous place to seek to prove one's manhood, what with plant closings, corporate layoffs, and downward mobility. Better to seek affirmation of manhood someplace safe, like as a father, husband, and an ethical man among men.

Promise Keepers ministers brilliantly to men's anxieties and needs, while promoting that masculine sense of entitlement that we believe is our birthright. The key words in their message are relationships and reconciliation. The organization's founding document proclaims the group's dedication "to uniting men through vital relationships to become godly influences in their world." Men have abdicated responsibility; at home, husbands are "not giving their wives the support they need," and are absent in the lives of their children or their friends. Among the "Seven Promises of a Promise Keeper" (also the title of their chief doctrinal book) are building strong marriages, families, and friendships, and working in the church.

Promise Keepers promotes a kind of soft patriarchy, male domination as obligation, surrender, and service—sort of "Every Man's Burden." There's lots of rhetoric about men becoming servants of Christ at home, ministering to their families as he did to his church. "A real man is one who accepts responsibilities and doesn't run away from them. He raises his family and takes a leadership role," says one rally-goer. Men are entitled to lead; expected to do it, soberly and responsibly. Masculine malaise, the search for meaning and community, is resolved by the reassertion of a kinder, gentler patriarchal control.

At one rally, Bill Bright, head of the Campus Crusade for Christ, opined that while men should respect women, the man "is the head of the household and women are responders." At Shea, the Rev. Ed Cole reminded the audience that "God's revelation comes through man," not women, and so the two genders can never be equal, and self-anointed "Bishop" Wellington Boone noted that "how you handle your wife" would reveal how you "handle the world." Boone relies on biblical inversion of biology—"woman came from man, not man from woman"—and describes his own conversion from absentee landlord to dutiful dad and husband. It's a form of competition, "spiritual warfare," a test of masculine strength, to do more at home than his wife does. "I'm never gonna let no woman out-serve me," he shouts to thunderous applause. In his essay in *Seven Promises of a Promise Keeper*, the organization's best-selling text, Tony Brown advises men to "sit down with your wife and say: 'Honey I've made a terrible mistake. I've given you my role. I gave up leading this family, and I forced you to take my place. Now I must reclaim that role.' Don't misunderstand what I am saying here. I'm not suggesting that you ask for your role back. I'm urging you to take it back. . . . [T]here can be no compromise here. If you're going to lead, you must lead." (For their part, women are urged to give it back, "[f]or the sake of your family and the survival of our culture.")

To some women, this traditional patriarchal bargain sounds a whole lot better than the deals they'd already cut. After all, the organization lists among its primary goals deepening "the commitment of men to respect and honor women." In return for submission, or being "responders," women are promised the respect and honor that went with the traditional patriarchal pedestal—and they get in return husbands and fathers who forswear drinking, drugs, smoking, and gambling, who lovingly support their families by steady work, and who even choose to go shopping with them as a form of Christian service. Not bad, perhaps—even if it does require that women remain absolutely obedient and subordinate to men. It's unclear to me whether having a job or even going to college fits into the picture. Some members want their wives home at all times; others say they still need the money. Perhaps we'll know soon enough: Promise Keepers has announced a women's organization, "Suitable Helpers," sort of its ladies' auxiliary, where, according to the Christian Coalition, women can "learn what it means to be a godly support and partner to man." In addition, an organization called Women of Faith is drawing thousands of women to its "Joyful Journey" rallies scheduled to happen in more than a dozen cities in 1998, using what seems to be a Promise Keeper model.

To some listeners, though, this message sounds like male supremacy with a beatific smile. "Promise Keepers are about the return of patriarchy in its Sunday best: spiffed up, polite, and earnest but always, and ultimately, in charge," noted Unitarian minister Rev. David Blanchard of Syracuse. The resolution of the crisis of masculinity cannot come at the expense of women. Though the Promise Keepers hear men's anguish, they offer a traditional patriarchal salve on a wound that can only be closed by gender equality.

The Racism of Racial Reconciliation

Promise Keepers' message of racial reconciliation is as compelling as it is troubling. On the one hand, reconciliation means that white people must take responsibility for racism and take the initiative in seeking fellowship with men of color. Noting that eleven o'clock on Sunday morning is the most racially divided hour of the week, Promise Keepers seeks to heal racial divisiveness by bringing black and white men together under the canopy of patriarchy. At Shea Stadium, it falls to McCartney—grandfather to two interracial children (both of Kristyn's lovers were men of color)—to sound the call for racial reconciliation. Racism is a white problem, he argues. A "spirit of white racial superiority" maintains "an insensitivity to the pain of people of color." Like harmony between women and men, which can be won only when men return to the home, racial harmony relies on white people's initiative. It is the privileged who must act.

Racial reconciliation is the organization's boldest move into the political arena, and it makes Promise Keepers one of the few virtually all-white groups in the nation willing to confront white racism. At Shea Stadium, that message energized the mostly white (I estimated about 80 percent) crowd. Rich, who is thirty-nine and white, is a single parent from New Jersey, who brought his two sons. He feels that the racial component is important. "In Christ we're all the same," he says. Daniel, a white twenty-seven-year-old, from a working-class neighborhood in Queens, came with another man from his Baptist Church, Joseph, a thirty-five-year-old black man originally from Ghana. "As a white person, you kind of take race for granted, you don't see it," Daniel says. "I'm not the one being hurt, but my people have done some terrible things to blacks. As a white person, it's important to take responsibility."

So, what's wrong with this picture of white people taking responsibility for racism, of men becoming more loving, devoted, and caring fathers, friends, and husbands? It's a nagging question that emerges once you begin to examine what lies outside the framing of each carefully orchestrated PK photo-op. For one thing, there's the message of reconciliation itself. Theirs is not a call to support those programs that would uplift the race and set the nation on a course toward racial equality. This is not about anti-discrimination legislation or affirmative action—heck, it's not even about integration. It's about being kinder and more civil. It's about hearing their pain, not supporting its alleviation. It's choosing to be nicer, but not about policies that force us to be fairer. In the PK world view, racial reconciliation is an individual posture, but not a collective struggle. Being less racist in one's personal life may be laudatory, but without a program of institutional remedies, it leaves untouched the chief forces that keep that inequality in place. Which is why it doesn't seem so strange to see who else is eagerly lining up to slap some high-fives on the Promise Keeper rank and file. Although McCartney and the Promise Keepers elite maintain a publicly apolitical position, there are increasingly ominous signs of connections between Promise Keepers and far-right religious organizations like Focus on the Family, Christian Coalition, and the Campus Crusade for Christ. James Dobson, founder of Focus on the Family, appears regularly at Promise Keeper functions, as does Bill Bright, whose Campus Crusade lent eighty-five full-time staffers to the Promise Keeper headquarters, and whose most recent book (sold at all Promise Keepers rallies) raves against the "homosexual explosion," the teaching of evolution, and abortion, as well as the laws against school prayer.

In addition to McCartney's well-publicized right-wing ties, other Promise Keepers maintain a "warm fellowship" with the far right. Mark DeMoss, the organization's national spokesman, worked for Jerry Falwell before serving on the advisory committee for Pat Buchanan's presidential campaign. In a sense DeMoss neatly encapsulates the three successive waves of the religious right in America—from Falwell's Moral Majority, to Reed's Christian Coalition, to a sanitized theocracy designed to appeal to Generation X. Promise Keepers is only the most recent example of a well-established and well-financed theocratic movement.

This movement promised that "America will be a Christian nation by the year 2000"—not a cheery prospect for Jews, Moslems, atheists, agnostics, and others (prophecies are not always accurate!). Urging his followers to "take this nation for Jesus," McCartney has made clear the political agenda: What you are about to hear is God's word to the men of this nation. We are going to war as of tonight. We have divine power; that is our weapon. We will not compromise. Wherever truth is at risk, in the schools or legislature, we are going to contend for it. We will win.

So much for the avowed apolitical stance of the organization. Theocracies are not known for their tolerance of difference, and their use of these earnest young minions is reminiscent of some New Left organizations, which were propelled from below by youthful idealism but steered from above by hacks who were not especially taken with the idea of participatory democracy. But the radical religious right is currently jumping on the racial reconciliation bandwagon, in part because it allows them to sound supportive of people of color, without actually having to support any of the political and social policies that would benefit people of color. Even Ralph Reed, Promise Keeper supporter and head of the Christian Coalition, protested the burning of black churches this past summer, only to be more than a little embarrassed when his organization floated overly racist mock-election guides to potential voters.

Such racial tokenism extends also to the black clergy who are part of the Promise Keepers team. Wellington Boone and other black speakers like E. V. Hill, from Los Angeles, and Pittsburgh's Joseph Garlington are also on the Steering Committee of the Coalition on Revival (COR), an extreme right-wing religious group that espouses biblical literalism and promotes "Christian reconstructionism." Boone himself was a consultant to Pat Robertson's presidential bid.

Though the Shea Stadium rally was endorsed by several prominent local black clergy, other prominent religious leaders, like the Rev. Calvin Butts of the Abyssinian Baptist Church in Harlem or the ubiquitous Rev. Al Sharpton, were conspicuously absent from the mutual love fest. Nationally, too, some black clergy are skeptical, to say the least. "It doesn't translate into how you bring black and white together," noted the Rev. Christopher Hamlin, pastor of the 16th Street Baptist Church in Birmingham, Alabama. "The barriers that are broken down in the stadiums are still there when people come home to their communities. I think most black pastors see it as being rhetoric, which is something most of the black community has heard for a long time."

Eventually, those black pastors who have innocently supported Promise Keepers' masculinist ministry will have to face the seamier political underside of their messages of hope. Though Promise Keepers was among the only white organizations to raise money for burned black churches in 1997 (they raised over $1 million), the traditional liberalism of black religious constituency, which favors welfare, civil rights, and women's right to choose, will sit uneasily with a right-wing theocratic evangelism. Through both sides agree that racism is a white problem, about the only policy issue they agree on is home schooling.

What is more, the inclusion of men of color comes at an exorbitant multicultural price—lopping off several bands of the rainbow through continued exclusion. Gays and lesbians, for example, don't even get near the pearly gates. Echoing familiar "love the sinner, hate the sin" rhetoric, McCartney and Dr. Raleigh Washington sidestep the question at the rally's press conference. "It's like lying," says Washington. "God doesn't like lying but he loves liars." Perhaps, but would God support a constitutional amendment banning marriages between liars? Would God sanction discrimination against confessed liars? Though rally-goers barely heard a word about it, homosexuality is a hot topic among both rank and file and PK leaders. It's the hottest topic on Promise Keepers' web site. Since the Bible never uses the term, or clearly defines homosexuality, these biblical literalists are forced to struggle with interpretations. The leaders see no ambiguity nor any need for equivocation. When he pronounced homosexuality "an abomination against Almighty God," McCartney was a board member of Colorado for Family Values, the statewide coalition of right-wing religious groups that sponsored Amendment 2, the unconstitutional Colorado initiative that would have permitted discrimination against gays and lesbians. Later, McCartney called homosexuals "a group of people who don't reproduce yet want to be compared to people who do." (One pities Bob and Elizabeth Dole and the Buchanans, as well as other non-breeders.) He's also addressed Operation Rescue rallies, calling abortion "a second Civil War." Given such obviously political positions, it would appear that Promise Keepers' notion of gender reconciliation is also an individual outpouring of concern, however heartfelt, for individual women, while ignoring collective efforts at building a new society together. Good, kind, decent men (and white people) can indeed develop better, more emotionally resonant and caring relationships with women and people of color, and then support precisely those policies that perpetuate their pain.

Male Supremacy as Racial Healing

Perhaps what we are witnessing in this strange alliance of right-wing evangelists and liberal black clergy is that the reassertion of male supremacy can serve as the foundation for both to sit down at the table of brotherhood. "What happened here is that the boys' club has expanded to include people of color," writes Chip Berlet, who is researching right-wing populism in America. "When push comes to shove, what's more important, race or gender?" Here, then, is a concept that both black and white clergy can unite behind. The resurrection of responsible manhood is really the Second Coming of patriarchy. Gender and racial healing is a more unified masculine entitlement. Such allies could even reach out to Louis Farrakhan, the black Muslim leader of his Million Man March, and invite him to the party, since he also excludes women and gay men and lesbians from the table of humanity.

Of course, like the Million Man March, the earnestness and sincerity of the movement's adherents—and a genuine alliance with wide range of black clergy—might in time outstrip Promise Keepers' right-wing political agenda. More likely, and more ominous, however, is the possibility that the repressive and censorious voices of theocratic authoritarianism will continue to whisper in the ears of the movement leaders, long after the shouts of the men themselves have died down.

Postscript, 1999–2009

One hears little about Promise Keepers these days. Membership has declined, and, at the organization's headquarters, staff have been quietly laid off. After two summers of half-filled stadiums, the number of large rallies has dwindled to single digits. After the massive rally in Washington, D.C., no more large-scale "non-political" events are scheduled.

Is the movement over? Has it failed? I think not. Promise Keepers is not dead. It's only sleeping.

For one thing, Promise Keepers has returned to its original mission of quietly reestablishing domestic patriarchy and resisting initiatives that promote gay and lesbian equality. Gone are the delightfully mediagenic photo-ops of white and black men hugging and high-fiving for Jesus. Racial reconciliation has proved relatively short-lived, especially since it was never intended to sustain a movement for racial equality.

Indeed, Promise Keepers was never a full-fledged social movement intended to sustain any policy initiatives, nor was its organization equipped to address movement sustenance issues. The organization's central figures consistently shied away from public political pronouncements, though their political views were easily known.

In effect, Promise Keepers offered Christian men a form of evangelical therapy, a vehicle by which they could understand that their traditional Protestant denominational churches could address what they experienced as palpably masculine spiritual issues. The success of Promise Keepers, then, is measured not by the size or visibility of its social movement organization, but by the extent to which it encouraged men to return to their parishes, from which they had become disaffected, and begin men's groups *within* their churches. Promise Keeper rallies began these men's retreat to their local communities—their churches and their families. Weekly church meetings of men inspired by Promise Keeper rallies provide the glue by which the evangelical movement will sustain solidarity in the coming decades.

Of course, Promise Keepers will continue to insist that such retreat is not a political position, but an individual search for spiritual community and redemption. And, of course, to the extent that they pay any attention anymore, the media will continue to swallow this position uncritically, instead criticizing feminists' discomfort with the therapeutic value of a personal theology of domestic patriarchy.

But efforts to capture home and church as men's havens in a secular world are political in the larger sense. Even God's minions need the comforts of home. Christian soldiers must always secure the domestic front.

10

Saving the Males
at VMI and Citadel

It is still dark and the courtyard at the center of the barracks is as quiet as the surrounding foothills of the Shenandoah Valley, dark and frost-covered. The late October air is cold and crisp. Dressed in a suit and tie, I am huddling under a balcony for warmth. "What the hell am I doing here?" I ask myself.

Suddenly, a siren goes off and a group of men start running along the top floor (called a stoop) of the courtyard. Doors fly open and nearly 300 young bleary-faced men come stumbling out of their rooms, all dressed in yellow sweatshirts and sweatpants. They snap to attention and then race down the stairs into the courtyard around which all the barracks are built.

There they are met by about 40 or 50 guys in uniform who instantly start berating them, screaming, nose-to-nose, hollering what appear to be commands. The young men start with calisthenics—push-ups, sit-ups, jumping jacks, running in place with their arms over their heads, squat thrusts—whatever the uniformed men demand of them. While they huff and puff in the chilly predawn light, the uniformed cadre stands over them, belittling them, calling them "skirts," "wimps," "wusses."

Near me, a young, heavy-set guy is straining to do his 40th push-up. His cadre is kneeling over his back, screaming directly in his ear, "What's wrong with you, skirt? There are women who can do more push-ups than you. When I was in the army, there was a woman who could do 100 push-ups. You can't even do 50."

Behind me, a young man is running in place—arms down, arms out, arms overhead—while his cadre is nose-to-nose with him, screaming at the top of his lungs, with no effort to keep from spitting into the face of his young charge.

Originally published in *Gender & Society* 14 (4) August 2000.

After forty-five minutes of this grueling pace, a bell goes off, the cadre disappears, and the young men stagger back upstairs to shower and prepare for their day. It is now 5:30 A.M. Welcome to college.

If this does not exactly sound like freshman orientation at your university, it is because what I have described is a very different kind of collegiate experience. I am describing my observations of the "rat line" at the Virginia Military Institute (VMI) in Lexington, Virginia. At the same moment, a similar scene is enacted in Charleston, South Carolina, at the Citadel. It was at those two schools that the most recent battles over gender discrimination have been fought, cases that were among our nation's most important legal cases for women's equality, the *Brown v. Board of Education* of gender discrimination.

These cases began in 1990, when the Civil Rights Division of the U.S. Department of Justice filed a suit against the state of Virginia and the VMI, an all-male, state-supported, military-type educational institution, for possible violation of the Fourteenth Amendment of the Constitution, which grants all citizens equal protection under the law. The suit claimed that VMI's all-male admission policy violated women's equal protection, and the U.S. government demanded that VMI become coeducational. VMI denied this charge and claimed that its unique educational methodology served vital state interests.

A year later, a young high school student in South Carolina named Shannon Faulkner applied and was admitted to the Citadel, after removing identification on her high school records that would show that she was a woman. (Because the Citadel had previously been an all-male institution, there was no place on its application form that asked the applicant's sex.) When she was subsequently rejected because of gender, she brought suit against that institution, also a state-supported, all-male, military-type institution. Her individual case, brought forward by the American Civil Liberties Union's section on women's rights and their pro bono litigators, was joined by the United States as plaintiff-intervener in a potential civil-rights violation.

Thus were the cases of VMI and the Citadel begun. I was invited by the Civil Rights Division of the Justice Department to participate in those cases as an expert witness, the expert on "masculinity" if you will. I testified in the remedial phases of both VMI and Citadel trials, which entailed site observations at all the schools involved; part of that testimony appeared as a footnote in Justice Ruth Bader Ginsburg's Supreme Court opinion in the case.

On the surface, these cases were obviously about the constitutionally protected rights of women to equal educational opportunity. Both the government and Shannon Faulkner's attorneys argued that such violations had occurred; VMI and the Citadel denied they had violated women's equal protection, claiming that, unlike race-based discrimination, their admission standards passed the criteria set forward by the Supreme Court that permitted discrimination against women.

I believe that such a reading of these cases—being about women's educational opportunity—only partially comprehends them. While such issues were certainly prominent in the court proceedings, and were the basis on which the legal decisions were rendered, I also want to suggest that there was a hidden subtext to these cases, a subtext that had less to do with women's educational opportunities and more to do with the making of men. In fact, the transparency of the claims made by VMI and the Citadel, refuted by both expert testimony and the legal opinions rendered in the case, allows us to see through this surface text about discrimination against women. VMI and the Citadel were, as they have always been, about men—or, more accurately, about masculinity. I will argue that these cases provide a unique meditation on the meaning of masculinity in the contemporary United States. In the words of the title of this article—the slogan that appeared on bumper stickers and buttons all over Charleston during the Citadel trial and that became the unofficial motto of the campaign to exclude women—the case may have originated as a question of equal rights for women, but to the institutions involved it was really about "saving the males."

In this article, I want to explore those decisions and suggest the relevance to sociologists, particularly sociologists of gender. To do that, I will focus on what these cases say about women, about men, about their questioning of the appropriateness of single-sex education, about gendered institutions, and about the relationship of difference and sameness to gender equality.

Discrimination, Difference, and Sameness

First, I will present a bit of theoretical background to help situate the discussion about gender discrimination. America's founding political theories were preoccupied with the relationship between difference and sameness, equality and inequality. It was, for example, a Lockean assumption that different talents, different motivations, and different abilities would lead to different, that is, unequal, economic and social outcomes. This is, of course, a bedrock principle of meritocracy. The harder you work, the more able you are, the higher you will rise. The inequalities at the end of the road are the natural outcomes of our differences.

By contrast, equality has always been confused with sameness. Historically, this was one of the cold war's ideological weapons against communism—to play on the fear that economic equality would mean that we would all look, talk, and dress alike; act exactly the same as everyone else; and perhaps most important, think the same things. Images of socialist societies always included large groups of indistinguishable people, often chanting or marching together; their message was that equality spelled the death of the individual. Similarly, antifeminists have historically played on fears of androgyny, which was imagined as

either gender inversion (masculinized women and feminized men) or a blending of masculinity and femininity into some rather unappealing amorphous
mush, to maintain traditional gender inequalities. In America, we believe that
difference leads to inequality and equality means sameness.

This is expressed in our legal system with the twin foundations of equal
protection. There are two ways you can discriminate in law: You can treat those
who are the same as if they were different and you can treat those who are different as if they were the same.

To treat alikes as unalike—treating sameness differently—is the basis for
most sex and race discrimination cases in the workplace or higher education. This
is the basis for *Brown v. Board of Education* in 1954 striking down separate but equal
as a way to maintain racial segregation. Separate cannot be equal. You cannot
treat people who are the same—Blacks and whites—as if they were different.

In addition, you cannot treat unalikes as alike, treat different people the
same. In a Supreme Court opinion in 1971, Justice Potter Stewart wrote, "The
grossest discrimination can lie in treating things that are different as though
they were exactly alike" (*Jeness v. Fortson* 403 U.S. [1971], 431, 442). In sexual harassment cases, for example, the traditional standard of harassment—Would a
reasonable person find the behavior objectionable?—has been replaced by a
"reasonable woman standard" (*Harris v. Forklift Systems, Inc.* 510 U.S. 17 [1993], 22).
Recognizing that there are some differences between women and men, the question has become not whether some abstract person would find it objectionable
but whether a woman would find it so. We cannot treat people as if personal
background or social characteristics were inconsequential. (This often has been
a basis for the sociological critique of American jurisprudence—it decontextual-
izes individuals from their social and historical roots.)[1] Discrimination is ignoring sameness when it is salient and ignoring difference when it is salient.

There are significant differences between gender discrimination and race
discrimination as a matter of law. Race discrimination receives what the courts
call "strict" scrutiny, that is, it is never justifiable under any circumstances
because, legally, Blacks and whites are the same. Gender discrimination receives
what is called "intermediate" scrutiny—it is usually wrong but you can discriminate only under some very well-defined circumstances. Such discrimination
has to (1) be based on real differences between the sexes, not on stereotypes;
(2) serve a legitimate state interest; and (3) be functionally and directly related
to the qualifications for the job, the so-called bona fide occupational qualification, or BFOQ.

So, for example, the Hooters restaurant chain successfully defended its all-
female waitstaff policy by claiming that "sex appeal" defined by large breasts
was a BFOQ and that since only women possessed that BFOQ (or, I suppose,
grammatically, those BFOQs) they could exclude men. By contrast, fire and
police departments have been unsuccessful in arguing that there were any

nonstereotypical differences that would make it impossible for some women to serve as police officers or fire fighters. Those issues of sameness and difference were very much in play in the VMI and Citadel cases, and the relationship of equality to both sameness and difference continues to reverberate through those institutions. To see that, it would be helpful to have some historical background on the cases.

The Historical Convergence of the VMI and Citadel Cases

VMI and the Citadel are not your typical educational institutions (Manegold 2000). Both provide a disciplined military atmosphere, although fewer than 15 percent of all graduating cadets pursue a career in the military. VMI and the Citadel are total institutions in which academic study, residential life (the barracks), and military training are all integrated into a closed system into which cadets are immersed from the moment they set foot on campus. Both use an educational methodology typical of a total institution; known as the "adversative method," the method deliberately introduces emotional and psychological stress to create "doubt about previous beliefs and experiences in order to create a mindset conducive to the values VMI attempts to impart," according to a 1986 institutional self-study at VMI (cited in *United States v. Virginia* 766 F. Supp. [W.D. Va 1991], 1421, hereafter *VMI I*). Each cadet is systematically stripped of his individual identity and then slowly and deliberately rebuilt in the corporate mold.

For first-year students, known as "rats" at VMI and "knobs" at the Citadel, the process entails a total shock to the system of beliefs. Heads are shaved (thus the nickname "knobs"); seemingly random and nonsensical orders are given and unquestioningly are carried out; and subordination to a training cadre of second-year students is relentless, merciless, and brutal. The rat line at VMI has been compared with Marine Corps boot camp in terms of the physical rigor and the mental stress of the experience. The brutality of the adversative system implants a deeply felt bonding among the men; solidarity among cadets is intense and loyalty of alumni is fierce. (This experience has even been explored in fiction. Pat Conroy's novel about his experiences at the Citadel, *The Lords of Discipline* [1983], offers a devastatingly critical view of the brutalities of male bonding. On the other side of the ledger, long before he played the role of president, Ronald Reagan starred in a film about VMI called *Brother Rat* [1938].)

This singular and unique educational methodology—and its appropriateness for women (but not its appropriateness for men)—was a central element in the legal cases. The VMI and Citadel cases proceeded separately on parallel tracks. Yet, each moment in one case had enormous ramifications for the other. Each was heard in a separate district court—VMI in the U.S. District Court for the Western District of Virginia in Roanoke and Citadel in the district court in

Charleston—but both appeals were heard in the U.S. Circuit Court of Appeals for the Fourth Circuit in Richmond. Eventually, only VMI was appealed to the Supreme Court.

In the liability phase of the case, the question before the court was whether VMI violated the Fourteenth Amendment by excluding women from a state-supported institution. In that phase (*VMI I*), Judge Jackson Kiser ruled in favor of VMI. His opinion claimed that the record showed

> that single-gender education at the undergraduate level is beneficial to both males and females [and that] key elements of the adversative VMI educational system, with its focus on barracks life, would be fundamentally altered and the distinctive ends of the system would be thwarted, if VMI were forced to admit females and to make changes necessary to accommodate their needs and interests. (*VMI I*, 1413)

Kiser argued that VMI met the three standards of intermediate scrutiny: (1) The exclusion of women was directly related to its mission, (2) it served a legitimate state purpose, and (3) it was based on real differences between the sexes. (VMI had argued that the state interest served by its exclusion of women was "diversity" in higher education in Virginia, offering one of several Orwellian moments in which the language of feminism or multiculturalism was used to perpetuate discrimination.) He further observed a Catch-22 in the Justice Department suit—to admit women to VMI would so alter the structure of the education that their very admission would transform the school into another institution; thus, their very entry would prevent them from getting the education they sought; and thus, by seeking equality as sameness, the women would get difference.

The U.S. Court of Appeals for the Fourth Circuit reversed that decision and found that VMI's and the Citadel's admission policies did, in fact, discriminate against women. The Circuit Court offered VMI several avenues by which it might remedy that discrimination: VMI could close, go private, admit women, or finance a program that would provide for women the same educational benefits that men receive at VMI. It was this last course that both VMI and the Citadel chose; the schools proposed to fund parallel programs in women's leadership at neighboring women's colleges. VMI would help develop the Virginia Women's Institute for Leadership (VWIL) at nearby Mary Baldwin College, whereas the Citadel proposed a South Carolina Institute for Leadership (SCIL) at Converse College, both small, private, all-women's colleges. While VMI would continue to use its adversative method of total immersion into rigid hierarchies, VWIL was to be a more nurturing and supportive educational atmosphere; each school would thus use the educational methodology most "appropriate" for the gender of its students (*VMI* 852 Fed. Supp. [1994], 484, hereafter *VMI III*). This was not to be a case of separate but equal, the schools claimed, but one of distinct but superior.

Several expert witnesses supported VMI's position, including sociologist David Riesman, who argued that VMI's adversative method would be "inappropriate" for women, and Elizabeth Fox-Genovese, who offered vigorous, if irrelevant, testimony that VWIL would offer poor and minority students an opportunity to receive a Mary Baldwin education to which they would have otherwise been excluded for financial reasons. Against this position, the Justice Department's expert witnesses, such as Carol Jacklin, Alexander Astin, and myself, suggested that VMI's contentions were based on stereotypes of what types of educational methodologies were appropriate to all women and that VMI's arguments were the same ones used historically to justify women's exclusion from entry into the public sphere for a century. VWIL's relationship to VMI was akin to a fictive program that one might imagine having been proposed for Vassar that was designed to keep West Point all-male.

Again, the district court judge bought VMI's argument. Judge Jackson Kiser ruled in favor of VMI's remedy of the VWIL program, claiming that VMI and VWIL were each appropriate for the gender they were to serve. But they were equivalent, he argued. "If VMI marches to the beat of a drum, then Mary Baldwin marches to the melody of a fife and when the march is over, both will have arrived at the same destination" (*VMI III*, 484), he wrote in his opinion—a rhetorical flourish that led the *New York Times* to write in an editorial on May 9, 1994, that "Judge Kiser Misses the Beat Again."

Hearing the Citadel case, the second district court judge, C. Weston Houck in Charleston, South Carolina, was not as easily persuaded. He ordered the school to admit Faulkner to its Corps of Cadets. The Supreme Court agreed. Eight justices heard the VMI case in January 1996. (Justice Clarence Thomas recused himself since his son, Jamal, was a cadet at VMI.) In its decision that June, the Court found, by a seven-to-one majority, that VWIL was but a "pale shadow of VMI" (*VMI* 1 16 S.Ct., 2285, hereafter *VMI V*). Three months later, on September 21, 1996, the VMI Board of Visitors voted nine to eight to admit women into the Corps of Cadets.

VMI's decision was preceded by the announcement that the Citadel would become coeducational, a decision reached within two days of the Supreme Court ruling on June 26. Thus, finally, did the last obstacles toward women's full equal educational opportunity tumble. In a case that many had regarded as women's equivalent of *Brown v. Board of Education*, women were now able to attend any state-supported educational institution in America.

What Were the Arguments Used to Exclude Women?

To argue, as VMI and the Citadel did, that their unique educational methodology was particularly suited to the educational needs of men and that their parallel programs would be more appropriate for women raises significant questions for sociologists of gender. What types of arguments were brought to support the educational separation of the sexes? How do we assess those arguments? and finally, What are the political and legal implications of these cases for students of gender relations and the law?

Stated most concisely, VMI argued that women simply could not do what the men did, that the adversative educational methodology was simply inappropriate for women. Throughout the case, VMI returned to assertions of natural and intractable gender differences as the basis for gender discrimination. The adversative model, they argued, is only effective for males. The rat line, the barracks lifestyle, the rigorous honor code—these were simply too much for women's purportedly fragile constitutions to bear. Women, the school claimed, could not cut it. They were "not capable of the ferocity requisite to make the program work." They are "physically weaker . . . more emotional, and cannot take stress as well as men." The school cited more than 100 physical differences that resulted in a "natural hierarchy" between women and men, with men, of course, at the top. If admitted, VMI averred, female cadets would "break down crying" and suffer "psychological trauma" from the rigors of the system (*VMI I*, 1435; *VMI V*, Brief for Petitioner, 2264; see also Epstein 1997b: 108; Vojdik 1997: 85).

Such arguments joined a long history of using putative sex differences as the basis for discrimination. In the nineteenth century, women had been excluded from educational institutions, the workplace, and the voting booth because they did not have the physical constitution or mental toughness to handle it. In what was the best-selling book on higher education of the entire century, *Sex in Education* (1873), Edward C. Clarke, Harvard's first professor of education, predicted that if women went to college their brains would grow heavier and their wombs would atrophy. (His evidence for this? By misreading correlation for cause, Clarke pointed out that college-educated women had fewer children than non-college-educated women. He also noted that 42 percent of the women in Boston-area mental hospitals had college degrees, while only 16 percent of male patients had degrees. If college did not shrink their wombs, perhaps it made them insane! Today, of course, we might more parsimoniously interpret these findings as the result of both expanding opportunities and frustrated ambition, not shrinking wombs.) Perhaps the most eloquent expression of this position, though, comes from our own era. Opposing women's participation in the military, the former Speaker of the House of Representatives Newt Gingrich noted, "If combat means living in a ditch, females have a biological problem staying in a ditch for 30 days because they get infections. Males are biologically driven to go out and hunt giraffes" (cited in Messner 1998: 27).

Since discrimination is justified on the basis of difference, all VMI had to do was demonstrate those differences. Toward that end, they attempted to use feminist theorists to buttress their claims, co-opting arguments by Carol

Gilligan, Deborah Tannen, and others who claimed that women responded better to more nurturing and supportive educational methodologies. (It was one of
the more pointed ironies to hear lawyers defending these two bastions of
Southern, white, chivalric masculinity invoke what they saw as feminist essentialism in their schools' defense.) According to the Citadel's lawyers, men "tend
to need an environment of adversativeness or ritual combat in which the
teacher is a disciplinarian and a worthy competitor," whereas women "tend to
thrive in a cooperative atmosphere in which the teacher is emotionally connected with the students" (*Faulkner v. Jones* 858 F. Supp. 552 [1994], 1434). The
Citadel even asked Gilligan to testify for them, to which she responded with an
amicus brief filed on behalf of Shannon Faulkner.

In this case, the mean differences between women and men were applied to
all women and men, which is, of course, the essence of stereotypical thinking.
It is stereotyping to think that just because most members of a group share a
characteristic, all members of the group share that characteristic. And while it
may be true that most women prefer such a supportive and nurturing educational environment, so too, actually, do most men. The rigors of the adversative
system are attractive to only a small number of men to begin with, and probably
to an even smaller number of women.

Saving the Males

The Citadel took a slightly different—and far more revealing—tack to thwart
Shannon Faulkner's effort to enroll. After all, here was a woman who did seek
the adversative educational methodology offered by the Citadel. At VMI, there
was no live plaintiff who wanted to go there at the time of the first court hearings. While the Citadel agreed that women could do everything required of the
male cadets, as women had been doing at West Point and the other service academies since 1976, and even agreed that there might be some women who would
want to do it, the entry of women, they argued, would destroy the mystical bonding experience among the male cadets.

Women's presence would "dilute" the testosterone-rich atmosphere, pol-
lute it. One of the Citadel's expert witnesses, Major General Josiah Bunting III,
himself a VMI graduate and former Rhodes scholar who is now superintendent
at VMI, suggested that women would be "a toxic kind of virus" that would
destroy the Citadel. "Adolescent males benefit from being able to focus exclusively on the task at hand, without the intrusion of any sexual tension," he
claimed (cited in Vojdik 1997).

The question of women's admission to an all-male school had become a
defensive struggle for men to preserve a pristine, homosocial institution. The
school's supporters sold light blue (the school color) buttons and bumper stickers that read "Save the Males," as if one woman represented a deadly threat to

an entire gender. Other slogans that appeared on T-shirts and bumper stickers after Faulkner's admission included "Citadel—1,952 Bulldogs and One Bitch" and "Save the Males, Shave the Whale."

This argument, too, replayed earlier debates. At the turn of the century, opponents to coeducation argued that women's presence would dilute the rigor of the curriculum and, more important, feminize the boys. Psychologist G. Stanley Hall, whose 1904 book *Adolescence* named and defined that transitional period of life, predicted that if they were educated together, boys and girls would "lose the mystic attraction of the other sex" and that, therefore feminized, the boys would become gay. This claim that heterosociality—coeducation—produces homosexuality is, of course, utterly disproved by the evidence. In fact, what Kinsey found in 1948 was that most of the 39 percent of men who had had at least one homosexual experience to orgasm had such an experience in a homosocial setting—single-sex summer camp, single-sex college, religious institution, or the military.[2]

Is masculinity that fragile that one woman can tear down an institution with such a celebrated 150-year history? Actually, the Citadel was already far from a homosocially pure institution. There already were significant numbers of women there. They cooked and served the food, cleaned the buildings, and taught classes as professors. Some women also attended classes. Prior to the legal cases, all veterans, women and men alike, were allowed to enroll at the school. There were also many women graduate students. The only thing women were not at the Citadel was cadets. It became clear, then, that the threat posed by women is not posed simply by their presence but by their equality. "Somehow when integration supports men's super-ordinate status there is no objection," notes Cynthia Fuchs Epstein, who was also asked to be an expert in the last phases of the Citadel trial. "Men cheerfully permit women into their workplaces when they are secretaries to their manager roles, nurses to their doctor roles" (Epstein 1997a: 206).

Even in their physical absence as cadets, women were rhetorically and symbolically omnipresent in the minds of the male cadets. Rats and knobs were constantly referred to with slang terms for women in general and women's genitals in particular. In fact, the absence of real women ensured the men that they had a constant symbolic other against which they were measuring themselves. "At least women couldn't do what I'm doing, I must be a man," they might be able to say to themselves. Women's exclusion seemed to be necessary for men to feel confident about their masculinity.

And saving the males did not mean all males. Assertions of categorical difference between women and men almost invariably accompany efforts to minimize the differences among men and among women. Any meditation about masculinity at VMI must bear in mind that of the variety of masculinities available to men, only the hegemonic version was to be reproduced. About one-fifth of all rats and knobs drop out during the first three weeks of their first year, and their names are not to be spoken again. Both schools vigorously deny that there are any gay men there, although Susan Faludi's article "The Naked Citadel" (1994) and one of my former students, a former Southern belle who said she "covered" for several gay cadets at various proms, testify otherwise. At the Citadel, I noticed a pamphlet on the coffee table in the counselor's office: "So You Think You Might Be Gay," it read. The counselor assured me that this was not for cadets but for graduate students. However, there is a counseling group for guys who feel they are not living up to the requisite standards of masculinity and feel they are too wimpy and feminine. It is called the "it group." Perhaps some males are not to be saved.

Thus, while VMI and the Citadel appear on the surface to be about men's natural superiority over women, they are, underneath, about precisely its opposite—the fragility of that hierarchy, the vulnerability to pollution and dilution, and the terror of emasculation that would be attendant on equality of opportunity.

Learning from West Point

If the experiences at the U.S. military academies are any indication, they need not have been so concerned. Over the past three years, two graduate students and I have been investigating these issues with different cohorts of cadets at the U.S. Military Academy (West Point), which first admitted women in 1976 under congressional mandate, and Norwich University, a private military college that voluntarily began to admit women in 1974. We have conducted interviews with virtually all the women in the first cohorts and a sample of women from a cohort from the late 1980s and the current cohort. This research tells us a lot, I think, about what women's experiences will be like at VMI and the Citadel.

For one thing, we found that the women and men did not differ significantly in their motivations for going to these military schools. Women said they wanted to place themselves "under stressful conditions, overcome obstacles, and succeed" (WP cohort I, interview 2).[3] Current female cadets summarized their cohort's motivations as follows: "I wanted to be in a place where I could live to the extreme," a West Point student said (WP II-6). "I like running around in the mud and doing that sort of stuff," a Norwich sophomore added (N III-8). "I wanted discipline and I wanted a military lifestyle," one twenty-two-year-old engineering major at West Point commented (cited in Schmitt 1997: 26).

But the experiences of the women and men diverged sharply once they arrived. Reliance on ideas of natural, biologically based sex differences placed women entering military education with the same dilemma as the women who have successfully entered every field of endeavor that was a traditional homosocial preserve of men—from the business world to medicine to law to the university: Women who seek military education cannot be real women. Military service is seen as gender-conforming for men and gender-nonconforming for women. In a sense, the phrase "woman cadet" was an oxymoron—one could not be both a woman and a cadet at the same time. Thus, women were trapped in a paradox: To the extent that they are successful cadets, women cannot be successful women; to the extent that they are successful women, they cannot be successful cadets. Either women are unsuccessful cadets or unsuccessful women; they cannot be both, and either way they lose.

Stereotypic assumptions about women were prevalent in the first years of coeducation at West Point. Like all tokens in institutions, they felt invisible as individuals yet hypervisible as members of their group. And they felt isolated from the others in their situation. "Obviously you stood out like a sore thumb," one female cadet from the first class at West Point commented. "You got longer hair and you got boobs. You're gonna stick out" (WP I-1). Another commented that "one minute we were supposed to do bayonet training. . . . You're screaming and yelling and you're in camouflage. And then the next half hour you're cleaned up. . . . But what's the real woman, what's the real girl?" (WP I-4).

And, of course, the military academies were concerned about the pollution of the homosocially pristine atmosphere, the dilution of the experience. Air Force Academy Superintendent Lt. Gen. Albert P. Clark argued that the environment of the Air Force Academy

> is designed around these stark realities [of combat]. The cadet's day is filled with constant pressure. His life is filled with competition, combative and contact sports, rugged field training, use of weapons, flying and parachuting, strict discipline and demands to perform to the limit of endurance mentally, physically, and emotionally. It is this type of training that brings victory in battle. It is my considered judgment that the introduction of female cadets will inevitably erode this vital atmosphere. (cited in Holm 1982: 307)

Army secretary Howard Callaway agreed. "Admitting women to West Point will irrevocably change the Academy. The Spartan atmosphere—which is so important to producing the final product [combat leaders]—would surely be diluted" (cited in Holm 1982: 308).

As tokens in a gendered institution, women cadets were constantly negotiating sameness and difference with each other, with male cadets, with faculty and staff, and with themselves. When they stressed sameness, they were seen as different; when they stressed difference, they were treated the same. Since so much was at stake, and both so fragile and fluid and so constantly scrutinized, the women were constantly "doing gender," negotiating publicly the meanings of femininity. What is typically left for backstage preparations had taken a very visible center stage.

We observed four gender strategies, ways of doing gender, adopted by the first cohorts of women at West Point and Norwich. One strategy, which we call emphatic sameness, involved downplaying gender identity as women in favor of being seen as cadets. To the extent that they were not seen as women, they could be seen as successful cadets. As one West Point graduate told us, "Once I was accepted as 'not one of those women' then I was O.K." (WP I-4). Emphatic sameness requires downplaying solidarity. They rarely appeared in public in groups of more than two, a strategy which seems to have developed in response to comments made by faculty, students, and administrators. "Literally, my class, we stayed away from other women"; one graduate said. "You didn't want to have more than two women together at one time, then somebody would make a comment" (WP I-1). "A group of women together was always seen as a cabal," one of West Point's first female cadets wrote (Barkalow 1990: 138). When some of the female cadets tried to initiate group lunches, the men would make derisive comments, as did one male instructor who said, "So what's going on? You plotting the revolution?" as he walked by.

A second gender strategy, strategic overcompensation, was developed because more than three-fourths of the women we interviewed believed that they had to work twice as hard to remain equal to the men. "You're put in a fishbowl here 'cause there's so few women in comparison to guys," one woman commented. "I think that maybe you do have to be a little bit tougher just because you are in the minority" (WP II-4).

Third, since formal networking was suspect and the first cohorts did not have upper-class women as mentors and role models, the first cohorts developed informal networks of support. "We really needed contact with women officers. We needed their experience, their advice, and their example," one cadet said. "We needed to be able to talk to them without suspicion or fear. We needed their empathy and their concern. We needed to be brought up the way men at the Academy had been brought up by their own for almost 200 years" (Barkalow 1990: 96). One woman made friends with the wife of one of the officers.

Finally, the first cohort of women cadets negotiated their contradictory experiences of femininity through strategic deployment of gendered display. Often, they asserted traditional femininity in social situations while they downplayed it in professional situations. Such minimizing and maximizing of gender difference, depending on the situation, is probably only an exaggerated version of what women do in virtually all public domains in which their participation is gender-nonconforming, from the legal and medical professions to institutions of higher learning and Wall Street investment houses.

Unfortunately, the military response was not nearly as subtle and differentiated as was the women's (see Greene and Wilson 1981). Concerned that military training would masculinize its women cadets, the institution responded initially by exacerbating the problem. The United States Military Academy

(USMA; i.e., West Point) offered its first women a class in how to apply and wear makeup (WP I-4). They produced a press release in 1979 to reassure the public that their cadets had not become masculinized. Its first two sentences read, "Female cadets here adopt traditional masculine personality traits to be accepted as leaders. They also want both marriage and a full-time military career" (cited in Rogan 1981: 201).

Institutional factors play a considerable role in the successful integration of women. Since tokenism is, in part, a function of proportions, not entirely of intention, the numbers of entering women will have a significant impact on their experiences. There were 81 women in the first coed class at the Naval Academy, 119 at West Point, and 157 at the Air Force Academy. The Citadel voluntarily admitted 6 women for its first coeducational entering class—1 percent of the entire class of 600 cadets. Without a critical mass of women, tokenism was far more pervasive and the women were somewhat less than fully welcomed. Two dropped out and sued the school for hazing violations. Less easily measured but equally important are the institutional measures, such as diversity training and a clear and enforced zero-tolerance policy on harassment, policies that might have ensured women's successful integration.

Much of the women's strategic maneuvering to reconcile being women and cadets was rhetorical. In the tortured, twisted, and often incoherent narratives offered by both first-cohort graduates and contemporary students, one hears most clearly and poignantly these efforts. One woman said, for example,

> I mean there's always going to be differences because there's differences between men and women. I hope I'm different from the guys. You know, I still like to be a woman, as well as a cadet. Especially outside. At the same time, you know, when I'm at school I don't want to get treated any different because I'm still a professional. I do the same things, so I don't want to get treated any different in that way. (WP II-3)

Equality, Sameness, and Difference

So, does equality mean sameness? Does equal treatment mean the same treatment? Many of the women who entered VMI and the Citadel think so. "If I thought VMI was going to change the fundamental things, I wouldn't have come here," an eighteen-year-old woman "rat" said. "I wanted the same experience that other Rats have gotten. I certainly didn't want a watered-down Ratline" (cited in Abrams 1998: B7).

On the other hand, in a gendered institution, does not treating differently situated individuals the same constitute another form of discrimination? In the Citadel case, the District Court judge held a special court session to determine whether the Citadel should be allowed to shave Shannon Faulkner's head the same way as they shave other knobs. Josiah Bunting III argued that it "would be demeaning to women to cut them slack" (Levit 1998: 95). On the other hand, I offered sociological testimony that to shave her head would be an additional form of discrimination. I suggested that, as Charles Moskos writes, "unisex standards are just a covert way to get women out" (Levit 1998: 95). I argued that "Shannon would become not only the cadet who doesn't look like a cadet but also, then, a woman who doesn't look like a woman." (The judge did not buy it and he ordered that the Citadel could shave her head. The school, however, decided that West Point's model of short hair would be acceptable.)

Let me give you one final example of how the failure to acknowledge difference—treating unalikes alike—is also a form of discrimination. One of the more ironic moments in sports history concerns a little girl who was a catcher on her central Florida Little League team. The league officials would not let her play because she did not wear a protective cup and the league rules, ungendered as they are, require, and I quote, that "all catchers must wear a protective cup." So, since she did not wear one, she could not play. She went to court. She lost. (So she wore it on her knee.) As one of the first cohorts of women at West Point said to my researchers, "They don't seem to understand that equality does not mean we all have to be the same" (WP I-6).

Are Single-Sex Schools Better for Women?

Another sociological question prompted by the VMI legislation concerns single-sex schools in general. Can separate be not only equal but better? VMI claimed, after all, that research had demonstrated that single-sex schools were better for both women and men. The district court agreed, holding that "substantial educational benefits flow from a single-gender environment, be it male or female, that cannot be replicated in a coeducational setting" (*VMI I* 766 F. Supp. 1407, 1426 [W. D. Va. 1991] vacated 976 F 2d. 890 [4th Cir 1992]). As they put it, "if VMI goes, there goes Wellesley." While that argument may be disingenuous and self-serving, it does highlight what appeared to be a case of feminist hypocrisy. The same year, 1990, that the United States first brought its case against VMI, the board of trustees at Mills College, a small, private, all-women, liberal arts college in Oakland, California, voted to admit men, in part to ensure the school's financial survival. And in 1994, as VMI and the Citadel were in their remedial phase, the regents at Texas Women's University (TWU) decided to admit men. Similar to the men at VMI, the women students were outraged and alumnae threatened to withdraw their support. Their protests made front-page news. Students were photographed weeping over the decision to become a coeducational school. Women at TWU carried signs that read "Better Dead Than Coed" and "Raped by the Regents." "We're not anti-man," one TWU student told a reporter. "We're for preserving this university's 91 years of tradition." (Sound familiar?) Feminist women cheered when the Mills trustees reversed themselves and decided to keep the school all-female.

And yet, did not those same women cheer when VMI was forced to admit women? At Mills, feminist women supported single-sex education; at VMI and the Citadel, feminists opposed it. Is what is good for the goose not good for the gander? Can feminists have it both ways? Or is there a difference between single-sex schools for women and single-sex schools for men?

Some earlier research found that single-sex colleges still held significant benefits for women. A study by Elizabeth Tidball in 1973 looked at the educational backgrounds of women listed in *Who's Who of American Women* and concluded that women's colleges with large numbers of women faculty provided the most beneficial environment for educating women (Tidball 1973). Subsequent research by Tidball and her associates found similar results in studies of women in medical schools and law schools and of women who earned doctorates in the natural sciences (see Tidball 1980).

Although it was true that most of the women listed in those volumes from the 1960s and before had gone to Vassar, Radcliffe, Bryn Mawr, Smith, and the other Seven Sisters colleges, Tidball's study had several serious flaws. Her data came from the 1960s, before any formerly all-male Ivy League and other prestigious all-male schools were opened to women, and the actual number of women in the study was so small as to defy efforts at generalization. Second, there were far more women's colleges at the time—nearly 300 in 1960 compared with just 84 in 1990. Third, women's colleges tended to be much smaller—and therefore more intellectually challenging and emotionally supportive—than were the coeducational schools. (Can one really compare educational outcomes of Vassar or Bryn Mawr with University of Minnesota or Michigan without controlling for size?) Finally, many of the women listed in *Who's Who* were there because of the accomplishments of their fathers or their husbands. They were not accomplished in their own right but only in their connection to a man, which could not have been the result of attending an all-women's college. (For example, until the 1980s, most women who were in the U.S. Senate, House of Representatives, or were governors of states were the daughters or widows of men who had held those offices [see Epstein 1991].)

Perhaps the most glaring error in Tidball's research was that she assumed that it was attendance at the single-sex college that led to wealth and fame. However, most of the women who attended such prestigious colleges were already wealthy and many had gone to single-sex boarding schools (or at least private preparatory schools). As one critic put it, these were women who "came from privileged backgrounds, had tremendous resources, and . . . were going to succeed no matter where they went. Yet these studies did not control for socioeconomic status" (Willinger 1994: 253). What Tidball had perhaps inadvertently measured was not the effect of single-sex schools on women's achievement but the correlation between social class and attendance at all-female colleges. Here was a reported gender difference that turned out not to be a gender difference at all. In fact, class turns out to be the better predictor of women's achievement than whether their college was single-sex or coeducational. Subsequent research found that coeducational colleges produced a higher percentage of women earning bachelor's degrees in the sciences, engineering, and mathematics (see Crosby et al. 1994; see also Epstein 1997a; 1997b). Ultimately, as two educational researchers summarized it, there is "little to indicate that attending a women's college has more than a trivial net influence on women's post-college educational, occupational, and economic attainments" (Stoecker and Pascarella 1991: 403).

There also has been some evidence that men's achievement was improved by attending a single-sex college. Again, many of these supposed gains in achievement vanished when social class and boys' secondary school experiences were added to the equation. In fact, when one discusses gender equality, the outcome of attending an all-male college, according to sociologist David Riesman, were "usually unfortunate. Stag undergraduate institutions are prone to a kind of excess" (Jencks and Riesman 1977: 298). Another study found that graduates of boys' schools were less likely to show concerns for social justice (Lee and Marks 1990: 585). While Jencks and Riesman "do not find the arguments against women's colleges as persuasive as the arguments against men's colleges," they conclude,

> The all-male college would be relatively easy to defend if it emerged from a world in which women were established as fully equal to men. But it does not. It is therefore likely to be a witting or unwitting device for preserving tacit assumptions of male superiority—assumptions for which women must eventually pay. So, indeed, must men . . . [who] pay a price for arrogance vis-à-vis women. Since they almost always commit a part of their lives into a woman's hands anyway, their tendency to crush these women means crushing a part of themselves. This may not hurt them as much as it hurts the woman involved, but it does cost something. Thus, while we are not against segregation of the sexes under all circumstances, we are against it when it helps preserve sexual arrogance. (Jencks and Riesman 1977: 298, 300).[4]

In short, what women may learn at all-women's colleges is that they can do anything that men can do. By contrast, what men learn is that they (women) cannot do what they (the men) do. In this way, women's colleges may constitute a challenge to gender inequality, whereas men's colleges reproduce that inequality.

Consider an analogy with race. One might justify the continued existence of historically all-Black colleges on the grounds that such schools challenge racist ideas that Black students could not achieve academically and provide a place

where Black students were free of everyday racism and thus free to become serious students. But one would have a more difficult time justifying maintaining
an all-white college, which would, by its existence, reproduce racist inequality.
Such a place would be more like "David Duke University" than Duke University.
Returning to gender, as psychologist Carol Tavris (1992: 127) concludes, "there is
a legitimate place for all-women's schools if they give young women a stronger
shot at achieving self-confidence, intellectual security, and professional competence in the workplace." On the other hand, since coeducation is based "on the
premise that there are few genuine differences between men and women, and
that people should be educated as individuals, rather than as members of a
gender," the question is "not whether to become coeducational, but rather
when and how to undertake the process" (Tavris 1992: 127; see also Priest,
Vitters, and Prince 1978: 590).

Single-sex education for men often perpetuates detrimental attitudes and
stereotypes about women, producing, as one expert put it, "men who feel that
they are superior to women" (Epstein 1997a: 101). At the same time, single-sex
schools for women may reinforce the idea that "by nature or situation girls and
young women cannot become successful or learn well in coeducational institutions" (Epstein 1998: 191). Even when supported by feminist women, the idea
that women cannot compete equally with men in the same arena, that they
need special treatment, signals an abandonment of hope, the inability or
unwillingness to make the creation of equal and safe schools a national priority.
"Since we cannot do that," we seem to be telling girls, "we'll do the next best
thing—separate you from those nasty boys who will only make your lives a living
hell." Law professor Nancy Levit (1999: 525) considers this "acceptance of boys'
behaviors of domination" one of the most disturbing consequences of the campaigns for single-sex education. "The single-sex remedy harkens back to a pro-
tectionist model of putting girls in a safe place, away from the male terrors,"
writes Levit. "Separation flatly ignores the problem of how males and females
are going to learn how to behave among one another."

Such proposals also seem to be based on faulty understandings of the differences between women and men, the belief in an unbridgeable chasm
between "them" and "us" based on different styles of learning; qualities of mind;
structures of brains; and ways of knowing, talking, or caring. John Dewey,
perhaps America's greatest theorist of education and a fierce supporter of
women's equal rights, was infuriated at the contempt for women suggested by
such programs. Dewey scoffed at "'female botany,' 'female algebra,' and for all
I know a 'female multiplication table,'" he wrote in 1911. "Upon no subject has
there been so much dogmatic assertion based on so little scientific evidence, as
upon male and female types of mind." Coeducation, Dewey argued, was beneficial to women, opening up opportunities previously unattainable. And, what's
more, coeducation is beneficial to men. "Boys learn gentleness, unselfishness,

courtesy; their natural vigor finds helpful channels of expression instead of wasting itself in lawless boisterousness," he wrote (Dewey 1911: 60).

Indeed, the historical evidence from West Point and Norwich suggests the benefits for both women and men and illustrates the sociological axiom that opportunity creates demand. At West Point, predicted drops in applications from men did not occur. In fact, when women were admitted to Norwich, for example, applications from men went up, as did alumni support.

After shaky starts, there were 23 women among the 384 cadets who entered their first year at VMI in 1998; 20 women attend the Citadel. After undergoing the grueling training of the rat line, both male and female cadets were surprised that the standards were not lowered and the treatment of the women and men was the same. "I'll be the first to admit I was not supportive of women coming to VMI," one male cadet commented.

> I felt that I would be getting a different VMI than the alumni had gotten before me. I didn't want that. It wasn't until October that I realized that it hadn't changed. VMI is about the honor code . . . the alumni network . . . the [mentoring] system, the big brother. It's about respecting those who have gone before you. If anyone tells you that VMI itself has changed, then they don't know what VMI is all about. (cited in Henry 1998: 8D)

A young, female cadet at the Citadel asked for no special treatment and got none. "You have to realize, for five or six people to crowd really close to your face, screaming, yelling, spraying spit all over you, calling you stupid, calling you a moron—that's normal," she said. "That's the harshness of the system here. But it's just the system." Sixty-four women applied to join the class that entered in fall 1999, a 3 percent increase over the previous year; the fall 2000 class saw about 5 percent more than that. There also has been an increase each year in applications from men (Gorman 1998: 90).

Conclusion

Once again, coeducation has disproved the stereotypes about women's inability to perform as well as men and also has disproved the stereotypes about a man's unwillingness or inability to perform adequately with a woman next to him. These twin successes raise the final comments I would like to make.

Women have succeeded in every single institution from which they had been historically excluded. Despite the dire predictions about what would happen to the women, to the men, and to the institutions themselves, women have proved that they can do it and that they want to do it for roughly the same reasons as the men. As I testified in the VMI case, I can think of no institutions where, after entering, women have said, "You know what? They were right all along. This isn't for us. Let's go home."

What this suggests, of course, is that gender identity is often not a good predictor of a person's motivation or talents. The gender of institutions does more to shape the behaviors of the people in them than the gendered identities of individuals who populate them. At VMI, as at West Point, both women and men "do" masculinity and appear to do it pretty equally well. Similarly, as the research on single fathers by Barbara Risman pointed out, in domestic life, single mothers and single fathers "do" mothering equally well (see Risman 1999).

That institutions are as gendered as the individuals who inhabit them leads to certain binds for tokens, for gender nonconformists. The dilemma in which women found themselves at West Point—that they cannot be both successful women and successful cadets at the same time—means that at the practical level, institutional mechanisms have to be developed to enable them to negotiate this paradox. At VMI—but not at the Citadel—the first cohorts of women cadets actually did not have to go it alone; the school had invited several upper-class women cadets from Norwich as exchange students for a semester or a year to act as role models and mentors to the first-year rats. The institution responded to the isolation and stereotypic assumptions that would accompany any token with an institutional arrangement that did not even upset their equation of equality and sameness.

But more, this equation also must be questioned, as we would, typically, from a sociological perspective. What a sociological perspective suggests, I think, is that the equality = sameness and difference = inequality dynamic is ill equipped to fully embrace the social dynamics of race, class, or gender.

Assertions of categorical sex difference create the possibilities that those putative differences can be used to justify discrimination against women. Because they exaggerate mean differences between the genders, they efface or obscure the far greater—and far more interesting—differences among women and among men. If VMI taught me anything, it is the dangers and potential disaster that may await proponents of difference feminism.

On the other hand, a liberal, egalitarian feminism, one that is based on the different abilities of individuals regardless of gender, also may be misguided. The notion that any individual can accomplish what he or she wants to, and ought not be handicapped by gender stereotypes, while true enough, also ignores the way in which these actors act in gendered institutions. In a sense, the gender of the institution is effaced, normalized. At VMI and the Citadel, it was assumed that the adversative method was a time-honored tradition that was effective and meritorious. As a result, the only question was whether women could be as violent as men, whether they could take the pressure without breaking down. The question of educational methodology, the question of the gendered institution, could not be raised. "There is almost something chemical about this place in its attraction for a certain kind of kid," Superintendent Josiah Bunting III explained about VMI. "They want to test themselves in ways that elude conventional measurements. They want to be tested, in short, to see if they measure up to being a 'real' man or woman" (cited in Abrams 1998: B7). When the task force, chaired by the dean of Mary Baldwin College, where VWIL was to be housed, claimed that "a military model and, especially VMI's adversative method, would be wholly inappropriate for educating and training most women for leadership roles," it was impossible to offer testimony that such an educational methodology also was inappropriate for most men (*U.S. v. Virginia* 852 F. Supp. 471,476 W.D. Va. [1994]). In such a construction, the institution's ability to provide such a test is unchallenged and unquestioned, although no educator of any stature would recommend the adversative method for men, let alone for women.

Perhaps there is one more lesson to be taken from the research on West Point and Norwich, where male and female cadets seem to have stumbled, inadvertently, on a cooperative strategy to accommodate gender difference within a context of the most rigidly hierarchical lines of authority and the absolute equality of all within the same rank. They are becoming family. "It's cooling here now," one current, female, West Point cadet observed. "There were real passions, but now we're like brothers and sisters. You can feel good about somebody and have it be friends" (WP III-9).

In our interviews, female cadets used family as a metaphor to describe what was good about their relations with male cadets. "The guys seem to look at the women as their little sisters," one current Norwich female cadet commented (N III-5). And it appears that some of the men, at least, agree. "It's almost like being brothers and sisters," a male cadet added.

At the Citadel, the family has become more than just a metaphor for the way differences can be accommodated within a hierarchy that also stresses equality. Mike Mentalvos, one of the Citadel's most decorated cadets, resigned from the school when his younger sister, Jenny, resigned after being sexually harassed in November 1997. The school's superintendent, appointed to steady an institution listing from so much adverse publicity, was Major General J. Emery Mace, the father of Nancy Mace, one of the first two women to graduate.

The family as political metaphor, of course, has a long history. For centuries, it provided the analogy for patriarchal political rule, theocratic domination, and misogynist familial life. But that family was always defined as the relations between father and "others," either wives or children. (At best, the more democratic family proposed relatively equal parents and their children.) As the father ruled the family, so too did the king. But the family also contains an alternative reading. Even within the structure of authority and hierarchy that is the relationship between parents and children, there is also the relationship among siblings, between brothers and sisters, each valued for his or her individuality, distinctiveness, difference, and yet each an irreplaceable part of the family, equally valued and equally loved (Imperfect taboos to the side, brothers do not typically torture, rape, and harass their own sisters, and parents do not abuse their authority by permitting one child to lord it over the others.)

On many campuses, this is the model promised but not delivered by fraternities and sororities, a model of familial equality among brothers and sisters that allows for the expression of individual differences among members of the group. And though the expression of those individual differences neither pollutes nor dilutes the purity of the stream from which familial sentiments spring, those sentiments are still based on fundamental, categorical, and often stereotypic assertions of difference between the members of the group and the rest of the school.

Consider, finally, an analogy from the field of metallurgy. If you want to make a metal stronger, you do not add more of the same metal. You add a different metal. You make an alloy. Alloys are stronger and more resilient than either metal could be on its own. So too, at VMI and the Citadel, in every arena from which women have historically been excluded. Integrating and embracing difference makes the institution stronger, more resilient. In a context of equality, the assumed differences between women and men will be revealed as stereotypes that help neither women nor men nor the institutions in which we find ourselves. We are neither Martians nor Venutians but Earthlings.

Today, I believe we are finding that only in the context of equality can the real differences—the vast array of different talents and interests among women and among men—finally flourish. It is a struggle to be taken together, by both women and men. The great British philosopher John Stuart Mill wrote that women will never achieve equality until some men "within the citadel of privilege" ([1869] 1997: 31) joined them in the struggle. This is equally true today: Gender equality is the only possible route, it seems to me, to "save the males."

NOTES

This article began its written career as the "Feminist Lecture" of Sociologists for Women in Society, 1999, before being published in *Gender & Society*. Several people helped me think about the issues discussed here, including Amy Aronson, Cynthia Fuchs Epstein, Susan Faludi, Nancy Levit, Lillian Rubin, and Val Vojdik. My collaborators on the research on women at West Point, Diane Diamond and Kirby Schroeder, also have provided helpful advice. I thank Christine Bose for helping me to shape the manuscript for publication. This article is dedicated to Michael Maurer and the pleasures of mutual mentorship.

   1. There is still considerable disagreement about this in the courts. Some cases have used the "reasonable woman" standard, most notably *Steiner v. Showboat Operating Co.* (25 F 3d 1459, 9th Cir. [1994]), *Burns v. McGregor Elec. Indus., Inc.* (989 F 2d 959,9 65, 8th Cir. [1993]), *Andrews v. City of Philadelphia* (895 F 2d. 1469, 1486 3d Cir. [1990]), and *Yates v. Avco Corp.* (819 F 2d 630, 6th Cir. [1987]). Other decisions upheld the "reasonable person" standard, including *DeAngelis v. El Paso Mun. Police Officers Association* (51 F 3d 591, 5th Cir. [1995]), *Bacon v. Art Institute of Chicago* (6 F Supp. 2d 762, 766, N.D. Ill [1998]), *Broom v. Regal Tube Co.* (881 F2d 412, 418, 7th Cir. [1989]), and *Radke v. Everett* (501 N.W. 2d 155, 166, Mich. [1993]). I am grateful to Nancy Levit for providing these cases.

2. See Alfred Kinsey et al., *Sexual Behavior in the Human Male* (Philadelphia: W. B. Saunders, 1948). As someone who began his college career at an all-male college and later transferred to a formerly all-female college that began to admit men, I could readily testify that men at the single-sex school were far more distracted by the absence of women than were the men at the coeducational school by their presence! With no women around, most of the young men could not stop thinking about them!

3. Interviews with cadets at West Point (WP) and Norwich (N) are identified by cohort and interview number. Cohorts included 1976–1978 (I), 1984–1986 (II), and current cadets (III).

4. Despite his own findings (see Riesman 1991), Riesman supported the continuation of VMI's single-sex policy.

REFERENCES

Abrams, A. 1998. "Changed, Yes, Different, No." *Newsday*, May 11, B7.

Barkalow, C. 1990. *In the Men's House: An Inside Account of Life in the Army by One of West Point's First Female Graduates.* New York: Poseidon.

Clarke, E. C. 1873. *Sex in Education; or; a Fair Chance for the Girls.* Boston: James Osgood.

Conroy, P. 1986. *The Lords of Discipline.* New York: Bantam.

Crosby, F., et al. 1994. "Taking Selectivity into Account: How Much Does Gender Composition Matter? A Reanalysis of M. E. Tidball's Research." *National Women's Studies Association Journal* 16(1): 107–118.

Dewey, J. 1911. "Is Coeducation Injurious to Girls?" *Ladies' Home Journal*, June 11.

Epstein, C. F, 1991. *Deceptive Distinctions.* New Haven: Yale University Press.

———. 1997a. "The Myths and Justifications of Sex Segregation in Higher Education: VMI and the Citadel." *Duke Journal of Gender Law and Policy* 4:185–210.

———. 1997b. "Multiple Realities of Sameness and Difference: Ideology and Practice." *Journal of Social Issues* 53 (2): 259–277.

———. 1998. "Multiple Myths and Outcomes of Sex Segregation." *New York Law School Journal of Human Rights* 14:101–118.

Faludi, S. 1994. "The Naked Citadel." *The New Yorker*, September 5.

G. I. Jane. 1997. Directed by Ridley Scott. 124 min. Lakewood, CA: Buena Vista Home Video. [Videocassette].

Gorman, M. O. 1998. "Front and Center." *Runner's World*, March.

Greene, B., and K. L. Wilson. 1981. "Exploring the New Integration of Women into the Military." *Journal of Political and Military Sociology* 9 (3): 241–254.

Hall, G. S. 1904. *Adolescence: Its Psychology and Its Relation to Physiology, Anthropology, Sociology, Sex, Crime, Religion, and Education.* New York: Appleton.

Henry, T. 1998. "VMI Cadets of Both Sexes Found 'Rat Line' Equal." *USA Today*, March 18.

Holm, J. 1982. *Women in the Military.* Novato, CA: Presidio.

Jencks, C., and D. Riesman. 1977. *The Academic Revolution.* Cambridge, MA: Harvard University Press.

Lee, V., and H. Marks. 1990. "Sustained Effects of the Single-Sex Secondary School Experience in Attitudes, Behaviors, and Values in College." *Journal of Educational Psychology* 82(3): 578–592.

Levit, N. 1998. *The Gender Line.* New York: New York University Press.

———. 1999. "Separating Equals: Educational Research and the Long-Term Consequences of Sex Segregation." *George Washington Law Review* 67 (3): 451–526.

Manegold, C. 2000. *In Glory's Shadow: Shannon Faulkner, the Citadel, and a Changing America.* New York: Alfred Knopf.

Messner, M. 1998. *Politics of Masculinities.* Thousand Oaks, CA: Sage.

Mill, J. S. [1869] 1997. *The Subjugation of Women.* New York: Dover.

Priest, R., A. Vitters, and H. Prince. 1978. "Coeducation at West Point." *Armed Forces and Society* 4 (4): 205–24.

Riesman, D. 1991. "A Margin of Difference: The Case for Single-Sex Education." In *Social Roles and Social Institutions: Essays in Honor of Rose Laub Coser,* ed. J. R. Blau and N. Goodman. Boulder, CO: Westview.

Risman, B. 1999. *Gender Vertigo.* New Haven: Yale University Press.

Rogan, H. 1981. *Mixed Company.* New York: Putnam.

Schmitt, E. 1997. "A Mean Season at Military Colleges." *New York Times,* Higher Education Supplement, April 6.

Stoecker, J., and E. Pascarella. 1991. "Women's Colleges and Women's Career Attainments Revisited." *Journal of Higher Education* 62(4): 394–411.

Tavris, C. 1992. *The Mismeasure of Woman.* New York: Simon and Schuster.

Tidball, M. E. 1973. "Perspective on Academic Women and Affirmative Action." *Educational Record* 54(2): 130–135.

———. 1980. "Women's Colleges and Women Achievers Revisited." *Signs: Journal of Women in Culture and Society* 5(3): 504–517.

Vojdik, V. 1997. "Girls' Schools After VMI: Do They Make the Grade?" *Duke Journal of Gender Law and Policy* 4:69–100.

Willinger, B. 1994. "Single Gender Education and the Constitution." *Loyola Law Review* 40:147–162.

11

Janey Got Her Gun

A VMI Postscript

Meet Erin Claunch. A high school honor student and cross-country runner from Round Hill, Virginia, Claunch enrolled at Virginia Military Institute (VMI) in 1997 "to test my limits and see how far I can go." A physics major, Claunch is preparing for a commission with the air force upon graduation, and she aspires to become an astronaut. She ranks fifteenth in her class of 298 and easily surpassed the uniform gender-neutral physical fitness standards: Sixty sit-ups in two minutes, five pull-ups, and a one-mile run in less than twelve minutes. (She did eighty-four sit-ups, fifteen pull-ups, and ran the course in less than eleven minutes.)

Quite a leap from Shannon Faulkner, who took on VMI's brother institution, the Citadel, in 1993 and waged a protracted three-year court battle to be admitted to its Corps of Cadets, only to leave the school in tears after a week.

The Supreme Court's 7-to-1 decision against VMI [in 1996] opened to women the last two all-male state-supported colleges in America. The schools' cynical last-ditch efforts to preserve their single-sex status—pale-replica "leadership training" programs at nearby women's colleges—were not to be understood, the schools tried to convince the courts, as separate but equal, but rather as "distinct but superior." (Imagine if West Point had tried to avoid coeducation by proposing that a few Vassar students march around in uniform once a week.)

In the four years since those barracks doors were thrown open, women haven't exactly poured into the formerly all-male bastions of Southern chivalry and military manhood. Rather, it's been a slow trickle. Today the U.S. military is about 15 percent female. VMI claims to be 16 percent and the Citadel is a scant 4 percent. The enrollment and retention problem has been cause for serious consternation for VMI's superintendent, Josiah Bunting III, who fought fiercely

Originally published in *The Nation*, June 19, 2000.

against women's entry but is now determined to make their "assimilation" a resounding success. On the other hand, nothing could make the Citadel administrators happier than ensuring that the school remain utterly inhospitable to women, turning a blind, if winking, eye away from their continued hazing. The difference between these two very similar schools makes for a fascinating story.

VMI and the Citadel are not your typical educational institutions. For one thing, they are both purposefully anachronistic Southern schools, looking back reverently to the Lost Cause, and they resent any federal official dictating on a state's right to determine its own educational policies. Both trace their histories to before the Civil War—the Citadel was established in 1842, on the heels of Denmark Vesey's ill-fated slave uprising, to insure Charleston's wealthy slave traders against any further "disturbances." VMI, founded three years earlier in the town of Lexington, sent its cadets directly into battle in a minor skirmish in 1864. Stonewall Jackson, a relatively unpopular and taciturn instructor of natural philosophy for a few months at VMI, is today worshiped as its greatest hero; the central barracks are named for him, his statue stands proudly at its entrance (cadets salute him as they enter), and his relics, including his moth-eaten stuffed horse, Little Sorrel, occupy hallowed space in VMI's museum.

Both schools provide a disciplined military atmosphere, although fewer than one-third of graduating cadets pursue a military career. VMI and the Citadel are what the great sociologist Erving Goffman called "total institutions," in which academic study, residential life (the barracks), and military training are all integrated into a closed system in which cadets are immersed from the moment they set foot on campus. Both employ what they call an "adversative method," which deliberately induces emotional and psychological stress. For first-year students, known as "rats" at VMI and "knobs" at the Citadel, the process entails a mixture, Laura Fairchild Brodie writes, "of bonding and bondage." Each cadet is systematically stripped of individual identity, then slowly and deliberately rebuilt in the corporate mold. Heads are shaved (thus the nickname "knobs"); seemingly random and nonsensical orders are given, to be carried out unquestioningly; subordination to a training cadre of second-year students is relentless, merciless, and brutal. One VMI alum claimed that the system prepared him to be a POW, not a soldier. "You don't really graduate from VMI," one daughter and sister of VMI grads said. "You survive it." Think of Marine Corps boot camp run by unsupervised teenage boys. Think of that tree house with the sign that says NO GURLS ALLOWED. If combat unleashes the dogs of war, VMI and Citadel cadets are its puppies.

Clearly, these are not schools for everyone—though virtually everyone who wants to attend can. Acceptance rates at both schools hover around 80 percent, ranking them among the nation's least academically competitive schools— albeit with the most fiercely loyal alumni (VMI boasts the highest per capita endowment of any publicly supported college or university). The brutality of the adversative method implants a deeply felt bonding among the men; solidarity among cadets is intense, and graduates join what they lovingly call the world's largest fraternity.

Two books take us inside these bastions of Southern manhood. Catherine Manegold's *In Glory's Shadow* offers an impressionist history of the school and its historical and cultural context as a citadel of Southern honor and male privilege. As an outsider with extensive access to historical documents and interviews with key players, Manegold, who covered the Citadel story for the *New York Times*, sees the school's resistance to Shannon Faulkner's admission into the Corps of Cadets as a morality play in miniature, a defining moment in the transformation of America. She provides an intricately detailed portrait of sadistic machismo, twisted by decades of insularity and insolent adolescence—a portrait that ends with the cadets' shamefully triumphant celebration at Faulkner's withdrawal, followed by a brief coda in which the school snarls and snaps at the prospect that others will take her place.

In *Breaking Out*, Laura Fairchild Brodie, an adjunct professor at VMI and wife of the school's band leader, writes from the inside, chronicling, with excruciating attention to detail, the deliberations and preparations for women's entry that followed the Supreme Court decision. VMI fought, valiant and bitter to the end, but when the end came, so too did its resistance. The difference between insider and outsider among the authors, though, is of less significance than the chronology each author unfolds—and the differences between two schools that on the surface appear so similar.

That surface gleams in the Southern sun like so many perfectly polished brass belt buckles, according to Manegold. The Citadel's public face is all honor, glory, and integrity, an antebellum world where men and women are addressed as "Sir" and "Ma'am." "The success of the Citadel is no mystery," observed Bud Watts, the superintendent of the school during the litigation. "It results from the benefits of a well-rounded education which develops cadets academically, morally, spiritually, and physically; all within a framework of a demanding, strict, disciplined military environment. This experience builds character and self-confidence, instills integrity and honor."

The shadow Citadel is something else entirely. Readers may recall Citadel alum Pat Conroy's description in *The Lords of Discipline*, his fictional re-creation of cadet life:

> We did not receive a college education at the Institute, we received an indoctrination, and all our courses were designed to make us malleable, unimaginative, uninquisitive citizens of the republic, impregnable to ideas—or thought—unsanctioned by authority. . . . It demanded limitless conformity from its sons, and we concurred blindly. We spent our four years as passionate true believers, catechists of our harsh and spiritually

arctic milieu, studying, drilling, arguing in the barracks, cleaning our rooms, shining our shoes, writing on the latrine walls, writing papers, breaking down our rifles, and missing the point. The Institute was making us stupid; irretrievably, tragically, and infinitely stupid.

(Conroy was one of Faulkner's staunchest supporters, sponsoring rallies in her support and eventually paying her tuition at a private college after she fled Charleston.)

In glory's shadow lie unspeakable cruelties, meted out by cadets, unpoliced by the administration. "They say all this stuff about honor and discipline," commented one cadet. "But it's not honor. It's boys taking boys and tearing them apart."

This sanctimonious sadism evolved over the years. At first, the Citadel looked back in anger at the South's defeat and ignominious humbling during Reconstruction. And for the next century and a half, smoldering Southern resentment fused with untrammeled adolescent masculinity. What was once a three-month hazing ordeal for freshmen gradually spanned the entire first year. None were spared the relentless torture; "in the end, they all broke." By the early seventies, the culture of cruelty was out of control. Injuries to cadets were "not only common, but expected, especially broken wrists caused by attempts on the part of the freshmen to deflect the swats of upper-class-men," wrote one cadet in the school paper. And reformers invariably met defeat. Adm. James Stockdale, brought in to clean the school up in 1979, left in disgust after a year of frustrated reforms, saying the place reminded him of the North Vietnamese POW camp he had endured for eight years. At the Citadel, the inmates ran the asylum, and they nearly ran it into the ground.

By the time Faulkner applied, enrollments had dropped almost as far as morale. Here was a chance for the school to reinvent itself, to enter the twentieth century in its last decade. Instead, the Citadel and its supporters—students, administrators, alumni, Charleston loyalists—used every conceivable subterfuge to ensure that Faulkner would not succeed. "Save the Males" appeared on bumper stickers and banners all over the state—as if one woman threatened an entire gender. (Well, Napoleon did apparently comment that "he who is full of courage and sang-froid before an enemy battery sometimes trembles before a skirt.")

Faulkner's case riveted the nation's attention on this largely forgotten educational throwback to that antebellum fusion of Southern chivalry and viciousness. And, recounting those terrible weeks, Manegold's book reveals for the first time why Faulkner really left. That Faulkner was reviled, scorned, and harassed routinely, mocked with obscene T-shirts worn proudly all over the state, is well-known. And the way she was shunned and isolated is testament, albeit a twisted one, that the Citadel system works. "A lone wolf will find it impossible to survive within the Corps," is the way the student handbook puts it. "Your classmates are your only companions. . . . These classmates are your sole source of support and aid at this time. They will be your friends for life."

Not Shannon Faulkner's friends for life. Frozen out, she had nowhere to turn for the support the school claims is essential for survival. The school wanted her to fail.

Much worse, though, is what actually happened. A few days before she left home for the Citadel, Faulkner was in a grocery store in her hometown when she was grabbed from behind by a man whose face she never saw. "I can't touch you while you're on campus," he said to her. "But I can get to your parents. I know a place where I can watch them burn." On her first day on campus, she heard that voice again, coming from a group of men near the entrance to the barracks. It was at that point that she lost her lunch and spent the rest of the week in the infirmary, unable to hold anything down. It wasn't that she was overweight, out of shape, or a girl; Shannon Faulkner suffered from battle stress.

Many observers thought Faulkner a failure who had demanded entry only to discover that she couldn't make the grade. But her persistence over those three years of constant torment and threat, her steadfast resolve, and impish sense of humor, suggested more courage than any of the male cadets at the Citadel would ever be called on to show. It was Faulkner—not the Citadel cadets—who had the right stuff, the stuff that makes for the honorable "citizen soldier." She opened the door for other women, who have followed her into the Citadel, seeking its particular brand of physical and mental torture as a way to test their limits and to cement bonds of friendship and love born of mutual—and equal—victimization.

Manegold tells this story deftly, with an effective mix of perverse curiosity and growing disdain and horror. Her journalistic reportage is crisp and clear, but it's mixed with moments when Manegold exults in her freedom from journalistic constraints. Occasionally, she lays on the metaphors thick as molasses, her prose becoming overladen with competing scents, like "mildew and magnolias," and coincidences are accorded a portentous historical significance. And in the book's finale, she relies on a series of anonymous, uncorroborated e-mail messages from a current cadet she identifies only as "V."

Compared with this, *Breaking Out* reads more like a required textbook, as Brodie recounts every deliberation, discussion, and debate that preoccupied VMI after 1996, when it was forced to admit women. "If we're going to do it, we're going to do it well—extraordinarily well," Bunting promised. "We will have to effect a cultural change, an attitudinal change, many of us in ourselves: doubt, skepticism, cynicism, sorrow are not a fertile soil in which to plant the seeds of a new coeducational VMI."

Some of the difference between the two schools can be traced to their leadership. The Citadel grumbled toward coeducation with indifferent and ineffective leaders, while VMI engaged one of its most illustrious alums. A Rhodes scholar and highly decorated Vietnam soldier, Bunting sees himself as a military figure cast in a classical, somewhat flamboyant mold, who leads his troops into battle by day and reads Ovid in the original by candlelight in his tent. He'd also been president of a women's college (Briarcliffe) and a men's college (Hampden-Sydney), and presided as headmaster of the transition from all-boys to coed at a private school in Lawrenceville (New Jersey). Having testified for both VMI and the Citadel at trial—it was Bunting who claimed famously that women would be "a toxic kind of virus" that would destroy the mystical bonding among the men—he now seemed to do a complete about-face. If women are coming, he said, we want them to be as fully assimilated into the corps as possible.

"Assimilated," however, does not mean integrated. The corps was not going to change one jot for these women. If they wanted VMI, they were going to get it. No holds barred. In the VMI view of the world, equality means sameness.

To make this coeducational VMI succeed, Bunting had to bring everyone along, some willingly, others kicking and screaming. That included the school's fiercely loyal alumni, who seriously tried to raise more than $200 million to take the school private rather than admit women; faculty, who largely welcomed the change; cadets, who feared the watering down of their training and thus their reputation as men (the last all-male class called itself LCWB, or Last Class With Balls); and groundskeepers, laundry workers, and food staff, all of whom would have to accept the new regime.

Committees debated endlessly. Topics ranged from the most central to the most trivial. Physical training requirements remained unchanged, and women struggled to make their quota of five pull-ups (West Point, using gender-norming, only requires women to do a flex arm hang). The honor code remained untouched; academics actually improved with the addition of new majors in psychology and criminal justice; and, most important, the brutal daily routines of the "ratline" were not altered at all.

Bunting prepared the corps to see women as the beneficiaries, not the cause, of the new regime. The brass instituted strict policies on sexual harassment, fraternization, and hazing, and also brought in women cadets from Norwich and Texas A&M to serve as mentors to the female rats. (In my research, the first women cadets at West Point identified the absence of role models and mentors as one of the more serious problems they faced.)

At the other end of the spectrum were the seemingly trivial details. Should the women's uniforms have breast pockets like the men's? (Too much attention drawn to anatomy or too different from men's uniforms?) What kinds of swimsuits should the women wear during compulsory swimming classes? (The school proposed baggy black sacks with padded cups for the bras, because they didn't want anyone embarrassed when they got cold leaving the pool. They settled on a modest compromise somewhere between *Baywatch* and Coney Island circa 1910.)

What about their hair? Should the women cadets also get their heads shaved? To shave the women struck some as "malicious compliance"—a vindictive, punitive equality of the sexes that makes the men look bald and the women look like freaks. Cutting the men's hair takes away their individuality, but not their manhood; for women it takes away their femininity and exaggerates their individuality. On the other hand, if equality means sameness, then what's good for the gander is what the goose is going to get, like it or not. (At the Citadel, three of the first four female cadets followed Demi Moore's lead in *G.I. Jane* and shaved their own heads.)

But if heaven is in the details, so, too, is hell. Some officials, Brodie writes, "seemed to want to create an environment in which they could spare the cadets the embarrassing moments that come with having a body." The all-male committees seemed utterly preoccupied—and woefully misinformed—about menstruation, for example. Should female rats be given medical leave during their periods? Would the women need private showers? (At the Merchant Marine Academy, the school installed private showers when women came, and the women promptly tore down the stall separators.) What about tampon machines in the bathrooms? (After all, the men didn't have them.) Should they be free or coin-operated? Images of once-modest women with blood trickling down their legs in gang showers were simply too much to bear.

Much of Brodie's book provides an exhaustive and exhausting catalogue of the elaborate discussions over every unbearably mundane item of clothing, training regimen, and dorm life. I'm not sure casual readers will be as engrossed as I was with the minutes of meetings to discuss shower stalls, but I was fascinated and occasionally appalled at the thorough—and occasionally thoroughly silly—attention to detail. By the end of the book I had developed a grudging but genuine respect for the school and for Bunting's resolve to preserve its traditions and have women succeed there. And, Brodie argues, it paid off. After just a few weeks of ratline training, one upperclassman said he only "saw a rat. I didn't see male or female; their gender was just transformed into one single rat."

VMI's tale of successful assimilation provides ample evidence to rebut Stephanie Gutmann's shrill and strident antifeminist polemic, *The Kinder, Gentler Military*. Gutmann argues that the costs of gender integration have been far greater than the benefits. Though one wants to ask, "to whom?"

Gutmann rehearses the three classic arguments that have been deployed against women's entry into every single public-sphere institution throughout our history. First, she claims, women just can't do it. The average woman cannot perform adequately and effectively; gender integration means a double standard. (This tired and untrue canard is reminiscent of Harvard education professor Edward Clarke's warning in 1873 that women are not mentally capable of withstanding the rigors of college education and that if women went to college their brains would grow bigger and heavier and their wombs would shrink.) Second, Gutmann argues that the presence of women pollutes the homosocial purity of military life, diluting the experience for the men (before the Tailhook harassment scandal, one pilot mournfully recalls, naval aviation was "a real brotherhood"). This leads to a softening of discipline and "unit cohesion"—that deep, binding, pure, and non-erotic sacrificial love that the men feel toward one another. Gutmann expresses sympathy for the "shamefully unmilitary situation" of one benighted sergeant who now has to "mentor" young recruits "instead of the manly pursuit of bellowing at boys." As a result, today's military is one of America's most politically correct institutions—overrun by GI Janes who can't do enough push-ups and by rules that prevent the most egregious excesses (she actually provides a ringing, if tinny, defense of Tailhook as just boys being boys).

These are the standard victim-blaming complaints, and Gutmann repeats them thoughtlessly, before adding another: The presence of women makes it harder to get men to join up. How are they going to prove their manhood with women around doing the same thing? (That warfare itself has changed doesn't enter into the discussion.) Her investigations turn up a host of career sailors and soldiers who agree that military heroism is attainable only after one passes through a training regimen of brutality and torture, of deliberately stripping away dignity and full-throttle spit-in-the face screaming at the young recruit. Gutmann seems unable to find any military personnel who think gender integration is a good thing.

Gutmann is afraid that the new kinder, gentler military is also softer and weaker, that men have become "feminized" in their forced adherence to the new rules of decorum. She isn't nostalgic for that world of Southern honor; she mourns the demise of military machismo, that brutal do-or-die-ism of the fiercest fighting force ever assembled. Phyllis Schlafly once called the Justice Department's case against VMI a "no-holds-barred fight to feminize VMI waged by the radical feminists and their cohorts in the Federal Government."

Such fears, though, have it exactly backward. Virtually all the research on women in the military—and women in every public arena formerly closed to them—finds the real problem to be the perceived masculinization of the women. Femininity is always questioned when women enter a new public arena, whether the military, the college classroom, the factory, or the corporation. As the old adage puts it, men are unsexed by failure; women are unsexed by success. "This is VMI," one female cadet put it, "where the men are men and so are the women."s

Of course, it's a done deal anyway, and women are in the military—and police forces, fire departments, VMI, and the Citadel—to stay. Gutmann recounts a telling exchange. During the Tailhook hearings, Barbara Pope, the only woman on the Navy's investigation panel, began to mutter about old-boy networks, foot-dragging, and clubbiness, all of which hampered the investigation. "What you don't understand, Barbara," Rear Adm. Mac Williams admonished her, "is that men in the Navy don't want women in the Navy." "Mac, you don't get it," she replied. "Yes, some men don't want women in the Navy. Things were easier when women weren't there. But if men can't accept women and integrate women into the military, then they shouldn't be there."

And increasingly, they aren't. Women are there, and the men are getting used to it. Just as those male journalists had to get used to women like Gutmann and Manegold in their ranks—though men had earlier issued dire warnings that women didn't have the nose for hard journalism and that women wouldn't be able to get a story because of the sexual tension with sources (who were, presumably, only men).

During one of my site visits to the Citadel, I had this exchange with a military captain, a woman who was on the staff of the psychological counseling services. She was describing her activities in the Air Force Reserves as a loadmaster on cargo planes during Desert Storm. When she began, her fellow reservists (male) were exceedingly chivalrous, giving her a wide berth, making sure not to touch or bump into her, and also did not include her in informal activities. She felt like an outsider. This, of course, made her uncomfortable, because she wanted to fit in.

Eventually, she said, their attitudes changed. "What caused this change?" I asked. "The fact that I was there, doing my job," she answered. "Has this been good for you, to be free of such excesses of chivalry and to be treated as equally competent?" I asked. "Yes." "And do you think it's a good thing for the men to have changed in this way, to now be able to look at you as an equally competent member of their reserve team?" "Of course," she said. "And do you think that they could have made such a change without your presence there, without your having been accepted into the reserves and willing to stick it out?" I asked. "No," she said, somewhat flustered.

New players and new rules may, however, be just what is needed down at the ol' PX (where soldiers buy stuff). The reality is that cruel and inhumane punishment as masculine initiation—whether in the Marine Corps or at the schools where boys play soldier with no consequences—may have been functional for Braveheart, but even by Vietnam it was an anachronism, made palpably evident by the filmic evolutionary throwback John Rambo. The wars of the present and the future—whether in the Persian Gulf, Kosovo, or somewhere else—will have far different rules of engagement and far different criteria for heroism.

Since the Supreme Court decision, life hasn't been easy for women at either school.

The Citadel remains beset with problems. Two of the first four women cadets left the school after their complaints of sexual harassment—they'd been doused with lighter fluid and then had matches tossed at their shirts, for one thing—were met with another circling of the wagons. And just recently Petra Lovetinska, the school's top-ranking female cadet, was demoted. Apparently, there is a time-honored tradition that knobs are commanded by seniors to pour ketchup or salad dressing on the shoes of other seniors. (This, like most

"traditions" at the Citadel, is probably no more than twenty years old.)
Lovetinska didn't particularly enjoy having the salad dressing poured on her, so
she wiped her shoes on the cadet's trousers. She—not the knob or the senior
who put him up to it—was disciplined by the school. In other words, she was
demoted for resisting this utterly sophomoric prank.

At VMI, it's been equally unpleasant for both women and men, and roughly
equal percentages drop out of the ratline. VMI accepted its defeat—if not exactly
gracefully, at least with a certain amount of resigned integrity, neither bowing to
"watered down" double standards nor resorting to vicious informal subterfuge. If
the Citadel has remained unreconstructed, continuing to fight a rear-guard
action like that rogue Tennessean Nathan Bedford Forrest, the Confederate general (and former wealthy slaveowner) who is credited with founding the Ku Klux
Klan, VMI has taken a more noble course, like that noble son of Virginia, Robert
E. Lee, whose dignity in surrender provided a model of Southern honor for generations of young boys, North and South, to emulate.

And Erin Claunch? Well, just as Petra Lovetinska was being demoted at the
Citadel, Claunch was selected as one of two battalion commanders at VMI, the
second-highest military position at the school, leading half the Corps of Cadets.
Was she selected because she was a woman? Hardly. After outperforming most
of the men in the unchanged VMI physical fitness regimen, running cross-
country, and maintaining a 4.0 average, "it was just a matter of her being qualified for the job," commented one of the male cadets who was on the selection
board. Gender, insists Derek Bogdon, the cadet selected as the other battalion
commander, is no longer an issue at VMI. "They're our brother rats," he says.
"They went through the same thing that we did."

Citadel loyalists and their sycophantic feminine followers like Stephanie
Gutmann could learn a thing or two from Erin Claunch. Can women do it? Sir!
Yes Sir!

NOTE

This review essay appeared in *The Nation*, June 19, 2000, and covered three books
about the VMI and Citadel cases, and women in the military in general:

Breaking Out: VMI and the Coming of Women, by Laura Fairchild Brodie (New York:
    Pantheon, 2000).

*The Kinder, Gentler, Military: Can America's Gender-Neutral Fighting Force Still Win
    Wars?* by Stephanie Gutmann (New York: Scribner's, 2000).

In Glory's Shadow: Shannon Faulkner, the Citadel, and a Changing America, by
    Catherine Manegold (New York: Knopf, 2000).

PART FOUR

Resistance

Everywhere there are signs of change. Young men today assume that they will be equally involved parents with their wives and partners, that they will share parenting responsibilities and even, perhaps, increase their share of housework. In U.S. workplaces, some men are getting used to—and even enjoying—the equal presence of women. On campuses men are organizing around issues of gender equality, straight women and men are organizing gay-straight alliances, and U.S. youth are becoming increasingly accustomed to identities, practices, and ideas that might make their parents squirm.

That's not to be Pollyanna about this: the other side is still in full stride, aided and abetted, as I have argued throughout this book, by a well-organized and extremely well-financed media campaign to discredit gender equality as a calumny against men. Globally, many of those groups that have mobilized against the United States and Europe place resurgent gender inequality at their core. (Fundamentalisms of any faith rarely offer a good deal for women.)

I've suggested, in several of the essays in this book, that the real calumnies against men are offered by those who think we are nothing more than biologically propelled, testosterone-crazed, rapacious animals. Real men make choices, and an increased number of men are choosing to live in a more egalitarian world.

They don't tend to be especially ideological about it. Gender equality is both a movement and a set of practices, and it is in our homes, our families, our friendships, and our relationships that men are moving, slowly but inexorably, toward greater equality. We're doing it because it feels right to share responsibilities and rights. We're doing it because, well, someone has to do the dishes!

We're less likely to be groping toward equality because we know that greater gender equality is correlated with greater degrees of happiness—though that is true at both the national and the personal level. Honest: the higher the nation's ranking on the Gender Equality Index prepared annually by the World Economic Forum, the greater the amount of life satisfaction that citizens of that country enjoy (which is, true, also a function of level of economic development). Which is sort of the point: greater gender equality is associated with greater economic prosperity—again, both nationally and in our families. And we're not supporting gender equality because it is better for our children—although that is also true.

No, we're slowly feeling our way toward greater gender equality because we know ethically that it's right, because we feel better psychologically when all those we love feel equally valued and loved, and because we sense, however vaguely sometimes, that gender equality might just be the best thing that could ever happen to men. It's to that vision of equality, both personal and social, that my work has been dedicated.

12

Who's Afraid of Men
Doing Feminism?

Can men "do" feminism? Ought men to do it? What happens when they do? These are questions with which I am constantly confronted, in my pedagogy, and in both my public and private lives.

Each year, I'm invited to give about twenty or more lectures at colleges and universities all over the country. Usually, the invitation comes from a coalition of women's studies faculty, sociologists, and the occasional student organization that has actually heard of NOMAS (The National Organization for Men Against Sexism, of which I am National Spokesperson) or my work. (On rare occasions, the funding comes from both the Women's Studies and the Intrafraternity Council—often the first time those organizations have collaborated on anything!) The motives for the invitation are similar. In each case, the Women's Studies faculty tell me that they feel frustrated by the fact that their courses have roughly the same gender composition today as they had twenty years ago. Today, they tell me, they typically have only one or two men in a class, and they spend much of their time cringing defensively in the corner, feeling blamed for the collective sins of two millennia of patriarchal oppression. Colleagues who teach more general courses on gender issues like Sociology of Gender or Psychology of Gender report only slightly less skewed gender composition of their classes. These colleagues believe, as I do, that it is imperative to find ways to bring men into the conversation about gender issues that women have been having for more than two decades.

That, then, is the starting point for my standard college lecture. I try to explain why virtually every month there is a new name added to that growing list of men who have come to symbolize the gender issues currently in play. I began to work on that lecture the day after Clarence Thomas had been confirmed to his

Originally published in *Men Doing Feminism*, edited by Tom Digby. New York: Routledge, 1998.

appointment to the Supreme Court. I sat down to write a short op-ed piece for a local newspaper about the ways in which Anita Hill's testimony opened up an opportunity for men to rethink the ways we had been taught to treat women in our workplaces. I called that op-ed piece "Clarence . . . and Us," to suggest the ways in which what I believe Clarence Thomas did to Anita Hill is not as atypical as it might at first have sounded. In fact, what most middle-aged men probably were taught was "typical office behavior"—explicit requests for dates, implicit sexual innuendos, assumptions that seniority has its privileges of access to women, pornographic pinups on the walls or calendars—might now be called sexual harassment. I argued that it was about time men took on the issue of sexual harassment.

A few months later, I was invited to expand upon that op-ed piece in a lecture. Wave after wave of women had been coming forward in the aftermath of Anita Hill's compelling testimony, describing their experiences in the workplace. Suddenly men seemed so confused, so defensive and resistant to what they were saying. William Kennedy Smith and Mike Tyson were standing trial for date rape. It seemed another opportunity for us addled, middle-aged men to rethink what we had been taught as adolescents, for what I grew up calling "dating etiquette" or even just plain "dating"—to keep trying to get sex, to see sexual conquest as an entitled right, to wear down her resistance, to keep going despite that resistance—is now called date rape. Mike Tyson and William Kennedy Smith were not, it seemed to me, monsters, but men, assuming and doing what regular guys had been doing and assuming for a very long time. Here, again was an opportunity to rethink what we had been taught, and I was determined to raise these issues so that we could rethink our own behaviors and assumptions.

Then Magic Johnson announced that he was HIV positive, and that he had contracted the virus through unprotected heterosexual contact with any one of the more than 2,500 women whom he had "accommodated" sexually—that was his term for it—during his career as a sexual athlete.

Suddenly, it seemed that America was taking a crash course on masculinity—on masculine sexual entitlement, aggression, and abuse—and our instructors were Anita Hill, Patricia Bowman, Desiree Washington, and any one of those anonymous 2,500 women whom Magic Johnson had "obliged." Just as suddenly, American corporations, state and local governments, universities, and law firms were scrambling to implement procedures to handle sexual harassment. Many seemed motivated more by fear of lawsuits than a general concern for women's welfare, more interested in adjudicating harassment after the fact than in developing mechanisms to prevent it.

Many men reacted defensively. "Men on Trial" was a common headline in newspapers and magazines. And other men seemed interested in more of a defensive retreat, running off to the woods to chant, drum, and "bond" with other men. It hardly seems coincidental that 1991 was the same year that the American media discovered the "men's movement," and in which Robert Bly's *Iron John* and Sam Keen's *Fire in the Belly* soared to the top of the best-seller lists. Just when women had found a voice through which they could finally speak about their experiences, men declared themselves tired of listening, and then trooped off to the woods to be by themselves.

I tried to address these themes in that lecture, paying attention to what I saw as the possibilities for change that these cases presented to us, as men, possibilities to think about ourselves, and our relations with women in new ways. I titled that first lecture "Clarence, William, Iron Mike, Magic . . . and Us: Issues for Men in the 1990s."

Since then, I've given that lecture at over one hundred colleges and universities. And virtually each month I have to revise the title to reflect the steady stream of men's names that capture the issues with which I think we are struggling. By the end of the decade, the title might have been "Clarence, William, Iron Mike, Magic, Senator Packwood, Woody, Tailhook, the U.S. Military, Spur Posse, John Wayne Bobbitt, The Citadel, Tupac, O.J. . . . and Us." The students usually get the point.

In the course of the lecture, I point to the ways in which women's lives have changed in the past thirty years, and how these changes have forever transformed the landscape upon which gender relations are carried out. I try and cover a lot of ground: sexuality, date and acquaintance rape, AIDS, the workplace, the balance of work and family life, sexual harassment. In every case, I suggest that men should want to support feminist reforms: not only because of an ethical imperative—of course, it is right and just—but also because men will live happier and healthier lives, with better relations with the women, men, and children in their lives if they do. I take as an epigraph a line from a 1913 essay by the Greenwich Village writer Floyd Dell. "Feminism," he wrote, "will make it possible for the first time for men to be free."

When I'm finished, the reaction is almost always the same: a substantial contingent of feminist women students visibly and vocally appreciate my lecture. A smaller—much smaller—contingent of male students come up afterwards and thank me, usually asking what they can do on their particular campus. The Women's Studies faculty and sociologists are also usually pleased. I feel good, as though I've contributed to an opening of dialog between women and men on the campus.

Then the criticism comes—and always from two sources. First, there are what I've come to call the angry-white-men-in-training. These young men are defensive, angry, and fully resistant to anything that remotely hints of feminism. Armed with the latest platitudes from Rush Limbaugh, they proceed to offer the false stereotypes of feminist women that we've all come to know and detest. They whoop and holler as if the lecture had become a daytime TV talk show bashing feminism. (It is significant that a discussion of men is so easily transformed into another opportunity to trash feminist women.) In about one in five lectures, I experience something like the following, which happened recently.

A burly white male student, sitting in the back row, arms folded across his chest, the brim of his baseball hat turned around, raised his hand as the moderator for the evening's lecture announced there was time for one more question. "What makes you such an expert on men?" he began with a challenge masquerading as a question. "The way you talk about listening to women, and supporting feminism, you must be a faggot or something. You sure aren't a real man."

I shifted to a kind of mental remote control, and tossed his question back to him. I asked what was it about my support for feminism that made him think I might be gay. He declined to pick up the question and disengaged, mumbling inaudibly. The lecture ended.

No matter how many times I've been gay-baited, been rhetorically or literally called out, my manhood questioned, I'm still somewhat startled by it. Why would some people believe that supporting feminism is somehow a revelation of sexual orientation? I offer no clues to my sexuality in my lectures or in my writing, no references to the gender of a "friend," "partner," or a "lover." All I do is agree with women that inequality based on gender is wrong, and that women and men should be equal in both the public and the private spheres.

Does this make me less of a real man? The reviewer of one of my books, a collection of men's writings examining the feminist debate about pornography, called me a "traitor." Another wrote that anyone who supports equality for women or for gays must be a wimp.

The second critical reaction is more complex, and somewhat more troubling. One or two feminist women express their displeasure at my lecture by poking holes in my argument, revealing what they see as inconsistencies and contradictions. Their follow-up questions and the ensuing discussion unravel quickly to what one might call "patriarchy-baiting," trying to elicit some reaction, some slip-up, some element of defensiveness, some point of weakness which will reveal my own patriarchal biases. These are inevitably revealed, to which their response is a loudly triumphant "Aha, we knew it!" and a quieter, but no less pronounced sigh of relief. All men *are* the same, and that "same" is patriarchal.

What are these two groups so afraid of? Why can't men "do" feminism, or at least be seen to support feminism? After all, feminism provides both women *and men* with an extraordinarily powerful analytic prism through which to understand their lives, and a political and moral imperative to transform the unequal conditions of those relationships. Why should men be afraid of feminism? And why should some feminist women be afraid of pro-feminist men?

To address these questions, two caveats are in order. First, to address the former question, we must make a distinction between feminism as that analytic prism and feminism as a set of policy initiatives designed to remove obstacles to public sphere participation for women. After all, although most American men remain, at best, indifferent, and, at worst, openly hostile, to the term feminism, and especially dismissive of the term feminist, it is also the case that most men support every single element in what we might call a feminist political and social policy agenda when its elements are disaggregated and presented as simple policy options. And second, in addressing the latter question, I want to be clear that I do not intend to be a ventriloquist, explaining women's experiences for them. Instead, I speak from my experience as a man whose work is devoted to making feminism, as I understand it, apprehensible and, even, acceptable to men.

While I will want to address each of these fears of feminism separately, I want to pause to point out one significant similarity. In both cosmologies, pro-feminist men cannot exist. To the angry white men, pro-feminist *men* cannot exist, and so their effort is to unmask me as a fraud of a man. Hence the gay-baiting and wimp-baiting, which often amount to the same thing. To that small group of feminist women, *pro-feminist* men cannot exist, because such men are potential allies, not enemies. So often these women, like the angry white males, discredit the motives or intentions of the men who support them. To move feminism forward, both as a cluster of theories and as a political project, I believe that we will need to honestly confront both of these fears of feminism.

I begin by speculating about the fear that some feminist women have of pro-feminist men, based upon my conversations with several of these women who have challenged and pushed these issues. Each of their perspectives is doubtless true, but even taken together, they are not the whole truth.

To some women, fear of pro-feminist men comes from a fear of men in general. All men are men, monolithically constructed essences, incapable of change. In this model, some things are eternal verities, always signifying the same thing. Erections signify domination and nothing else. Men embody unmediated patriarchal oppression. To be a man means to be an oppressor.

Thus "we"—men who could support feminism—cannot be said to exist if the polar dichotomy by which they see the world is to remain in place. In some cases, of course, this is more complicated than a simple "women good, men bad" world view. Rather, I understand these women to say that since all men benefit from patriarchy in a myriad of ways, seen and unseen, it is not possible for men to renounce patriarchy and come over to the other side. Since privilege is indelibly inscribed onto men, and men embody it whether they choose to or not, then the only possibility for men to be redeemed is for them to renounce masculinity itself. One simply cannot be a man and support feminism. (This position is also echoed by some men, like political activist John Stoltenberg, who encourages men to "refuse to be a man" in his first book, and celebrates the "end" of manhood in his second.) We can always retreat if the going gets tough or dangerous. This would be especially true for heterosexual white men, who can slide seemingly without effort, into the arenas of privilege which often remain invisible to those who have it.

To others, it's simply too easy for men to declare themselves pro-feminist. They fear a syndrome among men which a friend of mine has labeled "premature self-congratulation," in which men declare themselves liberated by masculine fiat. To still others, the expression of a fear of pro-feminist men is triggered more by what I actually argue in my lecture than by anything I might be seen to embody. Although I suggest that the ethical imperative—that feminist reforms are right and just—should be the basis for men's support for feminism, I also argue that it is in men's interests to support feminism, that men will actually "benefit" from their support of feminism. I argue that men's efforts to end sexual harassment, date and acquaintance rape, to share housework and child care will actually enable men to have more fulfilling lives, more satisfying relationships with women, with children, and with other men. "Just what we need," one woman snorted derisively, "a feminism that will benefit men. Count me out."

One expression of this fear of feminism is a particular hostility to men who have embraced feminism in the academy and are using a feminist perspective to understand gender relations. No sooner do women get a foothold on a legitimate domain in the academy than men rush in to a new growth area, displacing women and setting up shop, much the way obstetricians and gynecologists displaced midwives at the turn of the century, or that men are entering nursing as other fields dry up.

There is, perhaps, some truth in this. But for every male academic who uses feminist analysis as the framework for their work, there are hundreds, even thousands, who remain resolutely and defiantly hostile to the idea of feminism as a theory in the first place. I do not purport to do this new academic practice called "Men's Studies," which sounds so defensively reactive, as if it were the academic wing of the men's rights movement. I simply "do" the sociology of gender. I do it from a feminist perspective, which takes as its starting point that gender relations are constructed in a field of power. And the gender that I study is men.

I believe that each of these positions seems partly true. Privilege is invisibly but indelibly conferred upon men, whether we renounce it or not. But there are also costs to men for renouncing it, costs that the anti-feminist men recognize more readily, if less enthusiastically, than these few feminist women. The reaction of men to feminism does, I believe, contain an angle of vision that needs to be addressed.

That issue concerns power. Feminism requires an analysis of power; indeed, one of feminism's central tenets is that gender relations are constructed in a field of power. At the political level, feminism addressed a symmetry in women's lives. At the aggregate level, women were not *in power*. Just look at those corporate boardrooms, those collegiate boards of trustees, those legislatures and executive mansions, feminist women said. It's evident that women are not in power. And, at the individual level, women did not *feel powerful*. Feminism, then, was a political movement to challenge women's social powerlessness and their individual feelings of powerlessness.

But that tidy symmetry breaks down when applied to men. Sure, men are *in power* at the aggregate level. Again, the gender composition of those legislatures, boardrooms, and boards of trustees don't lie. But ask individual men to "give up" power and you are more likely to get a blank, defensive stare, as if you were from another planet. "What are you talking about?" the men will respond. "I have no power. My wife bosses me around, my children boss me around, my boss bosses me around. I'm completely powerless!"

Several groups on the political front privilege men's experience of powerlessness and ignore the continued social aggregate power of men over women as groups. Anti-feminist purveyors of men's rights, like Warren Farrell, claim that male power is a "myth." "Feel powerless?" he seems to say. "Of course, you do. Women have all the power. Currently, we men are the real victims of reverse discrimination, affirmative action, custody and alimony laws. Let's get some of that power back from those feminists!"

Some of the followers of Robert Bly and other leaders in the mythopoetic men's movement also seem to privilege the personal feeling over the social and political analysis. If you don't feel powerful, then you're not powerful. "Come with us into the woods," they seem to say. "We'll go get some power. Here's the power chant, the power ritual, the power drumming." I remember a few years ago when mainstream American men, who were supposed to feel such renewed power under Reaganism, resorted to wearing power ties and eating power lunches to demonstrate their power—as if power were a fashion accessory. What better expression of political economic impotence than to be eating and wearing the signs of one's power!

Farrell frequently uses the analogy of the chauffeur to illustrate the illusion of men's power. Think about a chauffeur. He's in the driver's seat. He knows where he's going. He's wearing the uniform. So, you might say, he has the power. But from *his* perspective, someone else is giving the orders. He's not powerful at all. His power is a myth.

This analogy has some limited value: individual men are not powerful, at least all but a small handful of individual men. And most American men do not feel powerful. But they're right for the wrong reasons. What if we ask one question of our chauffeur, and try to shift the frame just a little, to reveal what is hidden by the analogy of the chauffeur. What is the gender of the person who *is* giving the orders? Who is sitting in the back seat?

When we shift from the analysis of the individual's experience of his position to a different, relational context, the interactions between and among men become clear as relations of power. Of course, men as a group do have power, and that power is organized against women. But some men also have power over other men. Pro-feminism, a position that acknowledges men's experience without privileging it, possesses the tools to bring those levels together, to both adequately analyze men's aggregate power, and also describe the ways in which individual men are both privileged by that social level of power and feel powerless in the face of it.

It seems to me that men's defensiveness reaches its zenith around the question of power, as if to identify and challenge men's power was to ignore men's pain. Such a trade-off is unacceptable politically, and, frankly, a non sequitur. Men's pain is caused by men's power. What else could it be? Would we say that the unhappiness of white people was caused by black people's power? The pains and sexual problems of heterosexuals were caused by gays and lesbians? Pro-feminism requires that both men's social power and individual powerlessness be understood as mutually reinforcing, linked experiences, both of which derive from men's aggregate social power.

For men to support feminism, it seems to me, means acknowledging men's experience of powerlessness—which often makes feminist women uneasy—while placing it within a context of men's aggregate power—the power of men as a group over women as a group, and the power of some men over other men. Disaggregating the term "masculinity" into its plural masculinities is one way to address that second dimension of power. Some men are disempowered by virtue of class, race, ethnicity, sexuality, age, able-bodiedness. But all men are privileged vis-à-vis women.

There is another dimension that must be addressed with men, and upon it pivots our political work as men who seek to support feminism and challenge other men. It requires adding another dimension to the discussion of power and powerlessness—the issue of entitlement. I recently appeared on a television talk show opposite three "angry white males" who felt that they had been the victims of workplace discrimination. The show's title, no doubt to entice a large potential audience, was "A Black Woman Took My Job." In my comments to these angry men, I invited them to consider what the word "my" meant in that title, that they felt that the jobs were originally "theirs," that they were entitled to them, and that when some "other" person—black, female—got the job, that person was really taking "their" job. But by what right is that his job? By convention, by a historical legacy of such profound levels of discrimination that we have needed decades of affirmative action to even begin to make slightly more level a playing field that has tilted so decidedly in one direction.

Men's sense of entitlement is the source of much of men's experience of powerlessness. Consider the work of Robert Bly. The reaction to Bly's *Iron John* was curious in at least one respect: Readers of the book, as well as virtually all the men I've observed at mythopoetic retreats—men who are, themselves, fathers, and, indeed, even grandfathers—identify with the young boy in the fairy tale. There are three other men in the story with whom one could identify—the boy's father (the king), the father of the woman that the boy eventually marries (another king), and Iron John himself (who turns out to also have been a king). Three kings and one little boy. And all these fifty-year-old men, fathers them- selves, identify as the boy, not as any of the kings. What are we to make of this?

Let us ask who exactly is the little boy. He is a prince—that is, he is a man who is entitled to be in power but who is not yet in power. He will be, he is enti- tled to it. But not yet. In short, he is entitled to power, but feels powerless.

It is from this place—shall we call it the "Inner Prince"?—that I believe men speak, a place of gnawing, yawning anxiety, a place of entitlement unfulfilled. No wonder men are defensive when we present feminism to them—it feels like they will be forced to give up their sense of entitlement. Feminism, to men, feels like loss—a loss of the possibility to claim their birthright of power.

And when men feel their entitlement being snatched from them, they are likely to lash out. Thus, for example, the media created mischaracterizations of feminist women as man-hating harpies seeking to dethrone academic stan- dards and demolish democracy and individual freedom. Feminists are, in fact, "reasonable creatures," as feminist essayist Katha Pollitt titles her book, capable of sound judgment, informed opinions, and justifiable outrage at continued injustice. They're feminists because they know that feminism will enlarge the arena of individual freedom for women and ensure their equality and safety under the law. Those ideals seem as American as apple pie and fatherhood. And feminist women do not hate men. Most of the feminist women I've met love us enough to believe in men's ability to change, despite the pain they have endured both institutionally and individually from a world dominated by men.

Much of this vilification of feminists as man haters coincides with men's fear of feminism. The media assassination attempt, after all, reinscribes men as the centerpiece of the feminist project. Feminism is not about empowering or protecting women (or, obviously, both); rather, feminism is about hating men. Men are, after all, still the center of the universe—as they are entitled to be. To characterize feminism as an ideology that is about men is to return the frame- work of political ideas to the position to which men are entitled. The world revolves around men, either positively or negatively charged. And, according to Harry Brod, much of men's fear of feminism is not that it is about men's loss of power, but that it is not "about" men at all. If men are redundant, irrelevant, or even insignificant to the feminist project, then the world as we men have come to expect it is no longer a familiar one.

Pro-feminist men become targets for such anger, just as feminist women do. When hegemonic manhood is threatened, it almost always lashes out sexually.

Thus do all the "others" become sexualized—black men, Latinos, Italians, become rapacious beasts, and pro-feminist men become feminism's court eunuchs, emasculated, pussy-whipped wimps. Our masculinity is questioned, usually by questioning our heterosexuality. Any man who supports feminism cannot be a real man, hence he must be gay. Thus does internalized homophobia often keep men from supporting feminism.

Contemporary men did not invent this equation. We are in good company. I spent five years researching the history of men who have supported women's equality in the United States. Since 1776, these "pro-feminist" men have included a pantheon of respected Americans who supported women's rights to equality in the workplace, the classroom, and the polling place, who believed that women had the right to control their own bodies, their own names, and their own property. Men like Thomas Paine, William Lloyd Garrison, Frederick Douglass, Walt Whitman, Wendell Phillips, Robert Dale Owen, W.E.B. Du Bois, John Dewey, Matthew Vassar, and Rabbi Stephen Wise. (The results of this research were published in *Against the Tide: Pro-feminist Men in the United States, 1776–1990*, a documentary history, published in 1992.)

Ever since the origins of the American women's movement, pro-feminist men have had their manhood questioned. Pro-feminist men were consistently vilified by other men, jeered as they marched in demonstrations, mocked in the media, and occasionally, even physically attacked. The day after he gave the rousing speech at the first Woman's Rights Convention that turned the tide toward the suffrage plank, Frederick Douglass was vilified in the Syracuse newspapers as an "Aunt Nancy Man," an antebellum term for wimp. Another recalled that when he marched in suffrage parades with the Men's League for Woman Suffrage, onlookers shouted, "Look at the skirts!"

When he marched in the great parades for woman suffrage in the first decades of the century, playwright George Middleton recalled being heckled with such cries as "Take that handkerchief out of your cuff" and "You forgot to shave this morning." And the anonymous author of a pro-feminist pamphlet called "How It Feels to Be the Husband of a Suffragette" noted that he did not wash the dishes in his home (neither did his wife), despite the fact that "something over 11,863 of you requested me to go home and wash them on the occasion of that first suffrage parade." Even the *New York Times* anticipated that male marchers would "be called endearing names by small boys on the sidewalk," but extended to the male suffragists their "sympathy and admiration."

Opponents of feminism always questioned the virility of any man who supported women's rights. In 1913, Rep. Thomas Heflin of Alabama (uncle of Senator Howard Heflin) made this charge explicit. "I do not believe that there is a red-blooded man in the world who in his heart really believes in woman suffrage. I think every man who favors it ought to be made to wear a dress."

Such sentiments contain two false equations. There's the implicit equation of manhood with oppression and inequality—as if real men support injustice. And there's the equation of supporting gender equality with effeminacy—as if only "failed men" could learn how to listen to women's pain and anger. But feminist women can also take a lesson here. Men do stand to lose something by supporting feminism—our standing in the world of men. There are some costs to our public position as pro-feminists.

What can we do to challenge these fears of feminism? One thing that seems necessary is to clearly and carefully demarcate men's relationship to feminism, particularly what ways men can support feminism. What is the best way for men to support feminism, and for feminist women to welcome men to the struggle? I believe that we might begin by considering ourselves the Gentleman's Auxiliary of Feminism. This is, to my mind, an honorable position, one that acknowledges that this is a revolution of which we are a part, but not the central part, not its most significant part.

It will be the task of this Gentlemen's Auxiliary to make feminism comprehensible to men, not as a loss of power, which has thus far failed to trickle down to most individual men anyway, but as a challenge to that false sense of entitlement to that power in the first place. Like all auxiliary organizations, I think we need to remain accountable to headquarters.

In the conclusion to an article in *The New Republic*, sociologist Orlando Patterson outlined an ineluctable feature of all social change movements. Speaking of the movement for racial justice, he wrote that

> the burden of racial and ethnic change always rests on a minority group. Although both whites and blacks have strong mutual interests in solving their racial problem, though the solution must eventually come from both, blacks must play the major role in achieving this objective—not only because they have more to gain from it but also because whites have far less to lose from doing nothing. It is blacks who must take the initiative, suffer the greater pain, define and offer the more creative solutions, persevere in the face of obstacles and paradoxical outcomes, insist that improvements are possible and maintain a climate of optimism concerning the eventual outcome.

So too, I would propose, with feminism. Pro-feminist men are, as we social scientists like to say, necessary but not sufficient elements in feminism's eventual success. We can be its cheerleaders, its allies, its foot soldiers, and we must be so in front of other men, risking our own fears of rejection, our own membership in the club of masculinity, confronting our own fears of other men. But what choice do we have—we, women and men, who embrace a vision of sexual equality and gender justice?

13

Profeminist Men

The "Other" Men's Movement

Cory Sherb didn't go to Duke to become a feminist. He was going to be a doctor, covering his bets with a double major in engineering and pre-med. But his experiences with both organic chemistry and feminist women conspired to lead this affable and earnest twenty-year-old Detroit native in a different direction. Now in his junior year, he still has a double major—Women's Studies and French. And he works with a group of men to raise awareness about sexual assault and date rape.

Eric Freedman wasn't a feminist either, when he arrived at Swarthmore three years ago. A twenty-year-old junior literature major from Syracuse, he became involved in a campus anti-racism project, and began to see the connections among different struggles for equality. At an anti-racism workshop he helped organize, he suddenly found himself speaking about male privilege as well as white privilege. This fall, he's starting a men's group to focus on race and gender issues.

Who are these guys? And what are they doing in the women's movement?

They are among a growing number of profeminist men around the country. These aren't the angry divorcées who whine about how men are the new victims of reverse discrimination; nor are they the weekend warriors trooping off to a mythopoetic retreat. They're neither white Promise Keepers nor black Million Man Marchers vowing to be responsible domestic patriarchs on a nineteenth-century model.

You might think of profeminist men as the "other" men's movement, but I prefer to consider it the "real" men's movement, because by actively supporting women's equality on the job or on the streets and by quietly changing their lives to create that equality at home, profeminist men are also transforming the

Originally published in *Ms.*, November–December 1997.

definition of masculinity. Perhaps this is the movement about which Gloria Steinem rhapsodized when she wrote how women "want a men's movement. We are literally dying for it."

Profeminist men staff the centers where convicted batterers get counseling, organize therapy for rapists and sex offenders in prison, do the workshops on preventing sexual harassment in the workplace, or on confronting the impact of pornography in men's lives. On campus, they're organizing men's events during Take Back the Night marches, presenting programs on sexual assault to fraternities, dorms and athletic teams, taking courses on masculinity, and founding campus groups with acronyms like MAC (Men Acting for Change), MOST (Men Opposed to Sexist Tradition), MASH (Men Against Sexual Harassment), MASA (Men Against Sexual Assault), and, my current favorite, MARS (Men Against Rape and Sexism). Maybe John Gray was right after all—real men *are* from Mars!

Feminism and Men's Lives

I first met Cory, Eric, and about a dozen other young profeminist men at the Young Feminist Summit Conference, organized by NOW, in Washington in April 1997. They were pretty easy to spot among the nearly one thousand young women from colleges all over the country. As we talked during an impromptu workshop, I heard them describe both the exhilaration and isolation of becoming part of the struggle for women's equality, the frustrations of dealing with other men, the active suspicions and passive indifference of other students.

It felt painfully familiar. I've spent nearly two decades in feminist politics, first as an activist in anti-rape and anti-battery groups, and later helping to organize the National Organization for Men Against Sexism (NOMAS), a network of profeminist men and women around the country. More recently, I've tried to apply the insights of academic feminist theory to men's lives, developing courses on men, debating with Robert Bly and his followers, and writing a history of the idea of manhood in America.

Of course, men like Cory and Eric are a distinct minority on campus. They compete with the angry voice of backlash, those shrill interruptions that scream, "Don't blame me, I never raped anyone! Leave me alone!" They compete with that now-familiar men-as-victim whine. Men, we hear, are terrified of going to work or on a date, lest they be falsely accused of sexual harassment or date rape; they're unable to support their scheming careerist wives, yet vilified as bad fathers if they refuse to keep them in Gucci and Donna Karan after the divorce.

In the public imagination, profeminist men also compete with the mythopoetic vision of the men's movement as a kind of summer-camp retreat, and the earnest evangelical Promise Keepers with their men-only sports-themed rallies, and the Million Man March's solemn yet celebratory atonement. All offer men solace and soul-work, and promise to heal men's pain and enable them to become more nurturing and loving. All noble goals, to be sure. But to profeminist men, you don't build responsibility and democracy by exclusion—of women, or of gays and lesbians.

And profeminist men compete with the most deafening sound coming from the mouths of American men when the subject is feminism: silence. Most men, on campus and off, exude an aura of studied indifference to feminism. Like the irreverent second child at the Passover seder, he asks, "What has this to do with me?"

A lot. Sure, feminism is the struggle of more than one-half the population for equal rights. But it's also about rethinking identities, our relationships, the meanings of our lives. For men, feminism is not only about what we *can't* do—like violence, harassment, rape—or *shouldn't* do, like leaving all the child care and housework to our wives. It's also about what we *can* do, what we *should* do, and even what we *want* to do—like being a better father, friend, or partner. "Most men know that it is to all of our advantage—women and men alike—for women to be equal," noted NOW president Patricia Ireland, in her Conference keynote address. Far from being only about the loss of power, feminism will also enable men to live the lives we say we want to live.

This isn't the gender cavalry, arriving in the nick of time to save the damsels from distress. "Thanks for bringing this sexism stuff to our attention, ladies," one might imagine them saying. "We'll take it from here." And it's true that some men declare themselves feminist just a bit too effortlessly, especially if they think it's going to help them get a date. (A friend calls it "premature self-congratulation," and it's just as likely to leave women feeling shortchanged.)

In part, this explains why I call them "profeminist" men and not "feminist men" or "male feminists." As an idea, it seems to me, feminism involves an empirical observation—that women are not equal—with the moral position that declares they should be. Of course, men may share this empirical observation and take this moral stance. And to that extent men support feminism as an ideal. But feminism as an identity also involves the felt experience of that inequality. And this men do not have, because men are privileged by sexism. To be sure, men may be oppressed—by race, class, ethnicity, sexuality, age, physical ability—but men are not oppressed *as men*. Since only women have that felt experience of oppression about gender, it seems sensible to make a distinction in how we identify ourselves. Men can support feminism, and can call ourselves "anti-sexist" or "profeminist." I've chosen profeminist because, like feminism, it stresses the positive and forward-looking.

In a sense, I think of profeminist men as the Gentlemen's Auxiliary of Feminism. This honorable position acknowledges that we play a part in this social transformation, but not the most significant part. It's the task of the Gentlemen's Auxiliary to make feminism comprehensible to men, not as a loss of power—which has thus far failed to "trickle down" to most individual men anyway—but as a challenge to the false sense of entitlement we have to that power in the first place. Profeminism is about both supporting women's equality, and other men's efforts to live more ethically consistent and more emotionally resonant lives.

A Glance Backward

Today's profeminist men are not the first to figure this out. "The interests of the sexes are inseparably connected and in the elevation of the one lies the salvation of the other," wrote the great social reformer (and Lucy Stone's husband) Henry Brown Blackwell in 1853.

In fact, American men have always supported feminism—or, rather, there have always been men who did. No matter the issue, when women sought to enter the public sphere—from education to the workplace, the voting booth to the union hall—there were some men who also mounted the barricades and stormed the hallowed halls from which women were excluded. Even before the Declaration of Independence, that celebrated radical Thomas Paine argued that that any formal separation from England should include women's rights, since women have, as he put it, "an equal right to virtue."

Supporting women's rights was a result of both "conscience and common sense," according to the great abolitionist Frederick Douglass. It was Douglass, remember, who made the passionate and decisive plea for the suffrage plank at the Seneca Falls convention in 1848 (a meeting co-chaired by Lucretia Mott and her profeminist husband, James). To these men, women were equal individuals, and therefore "equally entitled," said Douglass, their rights "unquestionable," said Ralph Waldo Emerson.

For others, though, women were not *as* moral but *more* moral, and equality was necessary to purify a system that had rotted from masculine vice and corruption. Feminism was a "detergent remedy for vice, crime and immorality," wrote one man; her role "*is* the home," observed another, but now she was compelled to engage in a kind of national housekeeping. Only women could clean up "the muddle we have made," as Frederic Howe, warden of Ellis Island, put it.

Some men supported feminism for its potential to liberate men. Several bohemian radicals clustered in Greenwich Village at the turn of the last century saw feminism as more than "a revolt of women against conditions which hamper their activities," as writer Floyd Dell put it, but "also a revolt of women and men against the type of woman created by those conditions."

For them, the personal was also political; they struggled to walk their talk. Max Eastman, a young philosophy instructor at Columbia, founded the Men's League for Woman Suffrage in 1910 to organize men's contingents for the grand suffrage parades; he and his wife, Ida Rauh, caused a scandal when they placed both names on the mailbox of their Greenwich Village apartment (she was a

"Lucy Stoner" who had kept her maiden name), and the post office refused to deliver their mail. William Sanger, arrested for distributing his wife Margaret's birth control pamphlets, was equally supportive at home. "You go ahead and finish your writing," she quotes him as saying, "I'll get dinner and wash the dishes." (She drew the curtains to their first-floor apartment when he did, lest passersby notice this emasculating gender reversal.) "Feminism," as Dell put it in a 1914 article, "will make it possible for the first time for men to be free."

Today's Profeminist Men

Each historical strain is visible among today's profeminist men. The ethical imperative of individual freedom remains the centerpiece of support for the ERA, reproductive freedom, opposition to sexual harassment, or women's admission to VMI or The Citadel. Though this egalitarian position downplays gender difference, other profeminist men embrace or even exaggerate that difference in their support of current feminist campaigns against prostitution and pornography.

But neither position requires that men actually change as a result of their participation. Individual freedom would enable women to claim rights already held by men; moralizing rhetoric would protect the victims of male excess, and perhaps constrain men more adroitly, but would also freeze men in positions of self-denial.

Only the third historical position avoids such a static view of men and acknowledges that feminism is about transformation, both personal and political, public and private—for both women and for men. Like a lot of men, Eric Freedman found that out when he started dating. "Sexism was hurting both of us," he said. "I'd been taught to do all these things—by other guys, by the media— that weren't right. What I'd been taught kind of scared me. Basically, we're taught to sexually harass women."

Listening to Eric reminded me of my own locker room socialization to manhood. What I learned from my peers was that on a date, the goal was to score— "it doesn't count unless you put it in" was the felicitous phrase used by one of my baseball buddies—and one was entitled to do whatever it took to make that happen. "If she says no, keep going," they said. "If she pushes you away, keep going. Don't stop unless she actually hits you."

If we men were really honest about it, then, we'd probably have to admit that our socialization to masculinity was a kind of basic training for sexual assault, a boot camp for predation. Most red-blooded American men are also "failed attempted date rapists." Only then we might have called it "dating etiquette." What was once called office behavior, or seen by some as the perks of professorship, is now called "sexual harassment"—everywhere, that is, except in Supreme Court confirmation hearings.

Who Are These Guys?

So who *are* these guys anyway? Was there some variable that "explained" this new generation of profeminist men? A feminist mother or sister, perhaps? A divorce? An especially nurturing, or especially distant father? Were they gay? Bad at sports?

All of the above. And none. There's no single factor that explains profeminist men—then or now. They're raised in two-parent and single-parent families, by nurturing and absent fathers. Some are gay and some are straight, and they major in everything from engineering to French. Some love and some hate sports.

Searching for a "cause" turns out to be the wrong question. As with earlier generations, most profeminist men sound more like Wilford Brimley in his Quaker Oats ad than like feminist theorists. It's simply "the right thing to do." Michael Messner, a forty-four-year old sociology professor at University of Southern California, and a leading thinker on masculinity and sports, called his "conversion" a rather intellectual process. "I did not have the terrible experience in right field, the abusive or neglectful father, or the strong feminist role model mother" that prevailing myths seemed to suggest. Instead, he says, "I was convinced that the world was unfair as it was currently organized." Supporting women's equality turned out to be in the best traditions of American democracy, the extension of "liberty and justice for all." It's men who *don't* support equality who ought to have their heads, and their patriotism, examined.

The routes taken by today's profeminist men are as varied as the men themselves. But most do seem to have some personal experience that made gender inequality more concrete. For some, it was mother. (Remember President Bill Clinton describing how he developed his commitment to women's equality when he tried to stop his stepfather from hitting her? Of course, one wishes that commitment had facilitated more supportive policy initiatives.) Max Sadler, a sixteen-year-old junior at Trinity High School in New York City, watched his professional mother hit her head on the glass ceiling at her high-powered corporate job—a job she eventually quit to start an all-female rival company. Max shared her frustration, and also felt ashamed at the casual attitudes of her male colleagues.

Shehzad Nadeem, a nineteen-year-old student at James Madison University, remembered the way his older sister described her experiences. "I could barely believe the stories she told me, yet something deep inside told me that they were not only true, but common. I realized that we men are actively or passively complicit in women's oppression, and that we have to take an active role in challenging other men." Together with half a dozen other JMU students, Shehzad organized MOST (Men Opposed to Sexist Tradition), which presents workshops on violence and sexual assault in the dorms.

Some men saw sexism up close as it was used against their wives. "Sexism had always been something of an abstraction," wrote former Labor Secretary Robert Reich in a 1989 article in *Ms.* magazine. Then his wife was denied tenure. His perspective changed; he began to notice things that had earlier eluded him. It "made me wary of my own limited perspective—the countless ways in which I fail to understand my female colleagues and students, and their ways of knowing the world." David Sadker, now a fifty-five-year-old American University professor, recalls that as a married graduate school couple in the late 1960s, he and his wife, Myra, "were attending the same classes, and were destined to receive the same degree, we were receiving two very different educations. My hand was quickly recognized in class, my comments repeated," while Myra's insights were often attributed to someone else. Collaborators and partners, their 1990 book's title, *Failing at Fairness*, captured both their personal experience and those of women in general.

Or perhaps it was having a feminist girlfriend, or even just having women friends, that brings these issue to the fore for men. "I grew up with female friends who were as ambitious, smart, achieving and confident as I thought I was—on a good day," recalls Jason Schultz, a founder of MAC at Duke, who now organizes men's programs to combat campus sexual assault. "When I got to college, these same women began calling themselves feminists. When I heard men call women 'dumb chicks' I knew something was wrong."

Other profeminist men credit feminist professors for igniting their interest and supporting their efforts. David Gutterman, a 1990 Duke grad who cofounded MAC in response to a series of sexual assaults on campus, calls Jean O'Barr, director of Women's Studies at Duke since its inception in 1983, "an inspiring mentor." Seeking to "bring men into the feminist conversation," as O'Barr puts it, is part of her mission, and the program provides a home for the school's course on masculinity, as well as MAC.

The Profeminist "Click"

But it has to be more than the presence of feminist role models, challenges from girlfriends, brilliant assignments, or challenging support from professors. After all, we all have women in our lives, and virtually all of those women have had some traumatic encounter with sexism. There has to be something else.

Feminists call it the "click"—that moment when they realize that their pain, fears, confusion, and anger are not theirs alone, but are shared with other women. Do profeminist men have "clicks"? Yes, but they don't typically come from righteous indignation or fear, but rather from guilt and shame, a gnawing sense of implication in something larger and more pervasive than individual intention. It's that awful moment when you hear women complain about "men" in general and realize, even just a little bit, that you are what they're talking about. (Much of men's reactive defensiveness seems to be a hedge against these feelings of shame.)

Suddenly, it's not those "bad" men "out there" who are the problem—it's all men. Call it the Pogo revelation. "We have met the enemy, and he is us."

That's certainly the way it felt for Jeff Wolf (not his real name). A sexually naïve college sophomore, he found himself growing closer and closer to a woman friend, Annie, during a study date. They talked long into the night, and eventually kissed. One thing began to lead to another, and both seemed eager and pleased to be with the other. Just before penetration, though, Jeff felt Annie go limp. "Her eyes glazed over, and she went kind of numb," he recalled, still wincing in the memory.

This is the moment that many a college guy dreams of—her apparent surrender to his desire, even if it was induced by roofies or alcohol. In fact, it's a moment when men often space out, preferring to navigate the actual encounter on automatic pilot, fearing that emotional connection will lead to an early climax.

As Annie slipped into this mental coma, though, Jeff stayed alert, as engaged emotionally as he was physically. "What had been so arousing was the way we had been connecting intellectually and emotionally," he said. After some patient prodding, she finally confessed that she'd been raped as a high school sophomore, and ever since, had used this as a self-protective strategy to get through a sexual encounter without reliving her adolescent trauma. Jeff, it seemed, was the first guy who noticed.

"Suddenly I realized that the world wasn't divided up neatly into good guys and bad guys. It was just guys. And I was one," Jeff says now. "I felt so angry that some guy had hurt Annie so much, and ashamed at how it would have been so easy to have continued, to not know about it, to pretend never to know."

Other men had similar stories. After a close friend was sexually assaulted, Josh Schwartz (not his real name) was appropriately compassionate, but she grew distant, distrustful. "How can I know you won't do the same thing to me?" she asked him.

For other men, the moment came in pieces, not all at once. Tony Chen, a graduate student at U.C. Berkeley, recalls a series of what he called "smaller, self-indicting realizations"—interrupting women more than men, staring at a woman in an objectifying way—that led him to question masculine socialization. Jachinson Chan, now a professor of Asian American Studies at U.C. Santa Barbara, remembers being surrounded by really smart female graduate students who included him in their discussions. But it wasn't until his sister accused him of not really listening to her that he began to realize that the feminist critiques of masculinity in part applied to him. Wayne Morris remembers always supporting feminism, but passively and without much conviction. Only gradually did he begin to see the connections between racism and sexism. "As a black man living in a racist society," he recalls, "I wasn't satisfied with people not doing anything against racism." Nor was he satisfied with his passive support of feminism. "I began to realize the harm that I had done to a lot of women—relatives, acquaintances, friends," he says, and he began to fuse his two interests. He now runs court-mandated therapy groups for men convicted of domestic violence.

Others say their click experience happened later in life. In the 1970s, psychologist David Greene was deeply involved in political activism, when he and his wife had a baby. "Not that much changed for me; I still went around doin' my thing, but now there was a baby in it." On the other hand, his wife's life was totally transformed by the realities of round-the-clock child-care. She'd become a mother. "After several weeks of this, she sat me down and confronted me," he recalls. "The bankruptcy of my politics quickly became clear to me. I was abusing power and privilege—I'd become the enemy I thought I was fighting against." They meticulously divided housework and child-care and David learned that revolutions are fought out in people's kitchens as well as in the jungles of Southeast Asia. Terry Kupers, a fifty-four-year-old psychiatrist, and author of *Revisioning Men's Lives*, remembers his wife initiating some serious talks in those years about the "unstated assumptions we were making about housework, cooking, and whose time was more valuable." Not only did Kupers realize that his wife was right, "but I also realized I liked things better the new way."

And some profeminists just bristled at masculine socialization, feeling that they just didn't fit in with other guys. Alan Chan (not his real name) remembered the day the swimsuit issue of *Sports Illustrated* arrived in his dorm. "All the guys gather around it, and started making these lewd comments about the women. I just kept feeling worse and worse, and finally had to walk away. I think I mumbled something about having a lab just to get out of there."

The nonconformity can easily arouse suspicion. Profeminist men have always been ridiculed, their masculinity questioned. Or it could arouse suspicion of their motives, on the other extreme. When Chris Butler, a nineteen-year-old physics and computer science major, began to get involved with the Feminist Union at Boston University, his friends were sarcastically dismissive, teasing him that "feminism is a great way to meet babes." Either way, though, supporting feminism is seen as a strategy for losers—either failures at the dating game who need better odds, or failures at heterosexuality and masculinity altogether.

Still, a significant number of men are swimming against the tide, and not only on campus. Virtually every women's issue finds men doing coordinate work. Every contemporary campaign for women's equality finds male allies. NOMAS members, for example, have been active in every major feminist campaign—from defense of abortion clinics from right-wing attacks, to programs organized to end men's violence against women, to exploring the links between homophobia and sexism, and even researching masculinity from a feminist perspective.

Profeminism Today—and Tomorrow

And just as sisterhood is global, so too are profeminist men active around the world. Men from nearly fifty countries—from Mexico to Japan—regularly contribute to a newsletter of international profeminist scholars and activists, according to its editor, Oystein Holter, a Norwegian researcher. Scandinavian men are working to implement a gender equity mandated by law. Liisa Husu, the head of Finland's gender equity commission, has developed a parliamentary subcommittee of concerned men. (When I met with them in 1999, we spent our day discussing our mutual activities, after which they whisked me off to their all-male sauna resort on the shore of an icy Baltic Sea for a bit of male-bonding after all that equity work.) Scandinavian men routinely take parental leave; in fact, in Sweden they've introduced "Daddy Days," an additional month of paid paternity leave for the men to have some time with their newborns after the mothers have returned to work. About half of Swedish men take parental leave, according to fatherhood expert Lars Jalmert at the University of Stockholm.

The world's most successful profeminist organization must be Canada's White Ribbon Campaign. Begun in 1991 to coincide with the second anniversary of the Montreal Massacre—when a young man killed fourteen women engineering students at the University of Montreal on December 6, 1989—its goal was to publicly and visibly declare opposition to men's violence against women by encouraging men to wear a white ribbon as a public pledge. "Within days, hundreds of thousands of men and boys across Canada wore a ribbon," noted Michael Kaufman, one of the campaign's founders. "It exceeded our wildest expectations—even the Prime Minister wore a ribbon." This year, WRC events are also planned for Norway, Australia, and several American colleges; in Canada, events include a Manitoba hockey team planning a skating competition to raise money for a local women's shelter. WRC organizers have also developed curricula for secondary schools to raise the issue for boys.

But just as surely, some of the most important and effective profeminist men's activities are taking place in American homes every day, as men increasingly share housework and child-care, reorganize their schedules to be more responsive to the needs of their families, and even downsize their ambitions to develop a family strategy that does not exclusively revolve around his career path. "Housework remains the last frontier" for men to tame, argues sociologist Kathleen Gerson in her book *No Man's Land*. For every chubby hubby or sensitive new age corporate executive trooping off to bond with his fellow weekend warriors, there are those who are learning how to nurture the old-fashioned way: by doing it. Call them Ironing Johns, not Iron Johns. These are the quiet expressions of a quotidian revolution, without much ideological commitment, and fewer speeches and books—men simply struggling to live lives of equality and intimacy.

It's often in these quiet ways, as well as the public and visible expressions of support, that feminism has slowly but irrevocably transformed men's lives. For every men who gets involved with NOMAS or the WRC, or every man who signs up for a workshop on campus, there are hundreds, maybe thousands, who are looking for ways to support the women in their lives, to make the world safer for their daughters, their wives, their sisters, their mothers, their friends—as well as their sons, their fathers, and their brothers. Not only safer, but more free—a place where women's and men's aspirations stand a better chance of being realized.

In the process, they will invariably bump up against the same forces that hold women back—the institutional discrimination and internalized assumptions about women's inferiority. But mostly they will bump up against other men. "Just as I seek to educate myself," wrote Robert Reich, "I must also help educate other men."

But the payoff is significant. If power were a scarce commodity or a zero-sum game, we might think that women's increased power would mean a decrease in men's. And since most men don't feel very powerful anyway, the possibilities of further loss are rather unappealing. But for most men, all the power in the world does not seem to have trickled down to enable individual men to live the lives we say we want to live—lives of intimacy, integrity, and individual expression. By demanding the redistribution of power along more equitable lines, feminism also seeks a dramatic shift in our social priorities, our choices about how we live and what we consider important. Feminism is also a blueprint for men about how to become the men we want to be, and profeminist men believe that men will live happier, healthier, and more emotionally enriched lives by supporting women's equality.

Part of profeminist men's politics is to visibly and vocally support women's equality, and part of it is to quietly and laboriously struggle to implement that public stance into our own lives. And part of it must be to learn to confront and challenge other men, with care and commitment. "This cause is not altogether and exclusively woman's cause," wrote Frederick Douglass in 1848. "It is the cause of human brotherhood as well as human sisterhood, and both must rise and fall together."

INDEX

abortion: choice asserted by male, 20; Promise Keepers and Operation Rescue and, 167; Scandinavian extremism and, 156
abuse, masculinity and, 210. *See also* domestic violence
acquaintance rape, 214
Adams, Michele, 32
ADHD, 32; gender disparities in, 26
adolescence, gendered power shifts during, 96
Adolescence (Hall), 182
adversative method, 129–130, 177, 181, 193, 198–199
affirmative action, racial, 53
African American styles, young white male appropriation of, 57–58
The African Queen (film), 39
age, as variable in mutual aggression, 101, 111–112
Agger, Ben, 138
aggregate social power, men's, 215, 216
aggression: and age, 101, 111–112; in domestic life, 113–115 (*see also* domestic violence); masculine, 210; mutual, age as variable in, 101; premarital *vs.* connubial, 120n.11; sexual, source of, 76
"aggressive" *vs.* "violent," 111
"aggrieved entitlement," 10, 125, 137, 138
Air Force Academy, 184, 186
Ajami, Fouad, 158
Alda, Alan, 41
alloy model, of institutional diversity, 194
Al Qaeda, 157
Amendment 2, Colorado, and Promise Keepers, 170–171
American Civil Liberties Union, 174
American Nazi Party, 148
And Keep Your Powder Dry (Mead), 137
androgyny, fears of, 175–176
"angel in the house" fantasy, 38
Angier, Natalie, 72
"angry dad" campaigns, 22
"angry white men," 8, 19; and profeminist men, 213
Aniston, Jennifer, 46
anthropology, postmodern men's tropes of, 55–56

anti-authoritarianism, 66
anti-feminism, ix, 21, 175–176; confuted by facts, 79
antiglobalization politics, 158
anti-intellectualism, 66, 97
anti-Semitism, 149, 152; Scandinavian, 155
Archer, John, 100
Aryans, *see* white supremacists
asexuality, of gay men on TV, 47
assault: physical, quantification of consequences, 109–111 (see *also* violence); sexual, 111, 112 (see *also* rape)
Astin, Alexander, 179
Atlanta Braves fans' Tomahawk Chop, 56
Atta, Mohammed, 126, 159
attitude formation, and racism, 50–51, 52
attitudinalization and disaggregation, 50–51
autonomy: *vs.* aggregate social behavior, 71; *vs.* intimacy, 84
Auvinen, Pecca-Eric, 141

Baby and Child Care (Spock), 31
Baby Boom (film), 45
Bacall, Lauren, 39
backlash, anti-feminist, 65, 217
Backus, Jim, 41
Bailey, Susan McGee, 97
Barber, Benjamin, 126
barbiturate use and homosexual offspring, 79–80
Baron, R. A., 107
battered partners, 9–10; violence by, 116 (see *also* gender symmetry)
beards, and women's public-sphere equality, 159
Beecher, Catharine Ward, 87
Begin, Menachem, 155
Bellah, Robert, 126
Bergman, Ingrid, 39
Berlet, Chip, 171
The Big Sleep (film), 39
bin Laden, Osama, 157, 158
The Birdcage (film), 46
Bjorkqvist, K., 107
black clergy, and Promise Keepers, 170–171
blackface, 56
Black men: "good" *vs.* "bad" in sports, 61; "irrepressible" sexuality of, 151; and the

Black men (*continued*)
  Million Man March, 126; validation
    through sports talk radio, 60; as white
    men's role models, 56–57
Blackwell, Henry Brown, 223
"A Black Woman Took My Job" (TV talk
  show episode), 216
Blanchard, David, 168
Blankenhorn, David, 24, 70, 77–78
Bliss, Shepherd, 55
Bly, Robert, 10, 22, 55, 126, 211, 215, 216–217
Bogart, Humphrey, 39
Bogdon, Derek, 206
bona fide occupational qualification
  (BFOQ), 176
bonding, male, *see* male bonding
Boone, Wellington, 167, 170
Bootboys (Norway), 154
bourgeoisie, ability to revolutionize, x
Bowman, Patricia, 210
Boy Code, 96
"boy crisis," 26–28; feminist solutions to,
  94–98; in schools, 2; Sommers analysis of,
  92–94
Boy Meets Boy (TV show), 5
boys: feminization of, 182; poisoned by
  inequality, 70; "rescuing" of, from
  feminist reforms, 9; white, as school
  shooters, 132; and the zero-sum
  school/masculinity tradeoff, 66–67
Breaking Out (Brodie), 199, 201–203
Bright, Bill, 167, 169
Brimley, Wilfrid, 225
Brod, Artemis Leah, 62n.9
Brod, Harry, 217
Brodie, Laura Fairchild, 198, 199, 201, 203
Brother Rat (film), 177
Brown, James, 15, 17
Brown, Tony, 167
Bryant, Kobe, 4, 61
Brzonkala, Christy, 139, 140, 142n.14
bullying, 10, 134
"Bullying Behaviors among U.S. Youth"
  (Nansel et al.), 132
Bunting, Josiah III, 129, 181, 187, 192–93, 197,
  201–202, 203
Bush, George W.: administration of, 4; and
  post-9/11 masculinity, 7
busing, school, to achieve racial
  integration, 53
Butler, Chris, 228
Butts, Calvin, 170
Bye Bye Love (film), 43

Callaway, Howard, 184
Campbell, Patricia, 97
Campus Crusade for Christ, 167, 169
campus culture, dominance of, 140
cancer, Freud's last work discredited by, 77
capitalism, far right ambivalence toward,
  150, 152
Carneal, Michael, 124
Carrey, Jim, 43
Casablanca (film), 39

Cavanagh, K., 108, 109
celebrity, culture of, 135
Centers for Disease Control and
  Prevention, 103
Chan, Jachinson, 227
chanting, men's, ix, 56, 128, 211, 215
Chase, Richard Volney, 49n.7
Chen, Tony, 227
Cheney, Dick, 8
Cherlin, Andrew, 26
child care, 31–33, 214
childrearing, as woman's role, 78
children in films, 43–44, 49n.6
child support, 25, 26
Cho, Seung-Hui, 124, 131–132, 137
Christian Coalition, 167, 169
Christianity: "muscular," 23, 165; revirilized,
  23–25
Christian Men's Network, 165
The Citadel, 10, 49n.5; arguments against
  admitting women, 181–183; coeducation
  at, ix, 197, 198; culture of masculinity at,
  128–130; in fiction, 199–200; and
  litigation, 4, 177; profeminist men's
  support for female admission to, 224;
  residual problems at, 205–206; resistance
  to female cadets at, 2, 200–201
Civilization and Its Discontents (Freud), 77
"Clarence. . . and Us" (Kimmel), 210; spinoff
  lecture from, 211–212
Clark, Albert P., 184
Clarke, Edward C., 180, 203
class, socioeconomic: and hip-hop culture,
  57; and housework, 30–31; solidarity
  across racial divide, 58; and white
  supremacy, 149, 150, 154, 160 (see *also*
  downward mobility); and women's
  achievement, 188–189
Claunch, Erin, 197, 206
Clayburgh, Jill, 42
"click," profeminist men's, 226–229
clinical data, exclusion of, 105
Clinton, Bill, 4, 7, 132, 225
coeducation: at The Citadel, ix, 197, 198;
  early 20th-century resistance to, 182; and
  presumption of minimal difference, 190;
  and stereotypes about tokens, 184; at VMI,
  ix, 197–198, 201–203
Cole, Ed, 165, 167
colleges and universities, as local
  cultures, 139
colonization, and problematizing of
  indigenous masculinities, 144
Colorado for Family Values, 170
Colson, Charles, 165
Coltrane, Scott, 32
Columbia Pacific University, 81
Columbine (Cullen), 123
Columbine High School, 135–137, 139
"common couple violence," 115
communication: inter-gender, in Gray's
  essentialist model, 84, 85–86; violence as
  means of, 105

comparable worth, 28

compassion, for victims of domestic violence, 115, 118

Confederate iconography, Scandinavian white supremacists' use of, 155

conflict tactics, 106

Conflict Tactics Scale, 67, 101, 104, 105–113, 121n.22

Connell, R. W., 114, 147

Conroy, Pat, 177

consumption: of Christian products, 164; of the "other"'s culture, 57, 63n.10

control: breakdown of men's, 114; and premarital violence, 112

convenience samples, advertising-generated, 105

Converse College, 178

Cooper, Justin, 43

covenant marriage, 147

crime victimization studies, 102, 103, 107, 112, 118

Crowley, Jocelyn, 25

Cruise, Tom, 4–5, 43

Cruising (film), 45

cultures: of celebrity, 135; of Columbine High School, 139; firearm-friendly, 135; of gender, local, 135; hip-hop, 56–57, 63n.10; identification and political alliance, 57; local, colleges and universities as, 139; of masculinity, at The Citadel, 128–130; political, and school shootings, 135

"culture lag," 41

Cusack, Joan, 46

Cusack, John, 4–5

cyberspace, as masculine "clubhouse," 22

"Daddy Days" (Sweden), 229

Danson, Ted, 43

Daoudi, Kamel, 158

Darwin, Charles, as "misandrist," 70

date rape, 4, 210, 214, 224

date violence, 111

dating etiquette, 9, 210, 224

Dawkins, Richard, 71

Day of the Sword, 150

Dean, James, 41

The Decline of Males (Tiger), 89

defensive resistance, male, 18

DeGeneres, Ellen, 48

DeLay, Tom, 132

Dell, Floyd, 211, 223

demasculinization, feminism read as, 151

democracy, small-town exclusivist, 148

DeMoss, Mark, 169

Den Hollander, Roy, 21

Details magazine, 4

detection of potential shooters, 135, 140

development, global, 143

Dewey, John, 190–191, 218

difference: denial of, 187; discrimination justified on basis of, 180; faulty understanding of, 190; of gender, vs. power differences, 85–86; and sameness, negotiation of, 184, between sexes, in

VMI/Citadel litigation, 178; used to justify discrimination, 192–193

difference feminism, 192

disaggregation and attitudinalization, 50–51

discipline, physical, of children, see violence: parental, toward children

Disclosure (film), 42

discrimination: difference offered as justification for, 192–193; gender, litigation of, 174; sameness vs. difference in adjudicating, 175–176, 186; workplace, 20

displacement, male, 146. See also migration

display, gendered, strategic deployment of, by female cadets, 185

"distance learning," synopsized, 81

divorce; and fatherhood, 24–26; restrictive laws on, 147

Dobash, R. D. and R. E., 108, 109, 114

Dobson, James, 169

Dr. Dre, 57

Dr. Laura (Schlessinger), 9, 70, 81–83, 87

domestic patriarchy, 146

domestic violence, 9–10, 20; asymmetric rates of, in crime victimizations studies, 103; causes and severity of, 109; conflict-motivated, 115; and the Conflict Tactics Scale, 105–113; context of, 106; control-motivated, 115; expressive, 113–115; by former partners, 112; gender symmetry argument, 20, 67, 99–102; initiation of, 106; instrumental, 115; intervention strategies, 118; measures of, 100 (see also Conflict Tactics Scale); public/private split, 107; retrospective studies, 107; against same-sex partners, 115–116

domination: erection as signifier of, 213 (see also phallus); male bonding through, 52

dot-com bubble, 6, 7

Douglass, Frederick, 218, 223, 230

Dowd, Maureen, 7

downward mobility, 149, 150, 154; among Islamic extremists, 158

Driscoll, Marc, 23

drumming, male, ix, 2, 56, 128, 211, 215

dual-career couples, 29–33

dual-carer parents, xi

Du Bois, W.E.B., 218

Dunne, Irene, 38

Dworkin, Andrea, 69–70, 89

Eastman, Max, 223

economic crisis, Iraq War era, 7, 8, 17. See also recession

economic prosperity, associated with gender equality, 208

education; adversarial method, 129–130, 181, 193, 198–199; arguments for excluding men, 187–191; arguments for excluding women, 179–183; development of boys, 26–27, 97; Dewey on coeducation, 190–191; funding cutbacks, 135; methodology, evaluating, 192–194; for restraint, 74 75; single-sex, 175. See also school

Ehrenreich, Barbara, 74, 158
8 Mile (film), 58
Eliot, T. S., 126
Ellen (TV show), 47, 48
emasculation, fear of, 160, 183
Emerson, Ralph Waldo, 223
Eminem, 57–58
emphatic sameness, as female cadets'
    coping strategy, 185
empowerment, women's, inspiring to
    men, 22
"end of manhood," 214
entitlement, male, 10, 19, 211; aggrieved, 125,
    137, 138; and collapse of public patriarchy,
    158; in Promise Keepers ideology, 166; to
    restore patriarchy, 148–149; and sense of
    powerlessness, 216; in sexuality, 40; to use
    violence, 110; white, 149
environmentalism, and white supremacist
    ideology, 156–157, 160n.4
Epstein, Cynthia Fuchs, 27, 95, 182
equality: gender (see gender equality); of
    opportunity, 42–44, 183; of rank, and
    gender difference, 193; as sameness, at
    VMI, 202
equal protection, in U.S. legal system, 176
Equal Rights Amendment, 224
equal unpleasantness standard, 206
erection, as signifier of dominance, 213.
    See also phallus
ESPN, male target demographic of, 59
essentialism, gender, 10; Gray's model,
    82–88
E.T. (film), 43
evangelical movement, 171
evangelical rallies, male, 2. See also Million
    Man March; Promise Keepers
Evans, Tony, 165
Everett, Rupert, 46
evolutionary psychology, 70–75
ex-partners, violence by, 112
extremists, right-wing, 10, 125, 126, 147–157;
    and reaction to globalization, 145–146;
    rural militias, 148–150

Failing at Fairness (Sadker), 226
Faludi, Susan, 6, 183
Falwell, Jerry, 23, 169
Families and Work Institute, 29
family, 24–26; men's attachment to, 77–79;
    as metaphor, at The Citadel, 193; and
    work, balance between, 29, 39
Family Conflict model of domestic
    violence, 118
family conflict studies, 102, 103–105
Fangen, Katrine, 154
fantasies: of power, men's, 22; of rape, in
    white male racists, 151; romantic, of "the
    angel in the house," 38
Farr, Katherine, 52
Farrakhan, Louis, 171
Farred, Grant, 60
Farrell, Warren, 80, 215
fashion, appropriation of, 57

fatherhood, 24–26; "absentee landlord"
    stereotype, 9; in films, 43–44; new, 77
Fatherless America (Blankenhorn), 4, 24,
    77–78
fatherlessness: attributed to feminism, 82;
    fear of, 77–78
fathers' rights groups, 25, 145
Faulkner, Shannon, 128–129, 174, 179,
    186–187, 199, 200–201
FBI report, on school violence, 132
fear: of androgyny, 175–176; and battle stress,
    201; of fatherlessness, 77–78; of foreign
    invasion, Scandinavian, 155; Freud's last
    work discredited by, 77; of shame, and its
    prevention, 134
Fein, Ellen, 87–88
Fellowship for Christian Athletes, 164–165
The Feminine Mystique (Friedan), 42
feminism, 79; allegedly misguided, 93;
    analytic, 213, 214; blamed for
    fatherlessness, 82; difference, 192; as
    engine of gender inversion, 151; and
    freedom for men, 211; "Gentlemen's
    Auxiliary" of profeminist men, 219,
    222–223; indicted for "war against boys,"
    92–94; male abreactions to, 3, 87 (see also
    anti-feminism); and men's lives, 221–223;
    and policy issues, 69, 213; reasonableness
    of, 217; right-wing's systematic assault on,
    8; as therapy for failing relationships, 89;
    and women's colleges, 188
Feminist Union, Boston University, 228
feminization: of American society and
    culture, 15; of boys, 182. See also
    demasculinization; emasculation
Ferber, Abby, 160n.1
Fiebert, Martin, 100–102, 104, 107
Fiedler, Leslie, 49n.7
Field of Dreams (film), 44
fields of power, gender relations embedded
    in, 214–215
films, 41; action, violent, 137; depiction of
    children in, 43–44; gay men as women's
    virtue guides in, 45–47; male weepie, 44;
    masculine redemption in, 39
fire departments: and BFOQs, 176–177; as
    masculine preserve, 6, 19; New York's
    predominantly white male, 6
Fire in the Belly (Keen), 4, 55, 211
The First Wives Club (film), 42
Florida Interklan Report, 151
Focus on the Family, 169
foreign invasion, Scandinavian fears of, 155
Forrest, Bedford, 206
Four Weddings and a Funeral (film), 46
Fox, James Alan, 116
Fox-Genovese, Elizabeth, 179
Frank, Archie Gunder, 143
fraud and scandal, corporate, and corporate
    masculinity, 6, 7
Freaks Talk Back (Gamson), 47
Freedman, Eric, 220
Freud, Sigmund, 77
Friedan, Betty, 42

functionalism, of 1950s, 80
fundamentalism: masculine, 163 (*see also* Promise Keepers); as resistance to globalization, 145
Furstenberg, Frank, 26

Gable, Clark, 39
Gamson, Josh, 47
gangbangers, 2
Garrison, William Lloyd, 218
gay-baiting, 10, 134, 212, 213
gay liberation, 45
gay marriage, xi
gay men: of color, 5; excluded from Promise Keepers, 53–64; as female surrogates, 49n.7; new visibility of, 5, 46; oversexed and hypermasculine, 76, 79, 151; and Promise Keepers, 170; sports radio jokes about, 59–60; at VMI and The Citadel, 183; as women's virtue guides in film, 45–47
Gelles, R., 117–118
gender: cost-benefit tradeoffs of integration in, 203–204; discrimination litigation, 174; feminism as engine in inversion of, 151; and globalization, 143; in militia ideologies, 150; problematizing of nonwhite others, 151; rendered visible by women, 39; strategies of, among female cadets, 185
gender differences: false, between girls and boys, 97; Gray's "Mars/Venus" model, 83–87; as innate and healthy, 93; mean, applied to all women and men, 181; in violence, 107
gendered display, by female cadets, 185
gendered institutions, 146, 175, 184, 186. *See also individual institutions*
gender equality, x–xi, 10–11; acceptance of, 28; backlash against (*see* backlash); conducive to richness, excitement, and complexity, 89; difference and sameness in, 175–176; discouraged by Gray, 87; equated with effeminacy, 218; and increased economic prosperity, 208; male solace from, 5–6; and masculinized women in film, 42 men's responses to, 3, 15–37, 18–21, 33–34, 130 (*see also* backlash); as only way to "save the males," 192–194; and sexual arrogance, 189; in workplace, 207
gender identity: downplaying of, by female cadets, 185; uncorrelated with motivations or talents, 192
gender inequality: and privilege, in adolescence, 96; resurgent, 207; women's colleges as challenge to, 189
Gender Inequality Index, 208
gender policies, state: Afghanistan, 158–159; U.S., 153
gender reconciliation, and Promise Keepers, 171
gender regimes, and gay visibility, 47–48
gender relations: capacity to revolutionize, x; in field of power, 214–215; transformation of, 41

"gender symmetry," in domestic violence, 20, 67, 99–102
"Gentlemen's Auxiliary of Feminism," 219, 222–223
Gerson, Kathleen, 229
G.I. Jane (film), 42
Gilder, George, 26, 75–77, 79
Gillette, Douglas, 55
Gilligan, Carol, 93–94, 96, 180–181
Gilligan, James, 134
Gingrich, Newt, 132, 180
Ginsburg, Ruth Bader, 129
Giovanni, Nikki, 138
globalization: as gendered process, 143; and Islamic extremism, 158; resistance to, 145
Goffman, Erving, 138, 198
Gooding, Cuba Jr., 43
Gottman, John, 33
Grant, Hugh, 46
Gray, John, 9, 44, 81, 83–87
Great Recession, *see* economic crisis, Iraq War era
Greene, David, 228
Green Jacket Movement (Denmark), 154
Griffith, Melanie, 42
Gronjakkerne (Denmark), 154
guilt, politics of, 11
gun culture, 135
Gurian, Michael, 93
Gutmann, Stephanie, 203, 204
Gutterman, David, 226
Guyland (Kimmel), 1, 19

Hackman, Gene, 46
Haddad, Richard, 19
Hale, Sarah, 87
Hall, G. Stanley, 182
Hamlin, Christopher, 170
Harris, Eric, 123, 124, 125, 131, 136, 137, 139, 140
Hassan, Nasra, 157, 158
Hayes, Sean, 47
Hayward, Fred, 25
hazing, 130
health, psychological, enhanced by men's child care and housework, 33
hedge fund racketeering, and corporate masculinity, 7
Heflin, James Thomas, 218
hegemonic ideal, 143–144
Hekmatyar, Gulbuddin, 157
Hepburn, Katharine, 39
Herbert, Bob, 137
heroism, changing criteria for, 205
Heston, Charlton, 148–149
heterosexism, 53
Hill, Anita, 4, 210
Hill, E. V., 170
hip-hop culture, white consumption of, 56–57, 63n.10
Hisb-e-Islami, 157
Hoffman, Dustin, 44
Hofstadter, Richard, 150
"Hokie Nation" (Virginia Tech), 137, 140
Holocaust deniers, 148

Holter, Oystein, 229
home: and emasculation, 42; and hearth,
accessed through minstrelsy, 56
homicide: gender and relation of victim to
killer, 110; of partners, 113, 116
homophobia, 10, 52, 58, 149, 218; Dr. Laura's,
82; organized "Christian," 54
homosexuality: Jews blamed for, 155; in
Promise Keepers' ideology, 54 (see also
gay men)
homosociality, male, 80
Hooters BFOQ defense, 176
Horn, Wade, 77–78
Houck, C. Weston, 179
housework, 29–33, 41, 214, 229
Howe, Frederic, 223
"How It Feels to Be the Husband of a
Suffragette" (pamphlet), 218
Hrdy, Sarah Blaffer, 71–72
Hudson, Rock, 38
humiliation: of female cadets, 128; gendered,
160; responses to, 125, 134; Westernization
as, 158
Husu, Liisa, 229

identity: essentialist gender models of, 10,
82–88; gender (see gender identity);
masculine, 16–17; non-racist, 50, 51; as
provider, 17, 24; racial identification with
the "other," 58
immigration, 149, 154
Imus, Don, 60
In and Out (film), 46
inclusion through exclusion, 53
"Indicators of School Crime and Safety
2000" (Bureau of Justice Statistics), 132
inequality: of class, 50; of gender, 65, 70, 96,
189, 207; racial, 50
In Glory's Shadow (Manegold), 199, 201
initiation: of domestic violence, 106; male
rituals of, 156, 205
inner city, consumption of, 57
innocence, of children and gay men, 47
instrumental use of violence, 106
intention and motivation in domestic
violence, 106
Intercourse (Dworkin), 69–70
intermediate scrutiny, 176, 178
intervention strategies, in domestic
violence, 118
intimacy, vs. autonomy, 84
"intimate terrorism," 115
intolerance, right-wing "Christian," 135–137
Ireland, Patricia, 222
Iron John (Bly), 4, 55, 211, 216–217
Islamic radical organizations, 157–159
"it group," The Citadel, 183
Ittihad-I-Islami, 157
Iverson, Allen, 61

Jacklin, Carol, 107, 179
Jackson, Thomas Jonathan ("Stonewall"), 198
Jalmert, Lars, 229
Jamiat-I-Islami, 157

Jane Eyre (Bronte), 38
Jarrah, Ziad, 158
"J-B-C Men," 23
Jencks, C., 189
Jerry Maguire (film), 43
Jesus: masculinizing of, ix; revirilization
of, 23
Jeter, Derek, 61
Jews, as threat to American male, 152
The Jim Rome Show (sports talk radio), 59
John Birch Society, 148
Johnson, Magic, 210
Johnson, M. P., 114–115

Kaufman, Michael, 229
Keaton, Diane, 45
Keaton, Michael, 41
Keen, Sam, 4, 55, 211
The Kid (film), 43
Kimmel, Michael, 195n.2, 210, 211–212,
213, 221
The Kinder, Gentler Military (Gutmann),
203–204
Kindlon, Dan, 92
King, Jacqueline, 27
Kinkel, Kip, 124
Kinsey, Albert, 40, 182
Kiser, Jackson, 178, 179
Kitwana, Bakari, 57, 63n.10
Klebold, Dylan, 123, 124, 131, 136, 137, 139,
140, 141
Kline, Kevin, 46
Kramer vs. Kramer (film), 44
Kreatrivistens Kyrka (Sweden), 154
Ku Klux Klan, 148, 155, 206
Kulish, Nicholas, 28, 29
Kupers, Terry, 228

labor migrations, 143, 146
Lane, Nathan, 46
language: foreign, acquisition of, and
English skills, 96–97; hip-hop, white male
appropriation of, 57; men's, and relations
of power, 85–86
Larkin, Ralph, 135–137
Lee, Robert E., 206
lesbians, and Promise Keepers, 53–64, 170
Levit, Nancy, 190
Lewis, R., 108, 109
Liar Liar (film), 43
liberalism, sexual, 77
Life Without Father (Popenoe), 4
Limbaugh, Rush, 81
Lipnicki, Jonathan, 43
litigation, 177
Little Sorrel, 198
Loow, Helene, 160n.2
The Lords of Discipline (Conroy), 177,
199–200
Loukatis, Barry, 124
love, women's, transformative power of, 39
Lovetinska, Petra, 205–206
Ludacris, 57
Luke, Tim, 140, 142n.17

Maccoby, Eleanor, 25, 107
MacDowell, Andie, 46
Mace, J. Emery, 193
Mace, Nancy, 193
Made in America (film), 43
Mad Men (TV show), 2, 16
Madonna (Louise Veronica Ciccone), 46
Magnificent Obsession (film), 38
Mailer, Norman, 7, 17
malaise, male, 1–2
male bashers, 70. *See also* anti-feminism
male bonding, 20, 210–211; and the
    adversative system, 177; cross-generational,
    59; cross-racial, 60; through domination,
    52; evangelical (*see* Promise Keepers)
male displacement, 146
male liberationists, 80
"malicious compliance," 202–203
Malone, J., 101–102
Manegold, Catherine, 199, 201
The Manhood of the Master (Sunday), 23
The Manliness of Christ (Sunday), 23
The Manly Christ (Sunday), 23
Mansfield, Harvey, 21
marginalization: as a coping strategy, 138;
    cultural, and school shootings, 134, 136–141
marriage: as civilizing force, 77; as covenant,
    147
Marrs, Tex, 151
Martino, Wayne, 96
Marx, Karl, x
Mary Baldwin College, 178, 179, 193
masculinists, 21, 22
masculinity, 17; adolescent, 10; alternative
    meanings of, 41; assumptions about, 129;
    author's socialization in, 224; as
    commitment to relationships, 127;
    equated with anti-intellectualism, 97;
    failed, and retreat into Islamic extremism,
    159; feminized, 165; hegemonic models of,
    7, 144–145, 182–183; heroic, rehabilitation
    of, 6–8; historical constructions of, 93, 95,
    97, 143; and Islamic extremism, 157–159;
    manipulated, 77–78; in the media, 3, 4, 8;
    military, 7, 49n.5, 175; misframing of, 3;
    myths of, rescue from, 93; problematic,
    in film, 49n.8; quicksanding of, ix;
    restoration of, 125–127, 153; right-wing
    ideologies of, 126; rituals of, 130 (see *also*
    mythopoetic retreats); state as betrayer
    of, 149; use of black men to validate, 51;
    and violence, 108, 110
masculinity politics, 147
Masoud, Ahmed Shah, 157
masturbation, female, 40
mate guarding, 72
Maxim magazine, 4
McCartney, Bill, 10, 23, 52, 53, 163–164,
    169, 170
McCartney, Kristyn, 164
McCormick, Eric, 47
McVeigh, Timothy, 126
Mead, Margaret, 137
Meade, Michael, 22

media: and construction of masculinity, 3, 8;
    gender representations, post-innocence,
    39; global culture, 141. *See also* films;
    television; *individual magazines and TV
    shows by title*
memory, methodological problem of, 107
men: "angry white," 8, 19, 213; anti-feminist
    contempt for, 9; breakdown of control
    over women, 114; defenses against gender
    equality, 15–37; essentialist visions of,
    82–88; evangelical sports stadium rallies,
    2 (see *also* Promise Keepers); and family
    life, 77–79, 82, 166–167; gay (*see* gay men);
    Gilder's diagnosis of, 75–77; Gray's
    essentialism, 83–87; and identity, 16–17,
    24, 50, 51, 58; liberated and profeminist,
    8, 22, 33, 41–44, 209, 213, 214; as monolithic
    oppressor, 213; mythopoetic retreats for,
    ix, 10, 21–24, 54–56, 210–211, 217, 221; as
    the new victims, 8, 9; power relations
    between and among, 216; provider role,
    17; responses to racism, 50–52; of rural
    militias, 148; social movements for, 3–4;
    Swedish, and parental leave, 229; women
    as competition for, 18
Men Acting for Change (MAC), 221, 226
Men Against Rape and Sexism (MARS), 221
Men Against Sexual Assault (MASA), 221
Men Against Sexual Harassment (MASH), 221
Men and Marriage (Gilder), 75–77
Men Are from Mars, Women Are from Venus
    (Gray), 83
Men in Groups (Tiger), 80
Men Opposed to Sexist Tradition (MOST),
    221, 225
men's groups, 171, 172
Men's Health magazine, 33
Men's League for Woman Suffrage, 218, 223
men's movements, 55, 126–127, 211, 215; for
    men's rights, 19–21, 20, 21, 145
Men's Rights Inc., 25
"Men's Studies," 214
menstruation, and female cadets, 203
Mentalvos, Jenny, 193
Mentalvos, Mike, 193
meritocracy, 21, 79, 175
Messner, Michael, 52, 225
"metrosexuals," 5
Middleton, George, 218
migration, labor, 146. *See also* immigration
migrations, labor, 143
Mike and the Mad Dog (sports talk radio), 58
military schools, motivations for attending,
    181–186
Militia of Montana, 148
Million Man March, 126, 127, 171, 221
Mills College (Oakland, CA), 187
minstrelsy, 56, 138
"misandrous" reforms, 9
misogyny, in Eminem raps, 58
Mnookin, Robert, 25
model-minority model, specious, 131–132
Modine, Matthew, 43
Montreal Massacre (1989), 229

Moore, Demi, 42, 202
Moore, Robert, 55
The Moral Animal (Wright), 72
Moral Majority, 169
Morris, Wayne, 227
Moskos, Charles, 187
Mott, Lucretia and James, 223
Moussaoui, Zacarias, 158
Mr. Mom (film), 41
Mrs. Doubtfire (film), 44
Ms. magazine, on Obama presidency, 8
Murrah federal building bombing,
    Oklahoma City (1995), 10, 148, 151
Murray, Charles, 70, 77
"muscular" Christianity, 23, 165
My Best Friend's Wedding (film), 46
mythopoesis, 126, 128, 215
mythopoetic retreats, ix, 10, 22, 54–56,
    210–211, 217, 221
myths, masculine, 22

Nadeem, Shehzad, 225
NAFTA treaty, 150
"Nanny State," 151
National Center for Fathering, 164
National Consortium on Violence
    Research, 116
National Crime Survey, 103
National Crime Victimization Study, 103
National Family Violence Survey, 103
National Fatherhood Initiative, 77
National Front (Sweden), 154
National Institute of Justice, 103
National Opinion Research Center, 40
National Organization for Men Against
    Sexism (NOMAS), 209, 221, 228–229, 230
National Survey of Adolescents in the United
    States, 111
National Survey of Families and Households,
    30, 104
National Vanguard, 153
National Violence against Women in
    America Survey, 103, 109–110, 112,
    115–116
Native American cultures, men's movement
    tropes borrowed from, 56
nativism, 149
*A Natural History of Rape: Biological Bases of
    Sexual Coercion* (Thornhill and Campbell),
    72–75
Nazism, and Swedish white supremacists,
    155
Neal, Mark Anthony, 56
Nelly, 57
Nelson, Mariah Burton, 20
neo-Nazis, 148
New Man magazine, 164
New Order, 152, 153
New World Order, as threat, 151
The Next Best Thing (film), 46
Niemala, P., 107
9/11, as watershed, 6. *See also* Islamic radical
    organizations
No Child Left Behind Act, 27, 135

"No Crime Being White" (Day of the Sword),
    150
No Man's Land (Gerson), 229
nonindustrial cultures, men's movement
    tropes borrowed from, 56
Nordic countries, white supremacists in,
    154–157
"normalization" of gay men and women, 47
Norsk Arisk Ungdomsfron (NAUF), 154
Norwich University, 183, 191; female cadets
    as VMI role models, 192, 202
NS Mobilizer, 151
NUNS 88 (Norway), 154
Nylund, David, 20, 59

Obama, Barack, 8, 17, 31, 51
O'Barr, Jean, 226
The Object of My Affection (film), 46
Oklahoma City federal building bombing
    (1995), 10, 148, 151
O'Leary, K. D., 101–102, 111, 120n.11
Operation Rescue, 171
opportunity, equal: and fear of emasculation,
    183; gendered, in film, 42–44
orgasm, women's faking of, 40
other: consumption of culture of, 57,
    63n.10; nonwhite, problematizing gender
    of, 151; racial identification with, 58;
    woman as, 160
Owen, Robert Dale, 218

Packwood, Robert, 4
Paglia, Camille, 79, 95
pain, men's, 216
Paine, Thomas, 218, 223
Palmer, Craig, 72–75
paramilitary chic, 135
paranoid politics, 148
parental leave, in Sweden, 229
parenting: dual-carer, xi (see *also* child
    care); gender-independent styles of, 86
patriarchy: biblically based, maintenance of,
    53–54; and indelible inscribing of
    privilege, 213; indigenous, restoration of,
    145–146; restoration of, 148, 171–172; "soft,"
    166; types of, 146–147
patriarchy-baiting, 212
Patterson, Orlando, 219
Pennington, Gary Scott, 124
People magazine, gushes over Rumsfeld, 8
"Peter Panic syndrome," 1
phallus, filmic possession of, by Demi
    Moore, 42. *See also* erection
Phillips, Wendell, 218
Pierce, William, 151
police departments, and BFOQs, 176–177
political alliance, and cultural
    identification, 57
Pollack, William, 92, 93, 96
Pollitt, Katha, 217
Ponzi schemes, and corporate masculinity, 7
Pope, Barbara, 204–205
Popenoe, David, 77
pop psychology, 70–75, 81–87

pornography, campaigns against: feminist, 224; right-wing Scandinavian, 156
Posse Comitatus, 148
Powell, Kevin, 57
power: corporate, women in positions of, 80; field of, gender relations embedded in, 214–215; lost, extreme right's trope of, 148; relations of, between and among men, 216
"The Power Team," 24
premature self-congratulation, 214, 222
Prison Fellowship Ministries, 165
probability samples, nationally representative, 105
problem students, 94. See also "boy crisis"
producerism, 148
profeminist men, 213, 217, 219, 220–230
proletarianization, of local peasantries, 143
promiscuity, Hrdy's mock-etiology of, 71–72
"The Promised Land" (Springsteen), 160
Promise Keepers, 10, 23, 53, 126, 127, 145, 163–172, 221
prostitution, campaigns against: feminist, 224; right-wing Scandinavian, 156
protest masculinity, 147, 156
psychological responses to structural problems, 51
psychology, evolutionary, 70–75
The Psychology of Sex Differences (Maccoby and Jacklin), 107
public office, women's candidacies for, 28
public patriarchy, 146, 148
public/private split, in domestic violence, 107
Purdy, Jedediah, 126
Putnam, Robert, 126

Quaid, Randy, 43
Queer Eye for the Straight Guy (TV series), 5
Quindlen, Anna, 19, 38

R-2, 149
Rabbani, Burhannudin, 157
Race Matters (West), 57
racial and sexual discrimination litigation, sameness and difference in, 175–176
racial healing, strategies of, 8; appropriation, 54–56; conversation, 58–62; inspiration, 56–58; reconciliation, 52–54
racial inequality, 50
racism, 149; and attitudes, 50–51, 52; and Black colleges, 189–190; of "good" vs. "bad" black athletes, 61–62; Promise Keepers' response to, 168–171; as restorative of masculinity, 153; in school shooting analyses, 132; and sexism, 227; suppressed on sports talk radio, 60; as white people's problem, 53
radio, 58–60
rage, male, against women and gays, 60
Raising Cain (Kindlon and Thompson), 4, 92
Ramsey, Evan, 124
rape: in evolutionary psychology, 73; as homosocial act, 74; as multidimensional phenomenon, 73

Rape Awareness Weeks, collegiate, 75
Rauh, Ida, 223–224
Reagan, Ronald, 177
"real boy" books, 4
Real Boys (Pollack), 4, 92, 93
"reasonable woman standard," 176
Rebel without a Cause (film), 41
recession, Iraq War era, 28. See also economic crisis
reconciliation: gender, under patriarchy, 54; as strategy for coping with racism, 52–54
redemption, male, in films, 43–44
Red Men, Improved Order of, 56
"red" states, preponderance of school shootings in, 135
Reed, Ralph, 169
Reich, Robert, 226, 230
Reinhold, Judge, 43
Reiser, Paul, 43
relationships: egalitarian, 28; failing, feminism as therapy for, 89; men's commitment to, 127; romantic, Gray's model for managing, 86–87
religion, as women's domain, 22–23
reproductive freedom, 224. See also abortion
reproductive success, and rape, 73–74
restraint: education for, 74–75; sexual, of men, by women, 80
retaliatory violence, 114, 121n.24, 134, 156
retreats, mythopoetic, ix, 10, 21–24, 54–56, 210–211, 217, 221
retrospection, 107
revenge, 137
revirilization of Jesus, 23
Revisioning Men's Lives (Kupers), 228
Richardson, D., 107
Riesman, David, 179, 189, 195n.4
"right to choose" asserted by male, 20
right wing: assault on feminism, 8; extreme (see extreme right); males in extremist organizations, 10; New Right sexual philosophy, 75–76; Promise Keepers' ties to, 169; racism and masculinity, 50–52
Riksfronten (Sweden), 154
Risman, Barbara, 33
Roberts, Julia, 46
The Rock (Dwayne Johnson), 4–5
role models for female cadets, 192, 202
Rubin, Lillian, 40, 149
Ruby Ridge, Idaho, standoff in, 148
The Rules (Fein and Schneider), 87–88
Rumsfeld, Donald, 7, 8

Sadker, David and Myra, 226
Sadler, Max, 225
sameness: vs. difference, in discrimination litigation, 175–176, 186; emphatic, as female cadets' coping strategy, 185; equality as, at VMI, 202
San Francisco (film), 38–39
Sanger, Margaret and William, 224
Sayyaf, Abdul Rasoul, 157
Scandinavian white supremacists, 154–157
Schafly, Phyllis, 204

Schindler, Oskar, 43
Schindler's List (film), 43
Schlessinger, Laura, *see* Dr. Laura
Schneider, Sherrie, 87–88
schools: academic success *vs.* masculinity,
    66–67; the "boy crisis" in, 2, 92–98;
    busing to achieve racial integration, 53;
    conducive to violence, 138; shootings in,
    2, 10, 123–124, 131–141 (see *also* detection);
    tolerant of bullying and harassment,
    135, 136; underfunding of, and the
    "boy crisis," 94
Schultz, Jason, 226
secularization, resistance to, 157
self-affirmation through violence, 134
self-indicting realizations, 227
The Selfish Gene (Dawkins), 71
Selleck, Tom, 46
Seneca Falls Convention of 1848, 218, 223
The Seven Promises of a Promise Keeper, 23,
    54, 167
Seven Sisters colleges, graduates of, 188
sex, teleology of, 73–74
sexes, differences between, genetic, 71.
    See also essentialism
Sex in Education (Clarke), 180
sexism, 52, 53, 149; and racism, 227
sexual arrogance, 189
sexual assault, 111, 112; groups against, and
    profeminist men, 221, 225, 226. *See also*
    rape
sexual coercion, 121n.22
sexual harassment, 20, 214, 224
sexuality: and entitlement, 40; of gay men,
    79; gendered, challenges to binary
    construction of, 45
sexual predation: alcohol-inspired, 1; and
    sports talk radio, 61
sexual regimes, intact, despite gay visibility,
    47–48
sexual revolution, 40
Sexual Suicide (Gilder), 75
shame, fear and prevention of, 134
Sharpton, Al, 60, 170
"sheeple," 151
Shehhi, Marwani al-, 158
Sherb, Cory, 220
She's Gotta Have It (film), 42
siblings, family model based on, 193–194
Siege magazine, 155
The Silence of the Lambs (film), 45
single parents, 86
single-sex schools: arguments for excluding
    men, 187–191; arguments for excluding
    women, 179–183
skinheads, 148, 156
Slotkin, Richard, 49n.7, 137
Smith, William Kennedy, 4, 210
Sobchack, Vivian, 49n.6
socialization, primary forces of, 3
social movements for men, 3–4
social sciences: deceptive distinctions in, 95;
    epistemic unreliability of, 70–71; reliable,
    102. *See also* psychology; sociology

sociology: aggregate behavior, and the
    autonomous individual, 71; of school
    shootings, 123–124
Sommers, Christina Hoff, 70, 77–79,
    93–94, 95
South Carolina Institute for Leadership,
    178–179
Sowell, Thomas, 132
"So You Think You Might Be Gay"
    (pamphlet), 183
Spielberg, Steven, 43
Spike TV (formerly TNN), 5
spiritual colonialism, 56
Spock, Benjamin, 31
sports: girls' participation in, x; stadium
    rallies, of evangelical men, 2; women's
    and girls' participation in, 20
Sports Illustrated swimsuit issue, 228
sports talk radio, 20, 58–61
spousal homicide, 110, 113
Sprewell, Latrell, 61
Springsteen, Bruce, 17, 140, 160
stalking, 115
state: as betrayer of masculinity, 149; gender
    policies, 153, 158–159
Steinem, Gloria, 93
stereotyping: assumed differences as, 194;
    from predominant majority's shared
    traits, 181
Stewart, Potter, 176
Stiffed (Faludi), 4
Stimpson, Catherine, 96
Stockdale, James, 200
Stoltenberg, John, 213–214
Storm magazine, 155
strategic overcompensation, by female
    cadets, 185
Straus, Murray, 105, 106, 107, 109, 110–111, 116,
    117–118
Streep, Meryl, 44
stress: battle analogy, 201; gendered
    responses to, 84
Striperella (cartoon), 5
"suffering," men's, 55
Suhayda, Rocky, 160
suicide bombers, profile of, 158
Suitable Helpers, 167
Sunday, Billy, 23, 165
Sundquist, Matti, 156
superiority, sense of, and male bonding
    sexism, 52
support networks, among female cadets, 185
Supreme Court: and all-male military
    academies, 4, 128, 129, 179; on sameness
    and difference, 176; vacates the Violence
    Against Women Act, 142n.14
Svastika (Swedish skinhead group), 156
Symons, Donald, 71

Tailhook harassment scandal, 4, 203–204
Take Back the Night marches, 221
Taliban, 147, 157, 158–159
Tannen, Deborah, 181
Tavris, Carol, 190

Taylor, Robert, 38
television, gay visibility in, 46–47
Ten Stupid Things Couples Do to Mess Up Their Lives (Schlessinger), 82
Ten Stupid Things Men Do to Mess Up Their Lives (Schlessinger), 82
Ten Stupid Things Women Do to Mess Up Their Lives (Schlessinger), 82
The Terror Dream (Faludi), 6
test scores, adolescents', 94–95, 96
Texas A & M, female cadets as role models at VMI, 202
Texas Women's University, 187–188
Thelma and Louise (film), 42
The Man Show (TV show), 4
Thomas, Clarence, 179, 209–210
Thomas, Jamal, 179
Thompson, Michael, 92
Thornhill, Randy, 72–75
Three Men and a Baby (film), 43
Tidball, Elizabeth, 188–189
Tiger, Lionel, 79–80, 89
TNN, reinvented as Spike TV, 5
Todd, John, 18
To Have and Have Not (film), 39
tokens, 184, 186
Tomahawk Chop, of Atlanta Braves fans, 56
Tootsie (film), 44
torture, sadistic homosocial, 1
total institutions, 177, 198
transformation: of men's lives, 41–44; outside agent required for, in film and TV, 48; of sexual relations, through gay liberation, 45; of women's lives, 39–40
The Truth at Last magazine, 149–150
The Turner Diaries (Pierce), 151, 152, 153
Tyree, A., 101–102
Tyson, Mike, 4, 210

unemployment, youth, 154
unilateralism, in American foreign policy, 7
An Unmarried Woman (film), 42

Vanilla Ice, 57
Varg (Norway), 154
Vassar, Matthew, 218
Vesey, Denmark, 198
Vice Versa (film), 43
Vick, Michael, 61
video games, violent, 137
Vigrid, 155, 156
Vikings: as archetype, 155; Norwegian white supremacist group, 154
Vineyard Christian Fellowship, 164
violence: defensive/retaliatory, 106, 114, 121n.24, 134, 156; estimations of use of, *vs.* victimization, 108; excuses for, 108; gendered patterns of, 107, 110; in Gray's essentialist model, 85; inherent in patriarchal systems, 146; as means of communication, 105; men more likely to use, 102; parental, toward children, 117; restorative, 137; in schools, 132, 135 (*see also* school shootings); witnesses'

reports and informants' perceptions of, 101
Violence Against Women Act, 142n.14
Virginia Military Institute, *see* VMI
Virginia Tech massacre (2007), 131–132, 137–140
Virginia Women's Institute for Leadership, 178–179
virtue, gay men guide women's return to, in films, 45–47
Vitt Ariskt Motstand (VAM) (Sweden), 154, 155
VMI (Virginia Military Institute), ix, 10, 49n.5, 173–174, 177–180, 191; adversarial method at (*see* adversarial method)
Vulcan Society, 6

wage equality, 28
wage gap, 20
Waiting to Exhale (film), 42
"war against boys," 92–98
The War Against Boys (Sommers), 4
WAR magazine, 147, 152, 153
Washington, Desiree, 210
Washington, Raleigh, 170
Watts, Bud, 199
weapons, use of, in domestic violence, 110
Weaver, Sigourney, 42
West, Cornel, 57
Westernization, resistance to, 157, 158
West Point, U.S. Military Academy at, 183, 184–186, 191
whimpering collapse, of blond male, 153
White Aryan Resistance (Sweden), 154, 155
White Aryan Resistance (U.S.), 147–148, 148
white males, young, inspired by authenticity of ghetto masculinity, 56–57
White Ribbon Campaigns (WRC), 11, 229, 230
white supremacists: British, 160n.4; Scandinavian, 154–157; sexualized image of women used to recruit, 156; U.S., 149–153
Whitman, Walt, 10, 218
Who's Who of American Women, 188
Wiest, Diane, 46
wiggers, 57
"wilding," 132
Will and Grace (TV show), 46, 47
Williams, Andy, 124
Williams, Mac, 204
Williams, Robin, 44, 46
Willis, Bruce, 43
Willis, Sharon, 49n.8
wimp-baiting, 213
Wipsatt, William "Upski," 57
Wisconsin Militia, 148
Wise, Stephen, 218
Wolfowitz, Paul, 8
women: absence of, and undergraduate obsession with, 195n.2; breakdown of men's control over, 114; as Bunting's "toxic virus," 181, 202; capacity for violence, 115–116; childrearing by, 78; civilizing role of, 78; on comparative

women (*continued*)
presidential sex appeal, 7; entry into hazardous occupations, 80; equal educational opportunity, 174; equality of, with men, 15 (*see also* gender equality); exclusion of, and confident masculinity, 182; faking orgasms, 40; gay men as role models for, 46; Gray's essentialism about, 83; increased presence in public arenas, 127, 204; as men's competition, 18; of New Order, 151; 19th-century exclusions, 180; as "others," 160; perceived masculinization of, 204; preoccupation of men's movements with, 127; public-domain behavior, 185; "reasonable" standard of, 176; role in tempering male sexuality, 77; sports radio jokes about, 59–60; as threat, 181–183; transformative, 39, 76; uncovered, and Islamic masculinity, 159; as victims of domestic violence, 110–111; in the workplace, 20, 39, 207
Women: An Intimate Geography (Angier), 72
Women of Faith, 167
Women's Rights Convention (Seneca Falls, 1848), 218, 223
Women's Studies departments: Columbia University, 21; gender composition of classes, 209

The Wonder of Boys (Gurian), 93
Woodham, Luke, 124
Woods, Tiger, 61
Woolf, Virginia, 38, 87
"Word of God" movement, Roman Catholic, 164
Working Girl (film), 42
workplace: discrimination in, 20; gender equality, numerical, 207; women in, 39
workshops, men's, 54–55
World Conference on Women (Beijing, 1995), 99
World Economic Forum's Gender Inequality Index, 208
Wright, Robert, 70, 72

Young Feminist Summit Conference (April 1997), 221
Youth Violence (Office of the Surgeon General), 132

Zawahiri, Ayman al-, 157–158
Zellweger, Renee, 43
zero-sum calculus, of school *vs.* masculinity, 66–67
Zionist Occupation Government (ZOG), 152, 155

ABOUT THE AUTHOR

MICHAEL KIMMEL is among the world's leading researchers on men and masculinity, author of *Manhood in America*, *Guyland*, and *The Gendered Society*, among other books. He is the founding editor of the journal *Men and Masculinities* and various book series. He is a professor of sociology at SUNY Stony Brook, and lives with his family in Brooklyn, New York.

CPSIA information can be obtained at www.ICGtesting.com
Printed in the USA
BVOW032346010312

284173BV00003B/1/P